# THE
# CHRISTMAS
# COOKBOOK

# THE CHRISTMAS COOKBOOK

*Shona Crawford Poole*

*Atheneum   New York*

*1979*

Library of Congress Cataloging in Publication Data


Poole, Shona Crawford.
  The Christmas cookbook.
  Bibliography: p.
  Includes index.
  1. Christmas cookery.   I. Title.
TX739.P6          641.5'66          79-63631
ISBN 0-689-11008-1

Published simultaneously in Canada by McClelland and Stewart Ltd.
Manufactured by American Book–Stratford Press, Saddle Brook, New Jersey
Designed by Kathleen Carey
First Edition

*To Jasper*

# CONTENTS

# ACKNOWLEDGMENTS

Christmas foods are made each year with so much love and warmth and nostalgia that in gathering this collection of recipes it has been hard to resist the temptation to include everything I found that fits the theme. So many people shared with me their traditions, their recipes, and their memories that the choices about what to leave out were the hardest to make. So to everyone who helped, thank you.

My gratitude goes especially to Rita Slack, Krystyna Lyskowska, Ava Markus, Erkki Toivanen, Katie Stewart, Per Adolf Antell, Violeta Comati, Eulalia Sancho, Philip Vega, Flavio and Tiziana Andreis, Victoria Omotosho, Gabriel Ronay, Jacques Dandel, George Lanitis, and Lois James.

I would also like to thank Elizabeth Cuthbert, Dr. B. Stillfried, Myrna Lazarus, Carmen Gumucio, Sir Alvin Braynen, Raquel Braune, Yves Mabin, Ghizela Ringrose, Thordur Einarsson, Theresa Sherman-Pennoh, Margarita Sierra, Ray Mountain, and Elizabeth Waldron.

For permission to write this book, I am particularly grateful to my employer, *The Times,* and its editor, William Rees-Mogg.

And for their good company, and for asking for so many second helpings, thank you friends, and thank you family.

# THE
# CHRISTMAS
# COOKBOOK

# INTRODUCTION

All Christendom celebrates Christmas with feasting. It is a time of traditional dishes as richly varied, as odd, and as pleasing as the peoples who have made them. Rituals and recipes have survived immense journeys through time and across great distances. Often they have evolved to meet the needs of modern living or transplantation to quite different climates. But in many places people cling to old and sometimes touchingly inappropriate eating customs.

The universal ingredients of Christmas celebrations everywhere are the preparation of special foods and the enjoyment of them in the company of as many members of the family as can gather for the occasion. Foods bought ready-made for everyday are now prepared lovingly at home. Family recipes are consulted, old methods honored, and ingredients which would be an unthinkable extravagance at any other season are generously used.

In the weeks before the festivities, evocative smells of Christmases long-forgotten waft from kitchens busy with homely sounds of mixing and baking, steaming, roasting, simmering and sizzling. It is all a great to-do for the cooks.

In some countries the choice of Christmas foods is made not from a traditional selection as it is in Europe and America, but from a general list of party dishes which can be served on any sufficiently festive occasion, and it is fascinating to discover why particular foods appear only on days of religious or personal celebration. Often the reason is the simple one that they involve hours of tedious preparation. Nigeria's *moyin-moyin,* small parcels of bean-flour dough enclosing meat and spices, take a great deal of hard work without an electric blender to reduce the hard, dried beans to a fine paste. *Baklava,* the Greek pastry made with nuts and tissue-fine sheets of phyllo, takes both time and skill when the pastry is made at home.

In the splendid wealth of the world's Christmas eating styles almost every imaginable delicacy is served. There is a precedent somewhere for serving dishes as simple or as elaborate as anyone's taste could run to or skill devise. Every recipe in this book is an essential part of Christmas for someone, although not everything included is in the class of such unbreakable traditions as Christmas pudding in England, rice pudding or porridge in Scandinavia, Italy's fruitcake *pannettone,* or Spain's almond-nougat *turrón.* These are sweet things without which Christmas wouldn't be Christmas in the countries where they are eaten.

Some of the recipes are for dishes peculiar to quite small regions, while others have been popular for so long or have traveled so far that it has been hard to choose a particular recipe from the apparently endless variations possible.

If selecting recipe variations was a problem, deciding what to leave out was a greater one. Written recipes are rare in large areas of the world, and it is usually in just such places that the foods chosen for Christmas celebrations are least governed by tradition. So rather than dip more or less at random into these cuisines, I have taken only short detours along unmarked tracks. At the opposite extreme there are so many customs and recipes woven across well-traveled European borders that disentangling them would be a historian's lifework.

What I have tried to produce is a practical cookbook, gathering between two covers an entertaining and useful collection of Christmas recipes for family meals and all kinds of Christmas parties. Some call for considerable skill and expensive ingredients; others cost little in time, effort, or cash.

Since I am a professional journalist and an incorrigible cook, writing this book has been a voyage of discovery for me. Not because I had not previously attempted to reproduce in my own kitchen the tastes and smells of meals remembered from faraway places or eaten in foreign restaurants, though there were many discoveries of that kind, too. I came across lots of new flavors, combinations, techniques, and ideas which have greatly enriched my own repertoire. But the really rewarding discoveries were of a different kind. The biggest was learning to trust my own judgment. In everyday cooking I adjust recipes constantly, adding more or less of some ingredients to improve the flavor, and cooking a dish for a longer or shorter time than the recipe stipulates because experience and common sense tell me when it is or isn't ready. And, like everyone else, I improvise for unexpected guests, or when the stores are closed and I have forgotten something, and often, simply for amusement.

So to every reader of this book, and especially to those whose cooking schools are their own kitchens, I want to say be brave and have fun.

# PRACTICALITIES:
## *A Tablespoon is Level*

To cook rice of the fresh harvest, says a recipe from Southeast Asia, add a little less water. Now where I live, rice of many kinds can be bought—loose or packaged, dry, precooked, boil-in-the-bag, heat-in-the-can, and take-out—anything but "of the fresh harvest." And I mention it here only to illustrate the plain fact that the magic of good cooking can never quite be pinned down, even in the most detailed recipes. There are just too many variables. Quite apart from matters of taste, which are another whole story, ingredients differ from one season to the next, one manufacturer to another, and between breeds and strains. They differ because of how they are grown, harvested, packaged, transported, and stored. One clove of garlic can weigh anything from one-tenth of an ounce to half an ounce, and its size is not all. Only your own nose and taste buds will tell whether the garlic in your kitchen, of whatever size, is pungent or mild.

In a book which draws its recipes from so many places there are inevitable difficulties in defining, and sometimes obtaining, ingredients. Peppers and chilies are as good an example as any. The attributes and subtle variations of members of the *capsicum* family are the subject of much discussion by initiates, and rightly a matter of great importance to those who use them daily. For those who do not, too much precision, beyond a knowledge of whether the varieties called for are mild or hot, is seldom essential to enjoyable cooking and eating.

Techniques of cooking vary widely, too, because they have evolved to meet local needs and conditions. So while standardizing the recipes, I have tried to preserve the methods used in the countries of origin wherever this is practical. Electric mixers and blenders are a boon to busy cooks, but not everyone has one, and not every machine copes well with every kind of job. So except where making a recipe by hand involves an unthinkable amount of work, this is the method I have described. Most of us know our own mixers and blenders well enough to work out timings, and a glance at the appliance handbook should resolve any uncertainties.

Finally, cup and spoon measures are *always level* unless otherwise stated.

# SOUPS

Almond soup is a Christmas Eve favorite in Spain where almonds often appear again in the meal in both stuffings and in the traditional sweets. This delicate milky white soup is served cold, garnished with white grapes, powdered cinnamon, or, more festively, with a scarlet rose petal floating in each bowl.

## SOPA DE ALMENDRAS
### Almond Soup

{SPAIN}                                            TO SERVE 8

*1 ⅓ cups blanched almonds*
*4 cloves garlic*
*4 tablespoons olive oil*
*Salt to taste*
*4 teaspoons wine vinegar*

**FOR THE GARNISH**

*White grapes, peeled and seeded (optional)*
*Cinnamon (optional)*
*Rose petals (optional)*

Crush the almonds with the garlic, olive oil, and salt to a smooth paste using a mortar and pestle, or an electric blender. Gradually add 10 cups water. Check the seasoning and chill.

Just before serving the soup, stir in the vinegar. Serve it in individual bowls with a garnish of grapes or a sprinkling of powdered cinnamon— or float a single rose petal in each dish.

Chestnut soup has been made for centuries throughout Europe. This version is adapted from an early nineteenth-century English recipe.

## CHESTNUT SOUP

{ENGLAND}                                                          TO SERVE 10

2 pounds chestnuts                     Powdered mace to taste
10 cups well-flavored                  Cayenne to taste
       poultry or veal stock           2 cups light cream
Salt to taste

Preheat oven to 400°F. Using a sharp knife, slit the shiny brown skin of each chestnut on the domed surface. Lay them, in a single layer, flat side down on a roasting tray. Pour 1 cup water into the tray, and roast them for about 8 minutes. Peel the chestnuts while they are still hot.

Put the peeled chestnuts into a large, heavy-bottomed pot, and cover them with the stock. Bring to the boil, skim, cover, and simmer for about 45 minutes or until the chestnuts are easily broken by pressing them with a wooden spoon. Strain the chestnuts and reserve the stock.

Rub the chestnuts through a fine sieve or reduce them to a purée in an electric blender with a small amount of the stock. Rinse the pot and return the chestnuts to it. Gradually stir in the stock and season with salt, mace, and cayenne.

Bring the soup to the boil, reduce the heat, and just before serving, stir in the cream. Serve the soup very hot, but do not boil it again once the cream has been added.

The flavor and sweetness of fresh chestnuts can vary. If the chestnuts are very sweet, the soup may be too sweet for some tastes. This can be modified by stewing the chestnuts in water rather than stock and adding fresh stock to the purée instead.

Another festive-looking soup is the Polish beet and mushroom con-sommé, *barszcz*, traditionally served on Christmas Eve with *uszka*, "little ears" of mushroom-stuffed dough which are poached and served in the soup, or deep-fried and passed separately. Both of the recipes which follow are equally authentic, but the first, which involves the advance preparation of a fermented beet stock, does have a finer flavor and is worth the little extra trouble it calls for.

## BARSZCZ
### *Fermented Beet and Mushroom Consommé*

{POLAND}                                      TO SERVE 4 TO 6

### FOR THE FERMENTED STOCK

*1 pound fresh, raw beets*
*½ cup dark rye bread, cubed*

About one week before making the soup, prepare the fermented beet stock. Peel and slice the beets. Put the slices into a large glass or pottery jar and cover them with 4½ cups water which has been boiled and allowed to cool to lukewarm. Add the cubes of dark rye bread and cover the jar with a lid of perforated paper. Leave it in a warm place (65°–68°F) for a few days. Strain the stock and use it immediately, or bottle the strained stock until you are ready to finish the soup.

### FOR THE SOUP

| | |
|---|---|
| *½ cup dried mushrooms, boletus type* | *2½ cups prepared fermented stock* |
| *½ pound mixed soup greens, chopped* | *Salt to taste* |
| *1 clove garlic, crushed* | *Pepper to taste* |
| *1 pound fresh, raw beets* | *Sugar to taste* |
| | *Lemon juice to taste* |

Soak the mushrooms in water for several hours, then cook them in the soaking water until soft. This usually takes about 2 hours, but the time can vary a great deal. Add the soup greens and garlic, and cook until they, too, are soft.

In a separate pot cook the beets until tender in as little water as possible, then peel and grate them coarsely. Do wear gloves to handle the cooked beets, as their brilliant juice stains fingers bright red.

Add about 4½ cups of water to the mushroom and vegetable mixture. Add the beets and bring the pot quickly to the boil. Strain the mixture and add the fermented stock. Season to taste with salt, pepper, sugar, and lemon juice. Reheat the soup.

Serve in soup cups with *uszka* (see page 12).

## BARSZCZ
### Beet and Mushroom Consommé

[POLAND]                                          TO SERVE 4 TO 6

¾ cup dried mushrooms,            Salt to taste
    boletus type                       Sugar to taste
2½ pounds fresh, raw beets        Lemon juice to taste
1½ tablespoons red wine
    vinegar

Cover the dried mushrooms with about 4 cups boiling water and leave them to soak for several hours. Cook them uncovered in the soaking liquid until tender. This takes about 2 hours, by which time the liquid will have reduced to about 6 tablespoons. Strain the mushroom stock through a fine sieve.

Peel the raw beets and grate them coarsely. Wear gloves for this colorful operation. Add 4½ cups cold water to the grated beets in a large pot, bring to the boil, reduce the heat, and simmer uncovered for about 10 minutes. Add vinegar and simmer partly covered for another 30 minutes. Strain the beet stock through a fine sieve, extracting as much of the juice as possible.

Combine the beet and mushroom stocks in a clean pot, and bring the consommé quickly to the boil. Season to taste with salt, sugar, and lemon juice.

Serve in soup cups with *uszka* (see page 12).

## USZKA
### *"Little Ears"*

{POLAND}                                          TO SERVE 4 TO 6

FOR THE FILLING

2 ounces dried mushrooms,          1 ounce white bread
   boletus type                   ½ cup white bread crumbs
1 small onion, chopped             Salt to taste
   fine                           Pepper to taste
1 tablespoon vegetable oil

FOR THE DOUGH

1¼ cups flour
1 egg

Cover the dried mushrooms with boiling water and leave them to soak for several hours; then cook until tender in as little water as possible. Fry the onion in oil until golden. Soak the bread in water and squeeze out the excess moisture. Strain the cooked mushrooms. Put the bread, onions, and mushrooms through the fine blade of a grinder. Add the bread crumbs and season to taste with salt and pepper. Fry the mixture, using a little more oil if needed, until it makes a smooth, pleasant-smelling paste.

To make the dough, sift the flour into a bowl. Mix the egg with ½ cup water and blend with the flour to make a ball of firm dough, adding more water if needed.

Roll out the dough as thin as possible on a well-floured board, and cut into circles about 2 inches in diameter with a plain-edged cookie cutter or the rim of a wine glass. Spoon a small dollop of filling onto the center of each piece of dough, moisten the rim with water, and fold the circles in half, sealing the edges firmly. Do not overfill the cases or they will burst when cooking. Now make the stuffed half circles of dough into "little ears" by bringing the points together around your finger and pressing to join them securely.

The prepared *uszka* can be deep-frozen at this stage for poaching later, in which case they must be defrosted completely before cooking.

To poach the *uszka,* drop them by handfuls into a large pot of boiling, salted water. Reduce the heat, and simmer each batch for about 5 minutes, or until the dumplings are tender and the dough cooked. Keep them warm in a covered bowl until all are cooked before arranging them in individual bowls and pouring the hot *barszcz* (see pages 10 and 11) over them.

To fry the *uszka,* heat a large pan of deep fat or oil to about 350°F. (At this temperature a 1-inch cube of day-old bread will fry to a crisp, golden brown in about 90 seconds.) Cook them in small batches until golden. Drain them on paper towels and serve immediately.

Fried *uszka* may be deep-frozen and reheated without defrosting on a baking tray in a hot oven at 400°F.

The Finns, too, are not content with soup alone and often serve it with *piirakkaa,* small, boat-shaped pies made with a rye crust and a variety of fillings. A clear soup or broth most frequently begins the elaborate Christmas meal. The following vegetable broth is full of flavor.

## KASVISLIEMI
### *Vegetable Broth*

[FINLAND]                                        TO SERVE 8 TO 10

| | |
|---|---|
| *1 medium carrot* | *12 radishes* |
| *2 medium parsnips* | *1 pound fresh peas,* |
| *1 pound Jerusalem* | *preferably in the pod* |
| *artichokes* | *1 small bunch parsley,* |
| *1 small beet* | *chopped* |
| *4 stalks celery* | *6 whole allspice berries* |
| *½ pound cabbage* | *6 black peppercorns* |
| *1 large onion* | *2 bay leaves* |
| *2 medium leeks* | *Salt to taste* |

Peel and chop the carrot, parsnips, Jerusalem artichokes, and beet. Roughly chop the celery, cabbage, onion (do not peel), and leeks. Put all the vegetables, herbs, and spices into a large stockpot. Cover with 12 cups of water, bring to the boiling point, cover, and simmer for about 2½ hours. Strain the stock and reserve the vegetables for another use.

Salt the vegetable broth to taste and serve it very hot in warmed soup cups or bowls with *juustipiirakkaa* (see page 110).

According to Sir Walter Scott, fat brose was once the Christmas Day breakfast soup or gruel of his compatriots, and it would certainly have kept out the raw chill Scottish winters. "In olden times, all, gentle and simple, had fat brose on Yule Day morning."

In *The Scot's Kitchen. Its Traditions and Lore with Old-Time Recipes,* F. Marian McNeill, writing in 1929, describes how this now almost extinct concoction was made. Half an ox head, a cow heel, or a good piece of hough (shank of beef) was covered with water and boiled until an almost pure oil floated to the top. A ladle full of this fat broth was poured over a handful of lightly toasted oatmeal and a pinch of salt in a bowl. The mixture was quickly stirred to form knots, returned to the pot for a minute or two to reheat, and served.

A comparable practice born of harder times survives in Sweden where *dopp i grytan,* dip in the pot, was traditionally eaten at midmorning on the day before Christmas with rye bread, schnapps, and pickled herrings. Today it more often appears as a token ritual item in the elaborate *smörgåsbord* served at lunchtime on the day before Christmas or as the first part of a longer evening meal. *Dopp i grytan* is the stock in which the Christmas ham and a variety of sausages for the *smörgåsbord* have been cooked. Pieces of rye bread are dipped in the pot or kettle of hot stock and eaten with the fingers.

It would be difficult to find a simpler soup than *aïgo bouïllido,* literally translated as boiling water, which begins the traditional Christmas Eve meal in Provençe. Two large cloves of garlic, 1 tablespoon olive oil, 1 bay leaf, and 1 tablespoon salt are boiled together with 4 cups of water for about 15 minutes. Two raw eggs are broken into a tureen, then the boiling liquid is poured over them and beaten with a wooden spoon.

*Aïgo bouïllido* is followed by *cardons aux anchois,* a vegetable of the artichoke family cooked and served with an anchovy sauce, and *cacalaus,* cooked snails with garlic mayonnaise or a fresh tomato sauce mixed with thyme, savory, and fennel, and garnished with thorns of the acacia or judas tree. The final cooked dish, eels, chopped bacon, and mushrooms simmered in white wine, is followed by a salad. Then come thirteen more traditional items: dates, oranges, apples, pears, mandarins, almonds, walnuts, raisins, figs, chestnuts, black nougat, white nougat, and *fougasse,* a circular, latticed loaf of flour and olive oil flavored with aniseed.

This meatless feast, evolved in the days when Christmas Eve was a fast day in Catholic countries, puts to excellent use the superb garlic and herbs which, grown in the dry sunshine of southern France, taste so much better than those cultivated almost anywhere else.

In Peru, a substantial fish soup often begins a meal that is otherwise modest by American and European standards of Christmas eating. *Antichuchos,* skewers of marinated bull's heart, are accompanied by *papa rellena* (see page 115), meatballs enclosed in mashed potato and fried till crisp and golden, and an escarole salad. A fruit compote usually completes the meal.

## CHUPE DE PESCADO
### Fish Soup

{PERU}                                                          TO SERVE 6

| | |
|---|---|
| *1 tablespoon butter* | *1 pound cooked crabmeat* |
| *1 clove garlic* | *or shelled shrimp* |
| *Salt to taste* | *Dash cayenne* |
| *2 medium onions, quartered* | *4½ cups milk* |
| *1 tablespoon tomato paste* | *6 small potatoes* |
| *2½ cups grated goat's* | *6 slices eel or lobster* |
| *cheese* | *1 tablespoon olive oil* |
| *¼ cup rice* | *1 red bell pepper* |
| *Marjoram or oregano to* | *6 eggs* |
| *taste* | |

Melt the butter in a large, heavy-bottomed pot. Crush the garlic with a little salt, and add to the pot with the onions. At 2-minute intervals add in the following order, tomato paste, half the grated cheese, rice, and finally salt and marjoram or oregano to taste. Cook this mixture gently for about 5 minutes. Add the crab or shrimp, and cayenne. Cover and cook over a low heat until the rice and onions are cooked to a mush. Add a little water if the mixture becomes too dry before the rice is completely cooked. Rub the mixture through a sieve. Rinse the pot and return the purée to it. Add the milk, stir well, check the seasoning and set the soup aside while the garnish is prepared.

Boil the potatoes in their skins until tender. Peel them and keep warm on a large plate in a very low oven. Brush the slices of eel or lobster with oil and broil them lightly. Keep warm in the oven. Trim and seed the pepper, and broil it lightly before scraping off the skin. Cut it into six pieces and keep warm. Finally, poach the eggs in boiling salted water, drain, and keep warm.

Bring the soup to the boil. Arrange a potato, a slice of eel or lobster, a piece of pepper, a poached egg, and a portion of the remaining goat cheese on each of six large, heated soup plates. Pour boiling soup over the garnishes and serve.

Soup is an indispensable element of the Christmas meal in Hungary. This one is delicious.

## HAL LEVES
### Fish Soup

{HUNGARY}                                                    TO SERVE 6

| | |
|---|---|
| Head, tail, liver, hard and soft roe of a large fish, such as pike or sturgeon | 2 tablespoons butter |
| | ¼ cup flour |
| | 6 tablespoons sour cream |
| | Salt to taste |
| 1 tablespoon salt | Lemon juice to taste |
| 1 bay leaf | ¼ cup rice |

Put the fish in a large, heavy-bottomed pot, cover it with cold water, add the salt, and bring to the boil. Skim the liquid, add the bay leaf, cover the pot, and simmer until the fish is tender. Strain the liquid and reserve it. As soon as the fish is cool enough to handle, remove all the bones, break the flesh into pieces, and keep it warm.

Rinse the pot and melt the butter in it over low heat. Stir in the flour and cook the *roux* for a minute or two without allowing it to color. Gradually blend in about 6 cups of the reserved fish stock and cook the soup over low heat until the mixture has thickened slightly. Stir in the sour cream, and season to taste with salt and lemon juice.

Wash the rice and add it to the soup. Simmer the soup, covered, until the rice is tender, stirring occasionally to make sure the grains are not sticking to the bottom of the pot.

To serve the soup, divide the pieces of reserved fish among six large, very hot soup plates, and pour the boiling soup over them.

Lighter fish soups are an excellent beginning to hearty meals of roast goose or turkey with rich stuffings, not to mention plum puddings, hard sauces, nuts, and brandy. Both the Edwardian recipe for lobster soup below and the older recipe for a traditional English oyster soup which follows it call for a good fish stock. A well-flavored fish stock is quickly prepared by boiling the bones and trimmings of any white fish, and a cod's head, if available, with 1 or 2 roughly chopped onions, carrots, and celery sticks, a bay leaf, a bouquet of fresh herbs, salt, and pepper. Cook the stock for about 20 minutes, then strain it through a fine sieve. It can, of course, be reduced by fast boiling for a stronger flavor.

## RICH LOBSTER SOUP

{ENGLAND}                                                    TO SERVE 6 TO 8

| | |
|---|---|
| 1 small, whole lobster, | Pepper to taste |
| cooked | 2 teaspoons lemon juice |
| 1/4 cup butter | 1/3 cup cornstarch |
| 1 bay leaf | 3 1/2 cups good fish stock |
| 1 sprig parsley | 1 1/4 cups light cream |
| Salt to taste | |

Remove the lobster flesh from the shell. Dice and reserve the claw meat for garnishing the finished soup. Set aside the coral and chop the remaining meat. Wash the shell, pound it with the butter, and put the mixture into a heavy-bottomed pot with the bay leaf, parsley, salt, pepper, lemon juice, and cornstarch. Cook these ingredients together very gently for about 10 minutes without allowing them to color. Add the fish stock, chopped lobster meat and coral, and simmer the soup gently for about 40 minutes.

Strain the soup very carefully through a sieve lined with cheesecloth, to make sure all the gritty shell fragments are extracted. Rinse the pot and return the strained liquid to it. Stir in the cream and reserved claw meat. Reheat the soup gently but do not allow it to boil again after the cream has been added.

Serve in warmed soup cups or bowls.

## OYSTER SOUP

{ENGLAND}                                                    TO SERVE 6

| | |
|---|---|
| 1 dozen fresh oysters | Pepper to taste |
| ¼ cup butter | 2 egg yolks, well-beaten |
| ⅓ cup flour | ½ cup milk |
| 3 cups good fish stock (see | ¾ cup light cream |
| page 17 | Lemon juice to taste |
| Salt to taste | |

Open the oysters, reserving the liquid in the shells. Separate the flesh from the shells, remove and reserve the beards (the darker piece of flesh around the edge), and cut the flesh of each oyster into four pieces.

Melt the butter in a heavy-bottomed pot. Stir in the flour and cook the *roux* for a few minutes without letting it color. Stir in the fish stock, oyster beards, the oyster liquid, and the seasonings. Simmer this mixture, stirring occasionally, for about 15 minutes before passing it through a fine sieve. Rinse the pot, return the sieved soup base to it, and add the egg yolks, milk, cream, oysters, and lemon juice. Cook very gently until the mixture thickens. Stir constantly and do not allow the soup to boil or it will curdle at once.

Serve in warmed soup bowls or plates with thin, dry toast or thin slices of lightly buttered whole wheat or rye bread.

For centuries thrifty housewives have been making splendid soups from giblets and carcasses of chicken, geese, turkeys, poultry, and game of all descriptions. Every family has its own favorite. There would be great disappointment in my own household if a robust soup of leek and potato, sautéed in fat skimmed from the stock and then cooked in the broth made by boiling the remains of a bird with a few soup vegetables, did not appear on the table within a day or two of serving roasted poultry. My mother's version is a much lighter affair, a clear, golden broth with rice and plenty of chopped fresh parsley added at the last minute.

No doubt the Greek housewives' version is that marvelously fresh and frothy egg and lemon soup, *avgolémono,* and cooks of all nations convert the giblets and carcasses of the Christmas birds eaten everywhere into soups of unimaginable variety. But because few of them appear on festive menus, they are seldom thought special enough for mention when Christmas food is discussed.

The Danish *kråsesuppe* of goose giblets, apples, and prunes, embellished as often as not with butter dumplings, *boller,* is a worthy exception.

## *KRÅSESUPPE*
### *Giblet Soup with Apples and Prunes*
[DENMARK]                              TO SERVE 6 TO 8

| | |
|---|---|
| 1 ¼ cups prunes | 6 peppercorns, crushed |
| Giblets, neck, wings, and | ½ teaspoon ground mace |
| feet of 1 goose | 1 pound cooking apples, |
| 2 large carrots, chopped | peeled and sliced |
| coarse | 2 tablespoons sugar |
| 1 large onion, chopped | 2 tablespoons butter |
| coarse | ¼ cup flour |
| 1 stalk celery, chopped | Sugar to taste |
| coarse | 4 teaspoons wine vinegar |
| Salt to taste | Pepper to taste |

Cover the prunes with boiling water and leave them to soak 2 to 3 hours, or preferably overnight. Pit the prunes, reserving the soaking liquid. Set both aside.

Wash the goose giblets. Divide each wing into two pieces, and the neck into three. Put the giblets, neck and wing pieces, and feet into a large pot, cover them with cold water, bring to the boil and skim. Add the vegetables to the boiling stock with salt, peppercorns, and mace. Cover the pot and simmer gently for several hours until the giblets are tender.

Strain the stock. There should be about 9 cups; if necessary reduce by fast boiling the proper amount and set it aside. Reserve the giblets and vegetables.

Cook the sliced apples with the prunes and 2 tablespoons of sugar in the soaking water until the fruit is tender. Strain and set aside fruit and juice.

Melt the butter in a large, heavy-bottomed pot. Stir in the flour and cook the *roux* gently for a minute or two without allowing it to color. Stir in the fruit liquid and the giblet stock.

Chop the vegetables and the meat from the goose giblets into small pieces. Add the meat, vegetables, and fruit to the soup. Check the seasoning, adding more sugar, salt, vinegar, and pepper to taste.

Serve in warmed soup bowls or plates with *boller* (see page 20).

## BOLLER
### Butter Dumplings

{DENMARK}                                        TO SERVE 6 TO 8

6 tablespoons butter            4 eggs
2 cups flour                    1 egg yolk
2 cups boiling water            Salt to taste

Melt the butter in a heavy-bottomed saucepan. Stir in the flour and cook
the *roux* gently for a minute or two without allowing it to color. Gradually stir in the boiling water, and continue to cook slowly until a
lump-free ball of dough is formed. Remove the pot from the heat and
beat in the eggs and the egg yolk one at a time. Add salt to taste. Shape
the dough into little balls, using two teaspoons.

The *boller* can be cooked in the soup, or separately in stock, or in
boiling salted water. Drop them into the boiling liquid a few at a time
so that it does not stop boiling, which would make the dumplings soggy.
They are ready when they rise to the surface.

Serve with *kråsesuppe* (see page 19) in warmed soup bowls or plates.


Hungarians take their soup-making seriously, too, as the earlier recipe
for fish soup and this one for a hearty chicken soup demonstrate.

## UJHAZI TYUK LEVES
### Chicken Soup with Liver Dumplings

{HUNGARY}                                        TO SERVE 10 TO 12

FOR THE SOUP

1 2½-pound whole chicken        2 medium parsnips, peeled
1 pound stewing beef                and chopped
1 pound beef bones              1 large onion, chopped
1 tablespoon salt               1 clove garlic, chopped
6 black peppercorns,            5 small mushrooms,
    crushed                         chopped
1 teaspoon paprika              4 ounces thin noodles or
1 tablespoon tomato paste           vermicelli
3 medium carrots, scraped
    and chopped

**FOR THE DUMPLINGS**

*½ pound chicken livers*      *Salt to taste*
*2 tablespoons butter*      *Pepper to taste*
*1 cup dry bread crumbs*      *2 large eggs, beaten*
*Chopped parsley to taste*

**FOR THE GARNISH**

*Fresh parsley, chopped fine*

Put the chicken, beef, and beef bones into a large stockpot and cover them with cold water. Add about a tablespoon of salt and bring to the boil. Skim the liquid and let it simmer for about ½ hour before adding the peppercorns, paprika, and tomato paste.

Add the vegetables to the stock and continue cooking until both the meat and vegetables are tender. Strain the stock, reserve the beef and chicken, and return about 12 cups of the liquid to the pot. Bring the stock back to the boil, add the noodles, and cook until they are tender.

While the noodles are cooking, bone the chicken, cutting the meat into small pieces to serve in the soup. (The beef can be eaten cold later or incorporated into another dish.)

To make the dumplings, first stiffen the chicken livers by frying them lightly in butter, and then pass them through the finest blade of the meat grinder or press them through a sieve. Combine the ground liver with the bread crumbs and season to taste with the parsley, salt, and pepper. Add sufficient beaten egg to bind the mixture. Take teaspoonfuls of the dumpling mixture and roll them into balls.

Drop the liver dumplings into the boiling soup and cook them for about 10 minutes. Then add the chopped chicken meat.

Serve the soup in warmed soup bowls or plates garnished with plenty of finely chopped fresh parsley.

In Italy quite small areas and even single towns have long held traditions of eating particular dishes on Christmas Eve, traditions of which their nearest neighbors are often virtually ignorant.

*Cappelletti,* little hats of pasta, are made with various stuffings. Tuscany, Umbria, Emilia, Romagna, and Rome all have their own characteristic fillings. The following recipe is from Perugia, where *cappelletti in brodo* are made for the Christmas Eve dinner.

Many Italian cooks who buy ready-made pasta for everyday meals make their own for special occasions, and to pasta lovers the delicious flavors of homemade stuffings fully justify the work of making the filled varieties. Making pasta does require patience and a fair amount of space. It is not something to do in a hurry or in a tiny kitchen.

## CAPPELLETTI IN BRODO
### Cappelletti in Broth

[ITALY]                                             TO SERVE 8 TO 12

### FOR THE FILLING

6 ounces lean pork
6 ounces lean veal
2 ounces ham
2 ounces veal brains,
  cleaned
1 small carrot
1 small stalk celery
2 tablespoons butter

4 tablespoons dry Marsala
  wine
½ cup grated Parmesan
  cheese
Salt to taste
Pepper to taste
Pinch grated nutmeg

### FOR THE PASTA

2¼ cups flour (hard gluten or baker's bread flour, if possible)
2 teaspoons salt
3 large eggs

These quantities make about 84 *cappelletti*. Allow at least 1¼ cups of well-flavored chicken or veal broth for each serving.

Chop the pork, veal, ham, brains, carrot, and celery fine. Melt the butter in a heavy-bottomed pot. Add the chopped meats and vegetables and cook gently for 5 minutes. Add the Marsala and cook for about 20 minutes more. Put the mixture through the fine blade of a meat grinder. Mix in the grated cheese and season with salt, pepper, and nutmeg. Set the mixture aside to cool.

To make the pasta, sift the flour and salt together and heap in a mound on a large pastry board. Make a well in the center and break the eggs into it. Fold the flour over the eggs and knead until a soft, elastic dough is formed.

To roll out the pasta, divide it into two or four pieces—smaller amounts are easier to manage unless you have a very large board and an extra-long rolling pin. Place the first piece of dough on a floured board and roll it lightly. Lift it, drape it over the rolling pin to stretch it gently, sprinkle it with flour and roll again. Continue to lift, stretch, flour, and roll until the pasta is extremely thin, almost like a piece of fabric. Lay it on a clean cloth on a table or over the back of a chair. Roll out the remaining dough using the same rolling and stretching technique.

To assemble the *cappelletti,* spoon teaspoonfuls of the filling onto one sheet of the rolled-out pasta at about 1½-inch intervals. Cover with a second sheet of pasta. Using a crimped or plain-edged cookie or pastry cutter about 1½ inches in diameter, or the rim of a wine glass of suitable size, cut through both layers of pasta, centering the cutter over each bit of filling, to form little circular parcels.

*Cappelletti* may be made the day before they are to be eaten. Lay them in a single layer on a large, floured board or dish and cover with a floured cloth. Keep in a cool place, but not in the refrigerator.

To cook the *cappelletti,* prepare a large pot of boiling chicken or veal broth. Drop the *cappelletti* carefully into the bubbling liquid, a few at a time so that it does not stop boiling. They are ready when they rise to the surface of the broth, which takes only about 4 minutes.

Serve *cappelletti* in their broth in large soup plates. Pass a bowl of freshly grated Parmesan cheese.


The nearest thing to an instant Christmas soup is Hungary's wine soup, which is served before the cold hors d'oeuvres. To serve 6 people, 6 egg yolks are beaten with 8 tablespoons of superfine granulated sugar until the mixture is light and foamy. About 4½ cups of good white wine is heated with the juice of 1 lemon, a piece of lemon rind, and cloves and cinnamon to taste. When the wine boils it is whisked into the egg mixture and then returned to a low heat and whisked until thick. Wine soup is served hot in cups.

# FIRST COURSES

Travelers, especially people who travel on business, eat few dishes which do not appear on hotel menus everywhere. The distinctly local character of freshly baked breakfast rolls can easily be the only sign that one is in one capital and not another, unless there is time and opportunity to explore further than the city's main street.

A selection of authentic recipes for dishes which have traveled far and are often poorly made seems a useful offering. Their association with Christmas is real enough, although the strength of that association varies. Christmas dinner without *tortellini* would raise eyebrows in Bologna, and *cannelloni,* the other pasta dish in this section, comes not from Italy but from Spain, where the Catalonians have evolved their own seasonal variation.

For those who can afford them, *foie gras*, oysters, lobster, and caviar are internationally popular openings to Christmas dinner, especially in the cities where older local traditions have loosened their hold. These delicacies are much too good and too expensive to spoil by careless presentation.

Many more dishes which can be served as a first course, or between soup and the main dish, are included in later chapters. On the infinitely varied buffet tables of northern and eastern Europe are dozens of dishes which could have been drawn into this section. But as *smörgåsbord* and buffet-table dishes are so often, with the addition of various hot items, a meal in themselves, these recipes will be found under other headings.

The *tamales* of Mexico and Ecuador posed much the same problem. In those countries they are eaten at the beginning of the Christmas meal, while versions made elsewhere are served at different times. So, as descriptions of how to make them are repetitive, and because we are perhaps more likely to make them for a Christmas party than for the main family meal, *tamales* and their relations can be found, fitting a little uneasily, in the chapter on pies.

## CANALONES
### Cannelloni

[SPAIN]                                                TO SERVE 8

**FOR THE FILLING**

*1 pound lean beef*
*½ pound chicken livers*
*4 tablespoons olive oil*
*2 medium onions, chopped*
*    fine*
*1 pound tomatoes*
*4 tablespoons tomato paste*

*4 cloves garlic*
*1 tablespoon wine vinegar*
*Marjoram or oregano to*
*    taste*
*Sugar to taste*
*Salt to taste*
*Pepper to taste*

*Cannelloni shells (allow 2 to 4 pieces per person*
*depending on the size of the tubes)*

**FOR THE BÉCHAMEL SAUCE**

*4 tablespoons butter*
*½ cup flour*
*3 cups milk*

*Salt to taste*
*Pepper to taste*
*Grated nutmeg to taste*

**FOR THE TOPPING**

*½ cup grated Spanish Manchengo cheese or Parmesan*
*Sprinkling of paprika (optional)*

To prepare the filling, first grind the beef and chicken livers, using the finest blade of the grinder. Heat the olive oil in a heavy-bottomed pot and fry the onions for a few minutes. Add the ground beef and chicken livers and fry them with the onions until both are lightly browned.

Peel the tomatoes (dip them in boiling water for a moment and the skins should come off easily), discard the seeds, and roughly chop the flesh. Add chopped tomatoes and tomato paste to the meat mixture. Fry over low heat for a few minutes more before adding the garlic, crushed with a little salt, the wine vinegar, and marjoram or oregano, sugar, salt, and pepper to taste. Cover the pot and simmer gently for about 1 hour. You may need to add a little water during cooking, but the finished consistency of the filling should be solid enough not to run out of the pasta tubes.

While the filling is cooking, boil the pasta according to the directions on the package.

To make the sauce, melt the butter in a heavy-bottomed pot and stir in the flour. Cook the *roux* for a minute or two before gradually adding the milk, stirring well. Stir the sauce over a low heat until it is thick and smooth, then season with salt, pepper, and nutmeg. Cover and keep warm so that it will pour smoothly over the assembled dish.

When you are ready to begin assembling the dish, preheat oven to 350°. First, spread a thin layer of the filling over the bottom of a well-buttered shallow, ovenproof dish. Ideally, the dish should hold all the *cannelloni* in one layer without too much space round the edges. Fill the pasta tubes with the meat mixture and lay them side by side in the dish. Pour the *béchamel* sauce over the *cannelloni,* sprinkle the dish with grated cheese, and bake for about 40 minutes. A very light sprinkling of *pimentón* or paprika over the cheese before the dish goes into the oven will give the finished dish those caramel-colored blisters which make cheese toppings look so appetizing.

A bowl of freshly grated Manchengo or Parmesan cheese can be passed separately.

Although *béchamel* sauce does not freeze successfully by itself, it seems to come to no harm when incorporated into pasta dishes like *cannelloni.* If you can spare a baking dish good enough to go to the table, this recipe is a candidate for advance preparation and freezing. Freeze it ready to go into the oven, but do thaw it completely before baking. The frozen pasta would not come to grief, but a favorite dish might.


Christmas dinner in Bologna, the town that gave the world sauce Bolognese, begins with *tortellini.* According to a romantic local legend, these little rings of deliciously stuffed dough were the invention of a lovelorn cook who, catching sight of his master's wife sleeping naked, cooked and served pasta fashioned in the shape of her navel as a token of his hopeless passion.

*Tortellini* are fun to make. For grand occasions they are served in a well-flavored broth or, as here, *ascuitta,* dry with butter and grated cheese. For everyday eating they may come with *ragù Bolognese,* a giant of a sauce compared with its pale and widely traveled imitator, and cheese.

## TORTELLINI BOLOGNESE

{ITALY}                                                TO SERVE 4 TO 6

**FOR THE FILLING**

| | |
|---|---|
| 3 ounces lean pork | 2 tablespoons butter |
| 2 ounces lean veal | Salt to taste |
| 2 ounces breast of chicken | Pepper to taste |
| or turkey | Grated nutmeg to taste |
| 2 ounces ham | 2 large eggs |
| 1 ounce mortadella sausage | ¾ cup grated Parmesan |
| 2 ounces veal brains, | cheese |
| cleaned | |

**FOR THE DOUGH**

4½ cups flour (hard gluten or baker's bread flour if possible)
1 tablespoon salt
3 large eggs

Chop the pork, veal, breast of chicken or turkey, ham, mortadella, and veal brains. Melt the butter in a heavy-bottomed pot, add the pork, veal, and chicken or turkey meat, and sauté gently until lightly browned. Add the ham, mortadella, and brains, and season to taste with salt, pepper, and plenty of nutmeg.

Cover the pot and simmer for about 15 minutes. Put the mixture through a meat grinder, using the finest blade, and add the eggs and grated cheese. Mix all the ingredients together to make a smooth paste.

To make the dough, sift the flour and salt and heap in a mound on a large pastry board. Make a well in the center and break the eggs into it. Fold the flour over the eggs and knead until a soft, elastic dough is formed.

To roll the dough, divide it into two or four pieces—smaller amounts are easier to manage unless you have a very large board and an extra-long rolling pin. Place the first piece of dough on the floured board and roll it lightly. Lift it, draped over the rolling pin, to stretch it gently, sprinkle with flour, and roll again. Continue to lift, stretch, flour, and roll until the dough is extremely thin. Lay the pasta, which should now be almost like a piece of fabric, on a clean cloth on a table or over the back of a chair. Roll out the remaining dough using the same technique. Cut circles of the rolled dough using a plain-edged cookie or pastry cutter about 1½ inches in diameter, or the rim of a wine glass of suitable size.

To assemble the *tortellini*, place about half a teaspoonful of filling on each circle of pasta. Then fold each circle in two so that the top edge lies just short of the under edge. Curling the pasta around a finger, bring the two points of each folded circle together to make a ring. Arrange the *tortellini* in a single layer on a floured board or dish and cover them with a floured cloth until needed. They may be made the day before they are to be eaten.

To cook the *tortellini*, prepare a large pot of boiling chicken or veal stock, or boiling salted water. Drop the *tortellini* carefully into the bubbling liquid, a few at a time so that it does not stop boiling. They are ready when they rise to the surface. Scoop them out with a slotted spoon as they bob up to the top of the pot, and keep them warm until all the *tortellini* are cooked.

Serve in a large, warmed bowl dotted generously with butter. Offer more grated cheese separately.

It is, to me, a wicked waste of caviar, and indeed of any of its delicious but less prestigious relations, to serve it on wilting canapes or even at table with the freshest of toast in a nest of crisp white damask. Only *blini* will do, and for my taste, only *blini* made with buckwheat flour at that. The nutty, yeast-raised pancakes are at their mouth-watering best whisked straight from the frying pan to the table, generally an impractical ideal which can be realized only at the most intimate of dinners.

By cooking them in two pans simultaneously, sufficient *blini* for, say, 6 people can be finished and kept warm in a fit state to outshine any toast. And as the prepared batter can be left standing for hours—even a day or more—what is a little last-minute frying between friends?

## BLINI
### Yeast-Raised Buckwheat Pancakes

[RUSSIA]                                                    TO SERVE 6

**FOR THE BATTER**

*2 cups all-purpose flour*          *Generous pinch sugar*
*2 cups buckwheat flour*            *2 large eggs, separated*
*2 teaspoons dried active*          *2 tablespoons melted butter*
   *yeast*           *Salt to taste*
*2½ cups lukewarm milk*

**FOR FRYING**

*6 tablespoons melted butter*

Sift the all-purpose flour into one large bowl and the buckwheat flour into a smaller one. Dissolve the yeast according to the package instructions, using a little of the milk heated to about 110°F and sweetened with a generous pinch of sugar.

Make a well in the all-purpose flour, pour in the dissolved yeast, and gradually mix in the flour. Beat the mixture with a wooden spoon, adding enough of the warm milk to make a thick, smooth batter. Cover the bowl with a cloth and leave the batter to rise in a warm place until it is light and bubbly and has doubled in bulk.

Beat in the buckwheat flour with enough of the remaining milk to produce a smooth batter with the consistency of heavy cream. Now beat in the egg yolks, melted butter, and salt to taste. Beat the egg whites until they are stiff, but not dry, and fold them into the batter. Cover the bowl with a cloth and leave the batter to rise again in a warm place until it has doubled in bulk.

At this stage the batter can be left for several hours at kitchen temperature. If it is to be kept overnight, put it in a refrigerator but remember to allow it plenty of time to come back to room temperature before cooking.

To cook the *blini*, heat one or more small, heavy frying pans and brush them lightly with melted butter. Pour batter to a depth of about ¼ inch into the pan, swirl it to the edges, and cook over a steady, moderate heat until the underside of the pancake is golden and small bubbles are bursting through on top. Flip it over and cook until the second side is golden, too. Grease the pans before each addition of batter, and continue in the same way until all the batter is used.

To keep *blini* hot, stack them on a plate over a pot of simmering water and cover them loosely with a clean napkin.

Preparing the traditional accompaniments for caviar and *blini*—the separate bowls of sour cream, finely chopped hard-boiled egg, and finely chopped onion—can help to while away the time the batter takes to rise. Only a small jug of melted butter needs last-minute action.

*Foie gras,* the liver of fattened goose, is especially popular in France where the famous and notorious geese of Strasbourg are subjected to force-feeding and killed for their overdeveloped and mouth-watering livers. *Foie gras* is on the Christmas table of every Frenchman who esteems it and can pay the always high asking price. There are few places outside France where uncooked *foie gras* can be obtained. But the familiar round cream-colored earthenware pots, and cans shaped like long, inverted loaves of bread, are in good food shops the world over. Preserved *foie gras* is sold in three basic grades: *au naturel* is natural cooked liver with a little seasoning; *bloc* means cooked *foie gras* pressed with extra fat or a little stuffing; *purée, mousse,* and *crème de foie gras* should be at least 75% cooked goose liver stretched with chicken or pork. Truffles are sometimes included with any of the three preparations.

Hot fresh toast may be served with all types of *foie gras* served straight from the pot, or, if it is canned, whole or sliced on a plate. *Foie gras au naturel* can be baked in a raised pie crust with a protective coating of additional filling, and all types can be baked inside a loaf of melting *brioche* dough.

Cured and smoked hams, eaten raw, are a much sought-after delicacy wherever they are still made by traditional methods. They are becoming progressively more difficult to find, however, even locally, and few ever reach the shops at all. In some villages in Cyprus an unusual ham, *hiromeri,* akin to Parma ham but with an even stronger flavor, is served at Christmas. A leg of pork is soaked in a wine brine for 4 to 6 weeks and then pressed to about a quarter of its original volume before being smoked in the chimney of the house all winter. *Hiromeri* is made in the autumn, and for Christmas it is the *hiromeri* from the previous winter's smoking that is enjoyed. Yellow melons, tied up and hung from the rafters since summer, are cut down to compliment the pungent ham for the Christmas feast.

To make the best of cured meats of all kinds, never serve them straight from the refrigerator, but always at room temperature. If you want to make up portions more than a few minutes before serving, cover each plate with clear plastic wrap or aluminum foil to prevent the slices from drying out.

Smoked salmon is not at its best either when refrigerated and should also be served at room temperature, with lemon wedges and thin slices of buttered rye bread.

Oysters, too, could not be simpler. Open them with an oyster knife, or any strong, short-bladed knife, starting on the hinged side and working around the shell. Serve them very cold on their half shells, with lemon wedges and buttered rye bread.

Cooked oysters are much more popular in America than in Europe, although there are many English recipes dating from the days when they were cheap and plentiful. Oyster patties, individual pastry shells filled with poached oysters and a thick *béchamel* sauce and capped with a pastry lid, were a Victorian favorite. The pastry shells and lids were baked before being filled and the assembled patties popped into a slow oven for only 5 minutes to heat through.

Eliza Acton, whose major work, *Modern Cookery,* was first published in 1845, has been an often unacknowledged source for many later authors. She gives the following directions for scalloped oysters.

"Large coarse oysters should never be dressed in this way. Select small plump ones for the purpose, let them be opened carefully, give them a scald in their own liquor, wash them in it free from grit, and beard them neatly. Butter the scallop shells and shake some fine bread-crumbs over them; fill them with alternate layers of oysters, crumbs of bread, and fresh butter cut into small bits; pour in the oyster-liquor, after it has been strained, put a thick, smooth layer of bread-crumbs on the top, moisten them with clarified butter, place the shells in a Dutch oven before a clear fire, and turn them often until the tops are equally and lightly browned: send them immediately to table.

"Some persons like a little white pepper or cayenne, and a flavouring of nutmeg added to the oysters; others prefer pounded mace. French cooks recommend with them a mixture of minced mushrooms stewed in butter until quite tender, and sweet herbs finely chopped. The fish is sometimes laid into the shells after having been bearded only."

Miss Acton's instructions need no amplification. Small ramekins may, of course, be substituted for scallop shells, and in a modern gas or electric oven, the cooking time would be about 5 or 6 minutes at 400°F.

While on the subject of shellfish, Eliza Acton's recipe for potted lobster would be hard to better. This splendid dish, seldom seen on restaurant menus or at gourmet counters, makes the most of the lobster's own marvelous flavor.

"Separate carefully the flesh of fresh-boiled lobsters from the shells, and from the tough red skin of the tails, mince the fish up quickly with a very sharp knife, turn it immediately into a large mortar, and strew over it a mixed seasoning of fine cayenne, pounded mace, lightly grated nutmeg, and salt: this last should be sparingly used in the first instance, and it should be reduced to powder before it is added. Pound the lobsters to a perfect paste with from two to three ounces of firm new butter to each fish if of large size, but with less should it be small; and the lobster-coral previously rubbed through a sieve, or with a portion of it only, should any part of it be required for other purposes. When there is no coral, a fine colour may be given to the mixture by stewing the red skin of the tails *very* softly for ten or twelve minutes in part of the butter which is used for it, but which must be strained and left to become perfectly cold before it is mingled with the fish. The degree of seasoning given to the mixture can be regulated by the taste: but no flavour should predominate over that of the lobster itself; and for all delicate preparations, overspicing should be particularly avoided. A quart or more of fine brown shrimps, if very fresh and quickly shelled at the instant of using, may be chopped up and pounded with the lobsters with excellent effect. Before the mixture is taken from the mortar it should be placed in a cool larder, or set over ice for a short time, to render it firm before it is pressed into the potting-pans or moulds. In putting to these, be careful to press it into a compact, even mass; smooth the surface, run a little clarified butter over, when it is only *just liquid,* for if hot it would prevent the fish from keeping—and send the lobster to table, neatly garnished with light green foliage; or with ornamentally-cut paper fastened round the mould; or with a small damask napkin tastefully arranged about it."

Potted lobster can be prepared well in advance. It keeps perfectly in the refrigerator for several weeks with a covering of clear plastic wrap or aluminum foil. It is also suitable for deep freezing. Serve it with fresh toast and a bowl of lightly salted butter.

Christmas dinner in Chile begins with bite-sized chunks of freshly cooked lobster or king crab served cold on a crisp bed of chopped lettuce and topped with a classic olive-oil mayonnaise. *Locos con salsa verde,* abalone with a green sauce of oil, vinegar, onions, lemon juice, and herbs, is a traditional alternative to lobster or crab. Also traditional is the table setting. The centerpiece is a bowl of red carnations and sweet basil set on a snow-white cloth.

# FISH DISHES

Fish has a much more important place in traditional festive cooking than in modern everyday eating. And the number of fish recipes in this section reflects the place it once held. Despite the year-round availability of many fish varieties, less popular ones can be difficult to find even in major cities. If you cannot buy live carp or fresh pike do not be deterred from trying some of these splendid recipes with a more familiar fish like sole or turbot. In some cases you may think the result an improvement.

Many of the recipes for cold dishes make excellent first courses or attractive buffet choices, and nearly all of them will be popular with people who have an eye on their waistlines. In this chapter the number of servings given at the start of each recipe should be taken only as a rough guide. How much of each dish people eat will depend not just on their infinitely varied appetites, but on whether the dish is served alone or with others, and on what is to follow. The Swedish and Polish fish salads, for example, usually appear on the buffet table which begins the Christmas meal, and several will be offered together.

Fish is the focal point of the Christmas meal in many places where dinner or supper on Christmas Eve is the principal family celebration. The custom usually stems from the fast-day regulations of the Catholic Church, which, for many centuries, forbade the eating of meat on Christmas Eve. Now the dishes are often eaten as much for their Christmas associations as in strict observance of religious dietary regulations.

Only strong sentiment could account for the survival of some festive fish recipes. The Scandinavian specialty, lye fish, which is soaked for many days in a strongly alkaline solution of potash, is, even its admirers concede, an acquired taste. And mixed feelings about carp are evident in the instructions for its preparation. "Muddy" is the most usual description of its flavor, a drawback also acknowledged in the widespread practice of buying the fish live and giving it the run of the family bath for several days to wash away the taste of pond and river.

## SILLSALLAD
### Herring Salad

{SWEDEN}                                    TO SERVE 6 TO 8

| | |
|---|---|
| *1 large salt herring* | *1 medium eating apple* |
| *¾ pound potatoes, boiled* | *4 tablespoons wine vinegar* |
| *¾ pound pickled beets* | *2 tablespoons sugar* |
| *2 ounces pickled gherkins* | *White pepper to taste* |
| *1 small onion* | *½ cup heavy cream* |

**FOR THE GARNISH**

*2 hard-boiled eggs*
*Chopped parsley*

Soak the herring in cold water for at least 12 hours.

Clean and fillet the fish and dry with paper towels. Dice the herring, potatoes, beets, and gherkins. Peel and dice the onion. Peel, core, and dice the apple. Mix all these carefully together.

Mix together the vinegar, 2 tablespoons water, sugar, and white pepper, and stir this dressing gently into the herring and vegetables. Whip the cream and fold it into the salad.

*Sillsallad* can be heaped in a bowl to serve, or molded and chilled. Either way, garnish it with sliced or chopped hard-boiled eggs and chopped parsley. Pass separately a bowl of stiffly beaten sour cream.

## ŚLEDZIE W ŚMIETANIE
*Herrings with Apple and Cream*

[POLAND]                                             TO SERVE 4 TO 6

| | |
|---|---|
| *1 pound salt herrings* | *Salt to taste* |
| *1 small onion* | *Sugar to taste* |
| *1 medium, hard eating apple* | *Lemon juice to garnish* |
| *¼ cup heavy cream* | *Chopped parsley* |
| *¼ cup light cream* | |

Soak the herrings in cold water for at least 12 hours.

Clean and fillet the fish and dry them with paper towels. Cut the filets into diagonal strips and arrange them on a dish. Peel and chop the onion fine. Peel, core, and coarse-grate the apple. Whip together the heavy and light cream. Mix the onion and apple with the cream and season the dressing to taste with salt, sugar, and lemon juice. Pour the dressing over the herrings and sprinkle the dish with chopped parsley. It is ready to serve at once.

## INLAGD SILL
*Pickled Salt Herrings*

[SWEDEN]                                             TO SERVE 4

*1 large salt herring*

**FOR THE DRESSING**

*1 small onion, chopped*
*6 white peppercorns, crushed*
*6 whole allspice, crushed*
*½ cup white wine vinegar*
*¼ cup sugar*

**FOR THE GARNISH**

*1 small onion, sliced in rings*
*Fresh dill or chives*

Clean and fillet the herring and soak it overnight in cold water.

Drain and dry the fish. Cut the filets into narrow, diagonal slices and reassemble the pieces on a shallow plate to look like the whole fish.

To make the dressing, mix the onion, peppercorns, and allspice together with the vinegar, 2 tablespoons water, and sugar. Pour the dressing over the fish and garnish the dish with onion rings and sprigs of fresh dill or chopped chives.

Allow the dish to marinate in the refrigerator for 3 or 4 hours before serving.

## SYLTESILD
### Pickled Herrings

{DENMARK}                                          TO SERVE 12 TO 16

*16 fresh herrings*  
*4 medium onions, sliced*  
*into thin rings*  
*1¼ ounces pickling spice*  
*mixture*

*3¾ cups white wine*  
*vinegar*  
*⅓ cup brown sugar*

Clean and fillet the herrings and soak the filets overnight in cold water.

Drain the fish and cut the filets into bite-sized pieces. Cover the bottom of a large earthenware dish with a layer of the herring pieces topped by a layer of onion rings. Sprinkle with pickling spice. Continue layering and seasoning until all the herring, onion, and spice are used up.

Combine the vinegar with 3¾ cups water and the sugar and pour over the fish. Cover the dish tightly and put it in a cool place for 3 days. On the third day, stir the herrings gently with a wooden spoon. Cover the dish again, and allow the fish to marinate for at least another day before serving.

These herrings keep well, and in Denmark large batches are often prepared at the end of November so that they will be at their best during the Christmas holiday.

To serve, drain as many pieces as are required and arrange them in a shallow dish.

## ŚLEDZIE MARYNOWANE
### Pickled Herrings

{POLAND}                                    TO SERVE 4 TO 6

*1 pound fresh herrings*
*Salt to taste*
*3 tablespoons vegetable oil*

**FOR THE MARINADE**

*1 bay leaf*                    *1 ounce carrot, sliced*
*1 teaspoon sugar*             *1 ounce parsley root, sliced*
*1 teaspoon salt*                *( or chopped parsley*
*½ cup wine vinegar*            *leaves)*
*1 ounce onion, sliced*

Fillet, wash, and dry the herrings. Salt the pieces of fish. Heat the oil in a heavy-bottomed pan and fry the herrings until the flesh is just firm and lightly cooked.

Boil together in a small pot ½ cup water, bay leaf, sugar, and salt for about 2 minutes. Remove the pot from the heat and add the vinegar and vegetables.

Arrange the herring filets in a glass or pottery jar and pour in the marinade to cover them. Leave the jar, covered, in a cool place for at least a week.

To serve the herrings, arrange the pieces of fish, either whole or cut into slices, on a dish and pour over them a little of the strained marinade.

## ŚLEDZIE W OLIWIE
### Herrings in Oil

{POLAND}                                    TO SERVE 4 TO 6

*1 pound salt herrings*
*2 tablespoons mild mustard*
*3 large onions, sliced into thin rings*
*½ cup olive oil*

**FOR THE GARNISH**

*Chopped parsley*

Soak the herrings in cold water for at least 12 hours. Clean and fillet the fish and dry them with paper towels.

Spread the herring filets with mustard. Roll each filet neatly and secure the roll with a wooden toothpick or cocktail stick.

Arrange the herring rolls and onion rings in alternate layers in a glass or pottery jar. Pour in olive oil to cover the herrings and onions, and leave them in a cool place for at least a week.

Serve the herrings from the jar with some of the onion and a garnish of freshly chopped parsley.

In Fiji, where open-air Christmas feasting centers on an enormous pit barbecue called a *lovo,* and the celebrations last well into the night, *kokoda* is one of the cold side dishes usually served.

## *KOKODA*
### *Marinated Raw Fish*

{FIJI}                                           TO SERVE 6 TO 8

*6 lemons*
*1 tablespoon salt*
*2 pounds white-fleshed fish*
*   —haddock or gray*
*      mullet*
*2 large carrots, grated*
*1 bunch scallions, chopped*
*      fine*

*1 large green bell pepper,*
*      seeded and chopped*
*      fine*
*2 large tomatoes, seeded and*
*      chopped fine*
*2 fresh coconuts, chopped,*
*      plus coconut milk*
*Cayenne pepper to taste*

Squeeze the juice from all 6 lemons and strain into a deep bowl. Add the salt.

Skin and bone the fish and cut it into slices about ¼ inch thick. Soak the fish in the salted lemon juice for at least 4 hours. Overnight is fine. Drain the fish and add the vegetables to it.

Make coconut cream by putting the chopped coconut flesh into a blender or liquidizer with the coconut milk and enough warm water to make 2 cups. Strain the resulting liquid through a fine sieve. Press through all the cream and discard the residue.

Add the coconut cream to the fish and vegetables and chill the mixture. Sprinkle with cayenne pepper before serving.

## KOCSONYÁS PONTY
### Jellied Carp

{HUNGARY}                                    TO SERVE 12 TO 16

| | |
|---|---|
| *6–8 pounds carp, preferably* | *3 large green bell peppers* |
| *a whole fish* | *3 large tomatoes* |
| *3 large onions, chopped* | *Salt to taste* |
| *coarse* | *3 eggs, hard-boiled and* |
| *1 tablespoon paprika* | *sliced* |

Clean and fillet the carp. Put the head, bones, and roe into a saucepan with just enough water to cover and bring the stock to the boil. Skim the liquid. Add the onions, the paprika, and 2 bell peppers and 2 tomatoes, seeds removed and roughly chopped. Add salt to taste and simmer this stock for about 15 minutes.

Cut the fish filets into pieces weighing about 5 ounces each, and poach them very gently in the simmering stock until they are cooked through.

Carefully lift out the fish and arrange the pieces on a shallow serving dish just big enough to present the fish in one layer without too much space around it.

Strain the stock through a fine sieve lined with two layers of cheese-cloth to remove the fat, and reserve the roe. Refrigerate.

When the stock is on the point of jelling, set aside enough to glaze the decorations, and pour the rest over the fish. Refrigerate the dish until the jelly has set firm before decorating it with slices of hard-boiled egg, green pepper, tomato, and pieces of the reserved roe. Melt the remaining jelly and glaze the decorations with it.

## SZCZUPAK W GALAIECIE
### Pike in Aspic

[POLAND]                                                    TO SERVE 6

2 pounds pike, preferably a          2 bay leaves
    whole fish                          5 black peppercorns,
1 large onion, chopped                   crushed
1 large carrot, sliced               Salt to taste

**FOR THE ASPIC**

2½ cups fish stock
1 tablespoon vinegar
2 egg whites
1 package gelatin

**FOR THE GARNISH**

2 eggs, hard-boiled and sliced
1 large carrot, cooked
2 tablespoons peas, cooked

Fillet the pike and cut the filets into slices about 1½ inches thick.

Put the fish trimmings in a large saucepan with 3¼ pints water and bring to the boil. Skim the stock and add onion, carrot, bay leaves, and peppercorns. Simmer the stock for about 15 minutes, then strain it. Salt to taste and return to the saucepan.

Poach the pieces of pike filet in gently simmering stock for 15 to 20 minutes. Cool the fish in the stock before lifting it out carefully and removing as many bones as possible without breaking the pieces. Arrange the fish on a shallow serving dish just big enough to present it in one layer without too much space around it.

To make the aspic, strain 2½ cups of stock through a fine sieve lined with cheesecloth into a saucepan. Add the vinegar and egg whites and whisk together. Slowly heat the mixture to the boiling point, then set it aside for about ½ hour.

Remove the froth from the aspic mixture and strain it again through a lined sieve. Dissolve the gelatin in a small amount of stock and add it to the mixture. Check the seasoning, adding more salt and vinegar to taste. Refrigerate.

When the aspic is on the point of jelling, set aside enough to glaze the decorations and pour the rest over the fish. Refrigerate the dish until the aspic has set firmly before decorating it with slices of hard-boiled egg, cooked carrot and peas. Melt the remaining aspic and glaze the decorations with it.

## KARP SMAŻONY
### Fried Carp

{POLAND}                                                    TO SERVE 4

| | |
|---|---|
| 1½ pounds carp, preferably a whole fish | Pepper |
| | Flour |
| Salt | Vegetable oil |

Scale and fillet the carp and cut the filets into diagonal portions. Sprinkle the fish with salt, pepper, and flour, and fry it on both sides in hot oil until the flesh is cooked through.

Arrange the pieces on a warmed plate in the shape of a whole fish, and serve it with boiled potatoes.

Traditionally, this is the main hot dish of the meal and is served after the cold fish dishes and soup. To avoid a midmeal dash to the kitchen, the fish is sometimes fried lightly on both sides until golden in advance and finished in a slow oven while the earlier courses are eaten.

In Austria carp filets are dipped in egg and bread crumbs before frying. The head, skin, and bones of the fish are used to make stock for a soup which, with additional vegetables and the fish roe, is another traditional Christmas Eve dish.


Eels are almost compulsory Christmas eating in parts of France and Italy, and there are many recipes for their preparation. Neapolitans eat them stuffed and fried accompanied by *insalata di rinforz* (see page 132). Steaks of skinned and filleted eel are flattened and stuffed with a mixture of hard-boiled egg yolks, butter, parsley, and onion, all bound with raw egg yolk. The steaks are then tied to hold the stuffing in, and fried in butter and lemon juice. When they have cooled, the threads are untied, and the pieces of eel are dipped in batter and fried in oil until golden.

In Rome they are more likely to be stewed with peas.

## ANGUILLE IN UMIDO ALLA ROMANA
### Roman Stewed Eels

{ITALY}                                                    TO SERVE 4

| | |
|---|---|
| 1 pound small eels | Pepper to taste |
| 3 tablespoons olive oil | 1 1/4 cups dry white wine |
| 1 clove garlic, minced | 1 tablespoon tomato paste |
| 4 tablespoons shallots or | 1 cup peas, fresh or frozen |
| onion, chopped fine | 2 tablespoons fish or chicken |
| Salt to taste | stock |

Cut the eels into 3-inch slices and discard the heads. Heat the oil in a heavy-bottomed pot and fry the garlic and shallots until lightly browned. Add the pieces of eel, season with salt and pepper, and simmer, uncovered, until the liquid from the eels has evaporated. Add the wine, tomato paste, peas, and stock and simmer the stew for about another 15 minutes, or until both the eels and peas are tender. Add more stock if needed during the final cooking.

Serve the stewed eels in warmed soup plates with plenty of fresh, crusty white bread.

The English language edition of *Larousse Gastronomique* gives more than fifty recipes for eels, including *anguille à la provençale,* a magnificent eel stew with tomatoes, garlic, and black olives. But for an older recipe for this traditional Christmas dish let us leave the great chefs and turn to Elizabeth David's *French Country Cooking* and her source, Madame Léon Daudet in *La France à Table,* 1935.

"In a sauté pan put a little olive oil with a few strips of bacon, and let them turn very lightly brown. Next add about 1 pound each of sliced onions and 1 pound of the white part of leeks cut in rounds. Let these brown slightly and then add 1 pound of tomatoes cut in pieces and 3 or 4 cloves of garlic crushed, a bay leaf, salt, pepper, and a good pinch of saffron. On top of this put a layer of sliced raw potatoes and the eels cut in thick slices. Add water or white veal stock to cover.

"Boil rapidly for 20 minutes, and season with a good measure of freshly ground pepper from the mill before serving. Pour the stock from the *catigau* over pieces of French bread in a deep dish and serve the eels and vegetables on another dish."

The unlikely combination of beer and gingerbread in this classic German recipe makes a rich, dark sauce which is slightly sweet. Traditionally, each member of the family sharing the Christmas Eve carp saves one of the fish's large scales to bring luck in the coming year. (German gingerbread is dark, dense, and fairly sweet.)

## KARPFEN IN BIER
### Carp in Beer

[GERMANY]                                          TO SERVE 6

| | |
|---|---|
| 1 3–4 pound carp | 2 cloves |
| 3 tablespoons white wine | Salt to taste |
|    vinegar | Pepper to taste |
| 2 medium carrots, chopped | 6 ounces gingerbread |
| 1 large leek, chopped | 3¾ cups dark beer or |
| 1 large onion, chopped |    brown ale |
| 1 bay leaf | 1 large lemon |

Clean the carp but do not scale it. Soak the fish in cold water with the vinegar for about 1 hour.

In a pot or casserole big enough to hold the fish, put the vegetables, the bay leaf, cloves, salt, and pepper. Add about 2½ cups of water, and bring to the boil. Cover, and simmer the stock for about 1 hour.

Break the gingerbread into cubes and soak it in one-third of the beer.

Drain the carp and put it into the simmering stock. Add the juice of the lemon, reserving the rind, and the rest of the beer. Cover and cook gently for about 20 minutes or until the carp is tender. Lift the fish out carefully and keep it warm on a serving dish.

Strain the stock and return it to the pot. Add the soaked gingerbread and boil this mixture briskly until it has reduced to about half the original quantity.

Strain the sauce over the carp and garnish it with curls of lemon rind.

Lye fish is a very old and much-loved Christmas food of Scandinavia. It is called Lipeäkala in Finland, Lutfisk in Sweden, and Lutefisk in Norway, and traditionally its preparation is begun in early December.

First dried cod, or sometimes pike, is cut into large pieces which are skinned and beaten. They are then soaked for a week in cold water. A lye solution, made of birchwood ash, and slaked lime wrapped in a cloth and placed in a large tub of water, is boiled up, cooled, and poured over the fish. The fish is left in this mixture for several days before spending at least another week in fresh cold water.

It must be a relief to modern housewives that lye fish is now prepared commercially, and even outside Scandinavia can sometimes be found in specialty food stores.

Note: Do not cook lye fish in an aluminum pot or serve it on silver as it will discolor both metals.

## KEITETTY LIPEÄKALA
### Holiday Lye Fish

{FINLAND}                                      TO SERVE 4 TO 6

2 pounds lye fish
2 tablespoons salt

**FOR THE SAUCE**

2 tablespoons butter          Salt to taste
1/4 cup flour                 White pepper, freshly
1 cup light cream, fish or        ground, to taste
    chicken stock

**FOR THE GARNISH**

1 teaspoon crushed allspice
1/2 cup melted butter

Cut the fish into serving pieces and tie loosely in a piece of cheesecloth or a tea towel.

Bring 5 pints of water to the boil in a large pot. Add the fish and the salt. When the water is boiling again, lower the heat to a simmer and cook the fish for about 10 minutes. Drain the fish and arrange it on a warmed serving dish. Keep warm.

To make the sauce, melt the butter in a small saucepan and stir in the flour. Cook the *roux* for a minute or two without allowing it to color. Gradually add the cream or stock, stirring constantly. Cook the sauce, which should be thick and smooth, on low heat for a few minutes. Season it to taste with salt and white pepper.

Sprinkle the fish with crushed allspice and serve the white sauce and melted butter separately.

Boiled potatoes and peas are the usual accompaniments for this dish, which can also be baked instead of boiled.

## LUTFISK KOKT I UGN
### Oven-Baked Lye Fish

[SWEDEN]                                           TO SERVE 6 TO 8

> *3 pounds lye fish*
> *1 tablespoon salt*

**F O R   T H E   S A U C E** (see above for preparation)

*4 tablespoons butter*          *Salt to taste*
*½ cup flour*                   *White pepper, freshly*
*1¼ cups milk*                     *ground, to taste*

**F O R   T H E   G A R N I S H**

*1–2 teaspoons crushed allspice*
*¾ cup melted butter*

Preheat oven to 400°F. Cut the fish into serving pieces. Place in a buttered baking dish and sprinkle with salt. Cover with aluminum foil and bake for 30 to 40 minutes. When it is cooked, pour off any liquid and serve it with a sprinkling of crushed allspice, melted butter, and white sauce.

The richest of the traditional carp dishes comes from Czechoslovakia, where it is prepared with dried fruits, almonds, and beer, and from Hungary, where it is baked with sour cream and potatoes.

## KAPR NA ĆERNO
### Carp in Black Sauce

[CZECHOSLOVAKIA]                              TO SERVE 4 TO 6

2 tablespoons sweet butter
1 stalk celery, chopped
1 large carrot, chopped
1 medium parsnip, chopped
1 large onion, chopped
2 tablespoons superfine
   granulated sugar
5 ounces red wine vinegar
2 bay leaves
Pinch thyme
5 black peppercorns,
   crushed
5 whole allspice berries,
   crushed
1 teaspoon chopped lemon
   peel

2 tablespoons red currant
   jelly
3 ounces light beer
4 gingersnaps, crushed
1 tablespoon light brown
   sugar
Salt to taste
6 carp steaks, about 1 inch
   thick
10 prunes, pitted and
   chopped
¼ cup sultana raisins,
   chopped
1 tablespoon almonds,
   slivered

FOR THE GARNISH

2 lemons, cut into wedges

Melt the butter in a heavy-bottomed pot. Add the vegetables, lower the heat, cover the pot, and cook gently for about 10 minutes.

In another heavy-bottomed pot dissolve the sugar in 1 tablespoon water over low heat, then bring to the boil and continue boiling until the sugar forms a dark caramel. Add the vinegar and keep the mixture boiling until it has reduced to about 4 tablespoons. Add 2½ cups water, bay leaves, thyme, peppercorns, allspice, lemon peel, red currant jelly, and the cooked vegetables. Bring to the boil, lower the heat, and simmer the mixture, partially covered, for about 30 minutes. Add the beer, gingersnaps, and light brown sugar. Increase the heat and cook the mixture, uncovered, for about 5 minutes, or until it thickens a little. Strain the sauce through a sieve, discarding any vegetables that cannot be pressed through easily. Add salt to taste.

Preheat oven to 375°F. Butter an oven-to-table dish large enough to take the fish steaks in one layer. Arrange the carp in the dish and pour the sauce over it. Sprinkle on the prunes, raisins, and almonds. Bake the fish for about 20 minutes or until just firm, basting once or twice during cooking.

Serve the fish directly from the baking dish garnished with lemon wedges.

Hungarian hospitality can have the overwhelming warmth of a hug from a friendly bear. You need to be hungry to enjoy it. Servings are usually substantial, as is demonstrated by the following recipe for a dish of Rascian carp as made by the renowned Hungarian chef Karoly Gundel.

## RÁCZPONTY
### Rascian Carp

[HUNGARY]                                                    TO SERVE 6

6 pounds carp, preferably
   a whole fish
¾ pound bacon
1 tablespoon salt
1 tablespoon paprika
2 pounds potatoes, parboiled
   and sliced
2 large onions, sliced into
   thin rings

2 large tomatoes, sliced
3 large green bell peppers,
   sliced
6 tablespoons melted butter
1½ cups sour cream
2 tablespoons flour

Preheat oven to 375°F. Scale and wash the carp and split it in two. Divide the fish into 6 pieces and score them deeply. Press thin slices of bacon into the gashes and sprinkle the fish with salt and paprika.

Butter an oven-to-table dish large enough to hold the fish in one layer. Cover the bottom with the sliced potatoes. Lay the fish on top of the potatoes and cover it with the sliced onion rings, tomatoes, and peppers. Pour over the melted butter and bake for 30 minutes, or until the vegetables are half cooked.

Mix the cream with the flour and pour this mixture over the fish. Sprinkle the top with a little paprika and bake it for another 30 minutes.

Serve the fish, which needs no accompaniments, straight from the baking dish.

Baked sterlet (a small sturgeon) or pike with a tarragon sauce is another favorite dish for Christmas Eve supper in Hungary. Fresh tarragon can be difficult to find in summer, never mind midwinter, but as its true flavor survives drying remarkably well dried tarragon will do quite well for this recipe. Whole tarragon leaves pickled in a weak solution of vinegar and packed in glass bottles can also be found in some specialty stores, and if you grow your own, tarragon leaves freeze very well, particularly when chopped and mixed with butter.

Trout baked this way is also delicious.

## TÁRKONYOS HAL
### Tarragon Fish

{HUNGARY}                                              TO SERVE 4

> 4 pounds sterlet or pike, preferably 2 whole fish
> Juice of 1 large lemon
> Salt to taste
> 4 tablespoons butter

**FOR THE SAUCE**

> 2 tablespoons butter            Tarragon to taste
> 1 tablespoon flour              Sugar to taste
> 1 cup fish or chicken stock     Salt to taste
> 2 tablespoons mild wine
>     vinegar

Preheat oven to 375°F. Lay the cleaned fish, complete with heads and tails (unless these offend you), in a buttered oven-to-table dish. Pour on the lemon juice, sprinkle with salt, and dot with butter. Bake the fish for about 30 minutes.

While the fish is baking make the sauce. Melt the butter in a small saucepan and stir in the flour. Gradually add the stock, stirring constantly. Stir in the vinegar and tarragon. (The amount of tarragon to use is very much a matter of taste. The herb's strong anise-like flavor will vary greatly according to the variety, where it was grown, and whether it is fresh, dried, frozen, or pickled.)

Season the sauce, which should be fairly thin, with sugar and salt to taste.

Pour the sauce over the fish and serve it straight from the baking dish. Floury mashed potatoes are the best accompaniment for this distinctively flavored dish.

Sea bream (porgy) is traditional Christmas Eve fare all over Spain and each region has its own special way of cooking the fish. In the Basque country it is grilled over a wood fire with lemon, olive oil, and garlic. In Asturias it will usually be cooked in a casserole with white wine, garlic, pine kernels, olive oil, lemon, onions, and parsley. Olive oil and garlic are essential ingredients in much Spanish cooking, and for the baked sea bream of New Castille, no substitute will capture the flavor of Spain.

## BESUGO ASADO A LA MADRILEÑA
### Baked Sea Bream

{SPAIN}                                          TO SERVE 3 TO 4

| | |
|---|---|
| 3 pounds sea bream (porgy), preferably a whole fish | 2 cloves garlic, crushed or minced |
| 2 lemons, preferably thin-skinned, sliced | Chopped parsley to taste |
| 4 tablespoons olive oil | 1 bay leaf, crumbled |
| ½ cup dry white wine or dry sherry | Salt to taste |
| | Black pepper, freshly ground, to taste |

Preheat oven to 350°F. Clean the bream and leave it whole. Make diagonal cuts at 1-inch intervals on one side of the fish and put a slice of lemon in each cut. Put about 1 tablespoon of the olive oil in the bottom of a shallow oven-to-table dish and lay the fish, cut side up, in the dish. Pour over the rest of the olive oil and the wine or sherry.

Sprinkle the fish with the garlic, parsley, bay leaf, and a generous seasoning of salt and freshly ground pepper.

Bake the fish for about an hour. Serve directly from the baking dish with fresh crusty bread and a crisp green salad dressed with olive oil and lemon juice.

So many people are impatient with fish cooked on the bone that we are sometimes wary of putting any fish in front of guests except the ubiquitous shrimp cocktail and its near relatives. Two splendid recipes from eastern Europe solve this problem beautifully. The first, a soufflé of pike, comes from Poland. It is ideal for small lunch or supper parties and may, of course, be made with almost any fish you choose. The second is the much better known Russian *kulebiaka*, a crusty fish pie that has the uncommon distinction of being elegant on a heroic scale—which is just as well, since the work involved is considerable.

## SUFLET ZE SZCZUPAKA
### Pike Soufflé

[POLAND]                              TO SERVE 4 TO 6

| | |
|---|---|
| *1 pound pike* | *6 tablespoons butter* |
| *½ teaspoon salt* | *¾ cup flour* |
| *A few black peppercorns,* | *3 large eggs, separated* |
| *crushed* | *A pinch nutmeg* |
| *1 bay leaf* | *Salt to taste* |
| *½ teaspoon ground mace* | *Pepper to taste* |
| *5 ounces milk* | |

Preheat oven to 400° F. Put the pike into a pot, cover it with water, and add the salt, peppercorns, bay leaf, and mace. Bring to the boil slowly, reduce the heat, and simmer the fish gently until it is cooked through, about 15 minutes. Strain and reserve the stock.

When the fish is cool enough to handle, remove as many of the bones as possible. Put the flesh in a blender with about 5 ounces of the reserved fish stock, and blend it thoroughly so that any small bones remaining in the flesh are rendered harmless.

Add another 5 ounces of stock to the milk. Melt the butter in a small, heavy-bottomed saucepan and stir in the flour. Cook the *roux* over low heat, stirring constantly for about 2 minutes before gradually adding the fish and milk mixture. Cook the sauce for another 2 minutes over low heat, then remove the saucepan from the heat.

Beat the egg yolks well, then beat them into the sauce with the puréed fish. Season the mixture well with nutmeg, salt, and pepper.

Beat the egg whites until stiff and fold them gently but thoroughly into the fish mixture. Turn the soufflé into a 2-quart soufflé dish which has been well-buttered and dusted with dry bread crumbs (this gives the mixture something to bite on as it rises).

Bake in the center of the preheated hot oven for about 45 minutes, or until the soufflé is well risen and golden.

Serve it immediately with a crisp green salad and crusty bread or rolls.

*Kulebiaka* is a creation for which literally hundreds of varying recipes exist. Like so many long-established favorites, they differ not only from region to region but from family to family. The following recipe is for a salmon *kulebiaka* made with shortcrust pastry and explains the method in detail. There are puff pastry versions, too, and any number of possible fillings, from an inexpensive and delicious everyday cabbage with hard-boiled egg and sour-cream mixture to the festive fish kulebiaka below.

## SALMON KULEBIAKA

{RUSSIA}                                              TO SERVE 8 TO 10

**FOR THE PASTRY**

*4 cups flour*
*1 teaspoon salt*
*1 cup sweet butter*
*6 tablespoons vegetable fat*
*4–5 ounces ice water*

**FOR THE FILLING**

1¾ cups dry white wine
4 medium onions
1 stalk celery, chopped
    coarse
1 large carrot, chopped
    coarse
10 black peppercorns,
    crushed
4 teaspoons salt
2½ pounds fresh salmon,
    preferably in one piece
8 tablespoons sweet butter
½ pound mushrooms,
    sliced thin

2½ tablespoons lemon juice
Black pepper, freshly
    ground, to taste
Scant ½ cup long-grain rice
1 cup fish or chicken stock
4 tablespoons fresh dill
    leaves, chopped, or 1
    generous teaspoon
    dried dill
3 eggs, hard-boiled and
    chopped

**FOR THE GLAZE**

1 egg yolk
1 tablespoon light cream

To make the pastry, sift the flour and salt into a large, cold bowl. Cut the butter and vegetable fat, which should preferably be chilled, into dice, and work the fats and flour together, using your fingertips or a pastry blender, until the mixture looks like fine bread crumbs. Sprinkle the mixture with 8 tablespoons of the ice water and gather it into a ball. If the dough seems too crumbly, add as much as required of the remaining ice water, a drop or two at a time. Divide the pastry into two equal balls, dust both pieces with flour, wrap them separately in waxed paper and refrigerate until firm, about 3 hours.

To make the salmon filling, boil together in a large pot 12½ cups water with the wine, 1 of the onions, coarsely chopped, the celery and carrot, the peppercorns, and about 2½ teaspoons of the salt. Lower the salmon into the boiling stock, reduce the heat to a simmer, and poach the fish until it is firm. This will take 8 to 10 minutes according to the thickness of the cut. Lift the fish out and, when it is cool enough to handle, separate it into small flakes, discarding skin and bones.

Now take a heavy frying pan and melt in it 2 tablespoons of the butter. Fry the mushrooms in the butter, stirring occasionally, until they are soft. Transfer the mushrooms to a bowl and mix them with the lemon juice, a pinch of salt, and a little freshly ground pepper.

Melt 4 more tablespoons of butter in the pan and all but 1 tablespoon of the remaining onions, finely chopped. Fry the onions until they are soft, but not brown. Season them with the remaining salt and a little pepper, and add them to the mushrooms.

Finally, melt the rest of the butter in the pan and fry the remaining tablespoon of finely chopped onion until it is soft, but not brown. Add the rice and stir it together with the onions until each grain is coated with butter. Now add the stock, bring the mixture to the boil, cover the pan tightly, reduce the heat to a simmer, and cook the rice for about 12 minutes or until the liquid is absorbed and the rice is tender. Remove the pan from the heat. Stir in the dill.

Combine the mushroom and onion mixture with the cooked salmon. Add the rice and the hard-boiled eggs. Mix them together gently with a fork and adjust the seasoning, remembering to season more generously if the pie is to be served cold.

To assemble the kulebiaka, roll out one ball of the pastry dough to about ⅛ inch thick on a floured surface, and trim it to a rectangle about 16 inches long by about 7 inches wide.

Butter a large, heavy baking sheet generously, and, lifting the pastry by draping it over the rolling pin, place it on the sheet, stretching it as little as possible. Mix the egg yolk and cream. Heap the salmon filling on to the pastry to within 1 inch of the edge and brush the bare edge with some of the egg-yolk and cream mixture.

Roll out the second ball of pastry dough to a rectangle about 18 inches long by about 9 inches wide and place it on top of the filling. Seal the edges firmly with your fingers, a fork, or a pastry cutter. Make 3 diagonal cuts in the top of the pie and decorate it with pastry trimmings. Brush the pie with the rest of the egg-yolk and cream mixture, and rest it in the refrigerator for about 20 minutes before baking.

Preheat oven to 400°F. Pour a teaspoonful of melted butter into each of the holes on top of the pie and bake it in the center of the oven for about 1 hour, or until the pastry is crisp and golden. (If it browns too quickly cover the pie loosely with foil for part of the baking time, but remove the covering for the last 10 minutes of cooking to crisp the pastry.)

Serve the kulebiaka immediately with a jug of hot melted butter or sour cream, or serve it cold with sour cream.

# ROASTS

Back in fifteenth-century England, swans and peacocks graced the festive tables of the rich and powerful. Dame Alice de Byrene was not, the records show, in the peacock-eating class, but 2 swans, 2 pigs, 12 geese, 2 joints of mutton, 24 capons, and 17 coneys were roasted for the feast she gave for 100 people on New Year's Day 1413. Maybe she did not like peacocks, for by all accounts they are not good eating.

Two hundred and fifty years later, for a Twelfth-Night feast held at Ingatestone Hall, the Essex home of Secretary of State Sir William Petrie, over 7 pounds of meat per head were served. The household books show that 100 diners were offered 9 pieces of boiled beef (about 20 pounds to a piece), 6 pieces of roast beef (30 pounds to a "livery" piece), a haunch and leg of pork, 2 legs of veal, a whole young pig, a loin and breast of veal, 2 rabbits, 10 beef, 2 mutton, and 4 venison pasties—all these were "very great"—3 geese, 2 capons, 2 partridges, a woodcock, 2 teal, and 12 larks, plus sauces, dressings, forcemeats, pastry, and bread. Caterers these days think in terms of 4- to 6-ounce portions.

Wild and tame fowl were both popular Christmas gifts and payments in the Middle Ages, and were often presented live to be kept in special pens and fed on such delicacies as raisins, white bread crumbs, and milk until they were needed in the kitchen. This custom, and the difficulties of housing and feeding, more than breeding stock of larger beasts through the winter months, set a pattern of Christmas eating which is followed to this day.

Roasting is an art few of us practice for everyday meals when time is short and large joints and big birds would break the family budget. So, to insure success, work out cooking times carefully by using the charts given with each group of recipes. The following checklist may also be useful.

- Roasting times are calculated for meat or poultry at room temperature, not straight from the refrigerator.
- Preheat the oven.
- Calculate cooking time on the oven-ready weight—this *includes stuffing*.
- Roasting is a dry-cooking method. Never cover a roast closely with foil or a lid which will prevent steam escaping. Even the largest turkey will not burn or dry out if it is covered with a double thickness of cheesecloth wrung out in water then dipped in melted butter and draped over the whole bird. Baste frequently, moistening the cheesecloth with pan juices every 15 to 20 minutes throughout cooking time.
- To test a roast, use a thin metal skewer and stick it into the thickest part of the meat. Pull it out and the color of the juices that flow from the hole will tell you whether or not it is done. Appropriate juice colors are given with the timing charts. Do not prick the meat too often or it will be less succulent.
- Rest roasts before carving. Leave them for at least 15 minutes in the oven with the heat turned off and the door open.
- Never overstuff poultry or it may burst in the oven.

No stuffing should be so aggressively flavored that it overwhelms the taste of the meat. In some cases the stuffing is intended only to flavor the flesh during cooking and not to be eaten at all. But usually the stuffing is food in its own right.

Recipes for stuffings have changed little over the centuries. Although white bread crumbs are specified in many recipes, crumbs from a whole-wheat loaf give a nuttier flavor and a rougher texture which you may prefer. An extra egg or two, beaten and added to a stuffing mixture, will bind it more thoroughly if a denser texture is wanted.

A trussed bird need not look as if it has been caught in a game of cat's cradle. Sew or skewer the large cavity firmly to prevent juices escaping, then tie the legs together with string and tie the string round the tail. Pull the neck skin gently down under the back and fasten it with metal skewers or wooden toothpicks. Cut off the wing tips for the stockpot.

Of all the domesticated birds, goose has the finest flavor. Its creamy white flesh cooks to a dark beige and has a rich, slightly gamey taste. One of the reasons the meat tastes so good is that goose is a fatty bird. Nowadays its fattiness is more often mentioned as a criticism, but it is an advantage, too. Goose is the original self-basting bird.

Turkeys have been around a long time in Europe, but geese are indigenous and their appearance on the Christmas table goes back still further. The Germans are especially attached to their festive goose, stuffing it with apples, nuts, raisins, and prunes. Irish and Polish cooks often use mashed potato stuffing flavored with onion and herbs (see page 62). Sage and onion stuffing (see page 62) is the best-known English recipe, and all these traditions have merged in American kitchens.

Although geese live to a great age, they are little use for eating when more than two years old. If you are buying a fresh goose, choose a young bird with soft feet and legs which still have a little down on them. Gray goose is favored in France, the larger white goose in England. Both are raised in North America where wild geese are still much more widely available than in Europe.

A goose usually weighs from 9 to 12 pounds. When shopping, allow about 1 pound per person. Frozen birds should be thawed slowly in the refrigerator for at least 24 hours.

I much prefer the slow-roasting method for goose. The meat is evenly cooked and more of the fat melts out. Prick the bird on the legs, sides, and lower breast with a sharp skewer or fork before roasting. Put it breast side up in a roasting pan for the first 15 minutes. Turn it breast side down for half the remaining cooking time, then breast side up again, raised on a rack, for the remainder. Basting is unnecessary. (Save the goose fat drippings for other dishes, especially a *cassoulet*.)

Your goose is cooked when the juices run a pale golden color. Test with a skewer inserted into the leg close to the body.

## TIMETABLE FOR ROASTING GOOSE (AVERAGE ONLY)

| WEIGHT OF BIRD (including stuffing) | SLOW-ROASTING METHOD 400°F          325°F | FAST-ROASTING METHOD 400°F |
|---|---|---|
| 6–8 pounds | First 15 minutes, then 3½–4 hours | 2½–2¾ hours |
| 8–10 pounds | First 15 minutes, then 4–4½ hours | 2¾–3 hours |
| 10–12 pounds | First 15 minutes, then 4½–5 hours | 3–3¼ hours |

Goose roasted in the fashion of the Normandy region of northern France is the finest recipe I have found. Blood puddings are a continuing part of French Christmas tradition, and this stuffing of black pudding, apples, and port makes a magnificent dish.

## OIE Á LA NORMANDE
### Goose with Black Pudding and Apples

[FRANCE]                                                    TO SERVE 6 TO 8

*1 8–10 pound goose*

**FOR THE STUFFING**

*1½ pounds blood (black)*          *5 tablespoons port wine*
    *puddings\**                       *Salt to taste*
*1 goose liver*                      *Black pepper, freshly*
*1–2 cloves garlic, crushed*            *ground, to taste*
*2 large eating apples, peeled*      *¾ cup oatmeal (optional)*
    *and cored*

\* Available at charcuteries or specialty food shops.

**FOR THE GARNISH**

*4 pounds eating apples, pealed and cored and chopped coarse*

Skin the puddings and break them into a large bowl, picking out any visible pieces of white fat. Add the goose liver and garlic and pound the mixture smooth. Grate the apples coarsely into the bowl. Add the port, season with salt and freshly ground pepper, and mix all the ingredients thoroughly together.

Blood puddings vary enormously in the amount of liquid they will absorb. If the stuffing mixture appears too mushy, add up to ¾ cup medium oatmeal (ground oatmeal, not oat flakes or rolled oats). This will swell during cooking, so it is particularly important not to overfill the bird if oatmeal is used.

Stuff the goose loosely with this mixture, truss, and roast as directed on page 57.

To make the purée, put the apples into a large pot, add ½ cup water, and bring to the boil. Cover and cook gently until the apples are tender. Blend, liquefy, or sieve the cooked apples and keep warm until needed.

Serve the goose on a bed of hot, unsweetened apple purée.

## GAASESTEG MED AEBLER OG SVEDSKER
### Goose with Apple and Prune Stuffing

{DENMARK}                                        TO SERVE 6 TO 8

1 8–10 pound goose
½ lemon

### FOR THE STUFFING

1½ pounds pitted prunes,          Salt to taste
   chopped                        Black pepper, freshly
2 pounds cooking apples,             ground, to taste
   peeled, cored, and
   chopped

### FOR THE STOCK

Giblets, neck, feet, and wing tips of 1 goose
1 medium onion, chopped
1 medium carrot, scraped and chopped

### FOR THE GRAVY

1 tablespoon cornstarch          Salt to taste
2 tablespoons red currant        Black pepper, freshly
   jelly                            ground, to taste

Remove any excess fat from the cavity of the goose and rub inside with ½ lemon. Mix the prunes and apples together with a seasoning of salt and freshly ground pepper, and pack this simple stuffing into the goose. Truss the bird and roast as directed on page 57.

Make the giblet stock while the goose is in the oven. Put the giblets, neck, feet, and wing tips into a large pot with the onion, carrot, and 2 cups water. Bring to the boil, skim, and reduce the heat. Cover and simmer gently for about an hour. Strain and reserve the stock. Discard the giblets, goose parts, and vegetables.

Make the gravy while the goose is resting after roasting. Pour most of the fat from the roasting pan into a bowl. Pour the reserved stock into the roasting pan, and stir over a low heat to dissolve any hardened pan juices. Stir in the cornstarch blended with a little cold water. Cook for 2 or 3 minutes, then stir in the red currant jelly. Season the gravy to taste with salt and freshly ground pepper. Strain it into a gravy boat.

Red cabbage and sugar-browned potatoes are the traditional accompaniments to the Danish goose.

A typical German recipe for a Christmas goose also includes apple.

## GÄNSEBRATEN MIT ÄPFELN, ROSINEN, UND NÜSSEN
### *Goose with Apple, Raisin, and Nut Stuffing*

{GERMANY}                                    TO SERVE 6 TO 8

*1 8–10 pound goose*

### FOR THE STUFFING

*1 cup seedless raisins*
*3 tablespoons butter*
*1 goose liver, chopped*
    *coarse*
*1 large onion, chopped fine*
*2⅔ cups soft white bread*
    *crumbs*
*3 medium cooking apples,*
    *peeled, cored, and*
    *chopped*

*½ cup blanched almonds or*
    *hazelnuts, chopped*
    *coarse*
*3 tablespoons chopped*
    *parsley*
*1 teaspoon dried marjoram*
*1 teaspoon salt*
*Black pepper, freshly*
    *ground, to taste*

Put the raisins in a bowl and cover them with boiling water. Set them aside to plump up.

Melt the butter in a small saucepan and fry the liver until it is just firm. Take the liver from the pan and set it aside to cool. Fry the onion in the butter remaining in the pan until it is soft and transparent. Do not let the onion brown.

Chop the liver very fine and put it into a large mixing bowl with the fried onion and butter. Add the bread crumbs, apples, nuts, drained raisins, herbs, and a generous seasoning of salt and freshly ground pepper. Mix these ingredients well and check the seasoning.

Stuff the goose loosely with this mixture. Truss and roast as directed on page 57.

Red cabbage, sauerkraut, or noodles are usually served with goose in Germany. In Czechoslovakia sauerkraut is used for the stuffing. Its sharp flavor goes well with the rich goose flesh.

### PECENA HUSA SE ZELIM
#### Goose with Sauerkraut Stuffing

[CZECHOSLOVAKIA]                                        TO SERVE 4 TO 6

*1 6–8 pound goose*

#### FOR THE STUFFING

*2 tablespoons butter*  
*2 medium onions, chopped*  
    *fine*  
*2½ cups sauerkraut, well-*  
    *drained*  
*½ teaspoon caraway seeds*  

*6 juniper berries*  
*1 large potato*  
*½ teaspoon salt*  
*Black pepper, freshly*  
    *ground, to taste*

Melt the butter in a small saucepan and fry the onions gently until they are soft and transparent but not brown.

Put the sauerkraut into a mixing bowl with the onions, butter, caraway seeds, and juniper berries. Peel the potato and grate it coarsely into the bowl. Season the mixture with the salt and pepper and combine all the ingredients thoroughly.

Stuff the goose with this mixture. Truss and roast as directed on page 57.

Dumplings are the traditional accompaniment to this Czechoslovakian goose.

## ROAST GOOSE WITH SAGE AND ONION STUFFING

[ENGLAND]                                    TO SERVE 4 TO 6

*1 6–8 pound goose*

FOR THE STUFFING

*¼ cup butter*
*1 large onion, chopped*
*   fine*
*1 goose liver, chopped*
*   coarse (optional)*
*4 cups fresh white or*
*   whole-wheat bread*
*   crumbs*

*4 leaves fresh sage, minced,*
*   or ½ teaspoon dried*
*1 teaspoon salt*
*Black pepper, freshly*
*   ground, to taste*

Melt the butter in a small saucepan and fry the onion gently until it is soft but not brown. If the goose liver is being included, fry until it is just firm and then chop fine. Mix the onions, liver, and butter with the bread crumbs and sage. Season the mixture with the salt and pepper.

Stuff the goose with this mixture. Truss and roast as directed on page 57. For a denser stuffing, bind the mixture with a beaten egg.

A potato stuffing for an 8–10 pound goose consists of 2 pounds of well-mashed boiled potatoes mixed with 1 large onion, chopped and sautéed briefly in 2 tablespoons of butter; the goose liver, lightly cooked and finely chopped; and a finely chopped celery heart. Season with chopped parsely or thyme, nutmeg, salt, and pepper.

Wild turkeys were still plentiful in New England when the Pilgrim Fathers caught some for their first Thanksgiving dinner in 1621. Domesticated turkeys had been found by explorers in Mexico and central America a century earlier and were first imported to Spain in 1498. The earliest written record of their success in England comes in 1541 when Archbishop Cranmer, attempting to limit the gluttony of the higher clergy, laid down a list of "greater fowls," among them turkey-cocks, of which only one was permitted in a dish.

Turkeys are easily raised by traditional methods of husbandry as well as by newer, more intensive methods of production. They should be properly hung to develop their full flavor—a process often skimped with frozen birds. This is one of the reasons fresh turkeys often taste better than frozen ones. If it must be a frozen bird, thaw it slowly in the refrigerator—48 hours for a large bird, 24 hours for a small one.

Turkeys can weigh anything from 4 pounds to 40 pounds, but few domestic ovens can cope with a bird of more than 20 pounds. When shopping, allow about ¾ pound per serving.

A perfectly cooked turkey is a rare bird, if for no other reason than the darker meat of the legs takes more cooking than the delicate white breast meat. The cheesecloth basting method described on page 56 goes a long way to solving the problem of dry breast meat. The slow-roasting method (see table below) is generally better if time permits. For very large birds, however, it is not always practical.

Set the turkey on a rack in a shallow roasting pan and baste it every 15 to 20 minutes throughout the cooking time. It is ready when the juices run clear. Test with a skewer inserted into the thickest part of the leg close to the body.

### TIMETABLE FOR ROASTING TURKEY (AVERAGE ONLY)

| WEIGHT OF BIRD (including stuffing) | SLOW-ROASTING METHOD 325°F | FAST-ROASTING METHOD 450°F |
|---|---|---|
| 6–8 pounds | 3–3½ hours | 2¼–2½ hours |
| 8–10 pounds | 3½–3¾ hours | 2½–2¾ hours |
| 10–14 pounds | 3¾–4¼ hours | 2¾–3 hours |
| 14–18 pounds | 4¼–4¾ hours | 3–3½ hours |
| 18–20 pounds | 4¾–5¼ hours | 3½–3¾ hours |
| 20–24 pounds | 5¼–6 hours | 3¾–4¼ hours |

Turkeys are now so widely available that in many parts of the world, especially in cities and larger towns, older Christmas eating customs are being forgotten. Chileans stuff turkeys with apples and walnuts. In Ecuador they are filled with rice, almonds, eggs, raisins, prunes, and peas; in Greece, with pork and chestnuts; in France, with chestnuts and truffles. There are chestnut stuffings for turkey from every continent and there is surprisingly little to choose among most of them. The best I have found is a Milanese stuffing. The ingredients may seem an odd mixture, but the flavor they produce is magnificent. (Canned whole chestnuts, even well-drained, are a bit too wet for most stuffings. Fresh chestnuts, boiled or baked, and peeled, of course, or reconstituted dried chestnuts, have better flavor and texture.)

## IL TACCHINO RIPIENO
### Milanese Stuffed Turkey

{ITALY}                                          TO SERVE 10 TO 12

*1 small black Perigord truffle*
*1 8–10 pound turkey*

### FOR THE STUFFING

*½ pound fresh Italian sweet*
*pork sausages*
*½ pound veal, ground*
*1 turkey liver, chopped fine*
*¼ pound Parma ham,*
*chopped fine*
*½ cup shallots or onions,*
*chopped*
*1¼ cups pitted prunes,*
*chopped coarse*
*2 pounds cooked chestnuts*,*
*chopped coarse*

*Truffle trimmings*
*¼ cup olive oil*
*⅓ cup grated Parmesan*
*cheese*
*1 tablespoon honey*
*¼ cup sherry*
*½ nutmeg, grated*
*1 teaspoon salt*
*Black pepper, freshly*
*ground, to taste*

### TO BASTE

*6 tablespoons melted butter*
*½ cup dry white wine*

Peel the truffle and slice it very thin. Reserve the trimmings. Using your fingers, gently loosen the turkey skin away from the breast and upper legs, being careful not to break the skin. Tuck slices of truffle between the meat and the skin.

To make the stuffing, skin the uncooked sausages and break them into a large mixing bowl. Add the veal, liver, ham, shallots or onions,

* For preparation of chestnuts, see page 9.

prunes, chestnuts, and truffle trimmings. Mix well. Put the oil in a large, heavy-bottomed pot over medium heat and sauté these ingredients gently together for about 10 minutes. Return the mixture to the bowl and add the grated cheese, honey, sherry, salt, and a generous sprinkling of pepper.

Stuff the turkey with this mixture, dividing it between the breast flat and the main cavity. Truss and roast as directed on page 63, basting every 15 to 20 minutes.

A very similar Spanish stuffing is made by adding 6 ounces each of dried peaches and pine nuts, and omitting the honey and shallots. Thyme, marjoram, basil, and bay leaf are also added to this Catalan recipe. Serve very plain vegetables with these luxurious birds.

Another rich stuffing, American this time, uses pork, veal, and cream to keep the meat moist, as well as chestnuts and truffles for a superb flavor.

## TWO-STUFFING TURKEY
{UNITED STATES}                                    TO SERVE 12 TO 18

*2 black Perigord truffles*
*1 10–14 pound turkey*

### FOR THE FIRST STUFFING

*1 tablespoon butter*
*1 turkey liver, chopped*
  *coarse*
*1 tablespoon brandy*
*1 pound ground pork*
*1 pound ground veal*
*1 pound cooked chestnuts**
*½ cup hazelnuts, chopped*
  *fine*
*½ cup fresh white bread*
  *crumbs*

*Truffle trimmings*
*1 cup heavy cream*
*1 tablespoon paprika*
*2 tablespoons chopped*
  *parsley*
*1 tablespoon chopped chives*
  *or scallions*
*1 teaspoon salt*
*Black pepper, freshly*
  *ground, to taste*

* For preparation of chestnuts, see page 9.

## FOR THE SECOND STUFFING

*½ pound cooked chestnuts*
*Salt to taste*
*Pepper to taste*

## TO BASTE

*1 cup melted butter*

Peel the truffles and slice them very thin. Reserve the trimmings. Using your fingers, gently loosen the turkey skin from the breast and upper legs, being careful not to break the skin. Tuck slices of truffle between the meat and the skin.

Melt the butter in a small saucepan over medium heat and sauté the liver for about 3 minutes or until just firm. Flame it with the brandy and put the liver and juices into a large mixing bowl with the pork and veal. Break up the chestnuts and add them to the meat. Add the hazelnuts, bread crumbs, truffle trimmings, cream, paprika, parsley, chives or scallions, salt, and a generous sprinkling of pepper. Mix the ingredients together thoroughly, and when they are well blended put this stuffing into the main cavity of the turkey. Sew or skewer the opening.

To prepare the second stuffing, simply break up the chestnuts, season with salt and pepper, and pack them into the neck end of the bird. Truss and roast the turkey as directed on page 63, basting with melted butter.

Bacon rolls, small pork sausages, cranberry sauce (see page 231), bread sauce (see page 230), brussels sprouts (see pages 126–127) and roast potatoes (see pages 116–117) are traditional accompaniments to turkey in the United States and Britain.


A very plain chestnut stuffing is easily made by rubbing cooked chestnuts through a coarse sieve and mixing them with salt and pepper. A beaten egg will bind the stuffing to give a firmer texture, and the addition of truffles, sliced or chopped, improves the flavor. Allow 4 to 6 ounces of chestnuts per pound of turkey.

The simplest turkey recipe I know is roasted without stuffing. Constant basting with honey and butter make it crisp and black on the outside, while underneath the flesh is very moist and white. The method was taken to England by the Romans, who cooked flamingos, herons, and other large birds in this way, and it is still used in the north. Butter and dark honey are melted together and painted over the bird several times until it is well coated. This turkey should be roasted at 400°F for the first 30 minutes, then at the slow-roasting temperature for the remainder of its cooking time. For a 16–20 pound turkey, use 1 pound honey and 1 cup butter.

Eggs, raw and hard-boiled, are used in this substantial Maltese stuffing recipe.

## DUNDJAN MIMLI
### Roast Turkey
{MALTA}                                              TO SERVE 16 TO 18

1 12–14 pound turkey

FOR THE STUFFING

2 pounds ground pork
5½ cups fresh white bread
    crumbs
¼ pound ham, chopped
    fine
½ cup grated Parmesan
    cheese
1 ounce shelled pistachio
    nuts

1 small onion
2 tablespoons chopped
    parsley
1 teaspoon salt
Black pepper, freshly
    ground, to taste
4–5 eggs, beaten
3 eggs, hard-boiled and
    chopped

Put the pork into a large bowl with the bread crumbs, the ham, the cheese, and the pistachios. Peel the onion and grate it into the bowl. Add the parsley and salt, and the pepper to taste. Stir the beaten eggs into the dry ingredients, mixing until they are well blended. Fold the hard-boiled eggs into the stuffing.

With your fingers, separate the skin from the flesh a few inches at the neck end of the turkey and stuff this space loosely to allow the mixture to swell during cooking. Use the remaining stuffing to fill the main cavity.

Truss and roast the turkey as directed on page 63.

*Peru a Brasileira* has a delicious dry neck dressing of toasted manioc meal, as well as a more conventional stuffing inside the bird, and it is considered one of Brazil's outstanding contributions to the culinary arts. Its preparation, however, presents two small problems: First, manioc meal can be difficult to find (other names for it are cassava meal and farinha). The second problem is persuading a butcher not to chop the neck off the turkey. You want a really big flap of neck skin to encase the dry stuffing.

## PERU A BRASILEIRA
### Roast Turkey Brazilian Style

{BRAZIL}                                        TO SERVE 16 TO 20

*1 12–16 pound turkey*            *1 sprig parsley*
*Turkey giblets and neck*         *½ teaspoon salt*
*1 stalk celery, chopped*
*  coarse*

**FOR THE MARINADE**

*1 medium onion, chopped*         *¼ teaspoon powdered*
*1 stalk celery, chopped*         *  cloves*
*1 medium carrot, grated*         *½ teaspoon salt*
*3 cloves garlic*                 *Black pepper to taste*
*4 tablespoons chopped*           *2 cups dry white wine*
*  parsley*                       *1 cup wine vinegar*

**FOR THE NECK STUFFING**

*4 cups manioc meal*              *1 portion giblets, cooked*
*5 tablespoons butter*            *5 drops Tabasco sauce*
*1 medium onion, chopped*         *20 green olives, pitted*
*2 medium tomatoes, peeled*       *3 hard-boiled eggs, chopped*
*  and chopped*                   *Salt to taste*
*  (optional)*                    *Black pepper, freshly*
*4 tablespoons chopped*           *  ground, to taste*
*  parsley*

## FOR THE SECOND STUFFING

| | |
|---|---|
| 6 cups fresh white bread crumbs | 4 tablespoons chopped parsley |
| ¾ cup milk | 1 cup giblet stock |
| 2 slices bacon | 1 portion cooked giblets |
| 1 large onion, chopped fine | Salt to taste |
| 2 medium tomatoes, peeled and chopped fine | Black pepper, freshly ground, to taste |

## TO BASTE

1 cup strained marinade
½ cup melted butter

The day before you plan to roast the turkey cook the giblets and leave the bird in its marinade overnight.

Wash the giblets and neck, and put them into a pot with 4 cups cold water and bring to the boil. Skim off the froth, add the celery, parsley, and salt. Cover the pot and simmer for about 1 hour. Cool the giblets in the stock.

Strain the stock and reserve. Chop the giblets very fine, divide into 2 equal portions and reserve them for the stuffings.

Prepare the marinade in a bowl or dish large enough to hold the turkey. Mix the onion, celery, and carrot with all the remaining marinade ingredients. Pour some of this mixture into the turkey, and, holding the bird over the bowl, turn to dampen the whole interior. Place the turkey in the bowl and turn it from time to time in the marinade. Leave overnight in a cool place.

To make the neck stuffing, preheat the oven to 350°F. Spread the manioc meal on a shallow baking pan and toast it for about 15 minutes or until it is a golden color. Melt 2 tablespoons of the butter in a large frying pan. Sauté the onion and tomatoes gently in the butter. Add the parsley, 1 portion of reserved giblets, and the Tabasco sauce. Fry together for another minute or two. Now add the remaining butter and when it has melted remove the pan from the heat and mix in the toasted manioc meal. When it is well blended, return the pan to the stove and stir the mixture over low heat until it is crumbly.

Add the olives and hard-boiled eggs and season the mixture to taste with salt and freshly ground pepper.

To make the second stuffing, soak the bread crumbs in the milk and set aside. Fry the bacon gently in a frying pan until the fat runs. Add the onion, tomatoes, and the parsley. Fry these together until the onion is golden brown. Add 1 cup of the reserved giblet stock and bring to the boil. Remove from the heat and press this mixture through a sieve into a large bowl. Add the remaining reserved giblets and the soaked bread crumbs. Season the mixture to taste with salt and freshly ground pepper.

Remove the turkey from the marinade and pat it dry. Stuff the neck loosely with the manioc stuffing and sew it up neatly. Any leftover stuffing can be served separately. Stuff the main cavity with the bread stuffing.

Truss, and slow-roast the turkey as described on page 63. Baste with a mixture of strained marinade and melted butter.

Hand-rearing capons for the table is still a wifely art in country districts in many parts of the world. Present-day Romans roast them for Christmas with a stuffing of sausages, cooked giblets, pecorino Romano cheese, and bread crumbs. Any of the turkey stuffings already described can be made in smaller quantities for a capon or chicken. A lemon and thyme stuffing —made like the sage and onion stuffing on page 62, but adding grated lemon rind and fresh or dried thyme or lemon thyme in place of the sage —is particularly fresh and delicious.

Game, furred and feathered, is at its best in northern Europe and North America during the Christmas season. Wild boar is still sometimes available in France, Germany, and further east, and saddle of venison is a popular choice in Germany for the main Christmas meal. Small game birds, from pheasant which will serve 2, to quail, 2 or 3 per person, are often served in the days before or after Christmas. These are seldom stuffed, although fruit, berries, and herbs are sometimes inserted to add flavor during roasting. Spit-roasting is a particularly good method for cooking well-hung birds. Remember to baste well. The following table gives oven-roasting times for the most popular game birds and lists their traditional accompaniments.

## TIMETABLE FOR ROASTING GAME BIRDS (AVERAGE ONLY)

| TYPE OF GAME | OVEN TEMPERATURE | COOKING TIME | ACCOMPANIMENTS |
|---|---|---|---|
| Pheasant | 400°F | 50–70 minutes | Fried bread crumbs, bread sauce, clear gravy, watercress, plus red currant jelly, cranberry sauce, roast or sautéed potatoes. |
| Teal | 425°F | 15–20 minutes | Strong clear gravy, orange salad, watercress. |
| Mallard | 450°F | 25–35 minutes | As teal. |
| Quail, partridge or bobwhite | 450°F | 15 minutes | Serve on toast with bread sauce and clear gravy plus red currant jelly and bacon rolls. |
| Wood pigeon, squab | 425°F | 20–25 minutes | Thin gravy and watercress. |
| Woodcock | 425°F | 15–20 minutes | Roast on toast. Fried bread crumbs, lemon wedges, and watercress. |

## REHRUCKEN MIT ROTWEINSOSSE

*Roast Saddle of Venison with Red Wine Sauce*

[GERMANY]                                    TO SERVE 6 TO 8

*1 5-pound saddle of venison*
*1 4-ounce slice pork fat*
*¼ cup lard*

## FOR THE MARINADE

*3 cups dry red wine*
*5 juniper berries, bruised*
*2 cloves, bruised*
*8 black peppercorns,*
*    bruised*

*1 bay leaf, crumbled*
*2½ teaspoons salt*

## FOR THE SAUCE

*2 medium carrots, chopped*
*    coarse*
*1 small onion, chopped*
*    coarse*
*2 scallions, chopped coarse*

*3 stalks celery, chopped*
*    coarse*
*2½ tablespoons flour*
*6 tablespoons heavy cream*
*1 teaspoon lemon juice*

## FOR THE GARNISH

*8 pear halves, poached or canned*
*4 tablespoons lingonberry or cranberry sauce (see page 231)*

The venison must marinate for at least 8 hours at room temperature, longer if the meat is not from a young animal. Marinating it in the refrigerator for 3 days or more will improve the flavor and tenderize the meat.

To make the marinade, put the wine in a large pot with 3 cups water and add the juniper berries, cloves, peppercorns, bay leaf, and the salt. Bring to the boil and set the liquid aside to cool. Put the venison in a dish just large enough to hold it and pour on the marinade. Turn the meat to wet it all over and marinate it, turning occasionally.

Remove the meat from the marinade and pat it dry. Strain the marinade and set the liquid aside for the sauce. Cut the pork fat into long, thin strips (lardons) and, using a larding needle, insert two rows of lardons along each side of the meat at approximately 1-inch intervals.

Preheat oven to 350°F. Melt the ¼ cup lard over high heat in the roasting pan on top of the stove. Brown the venison evenly on all sides. Transfer the venison to a dish. To prepare the sauce, add the vegetables to the roasting pan and cook them over medium heat until they are soft and slightly browned. Reduce the heat, sprinkle the flour over the fried vegetables, and cook the mixture gently to brown the flour a little. Pour in the reserved marinade to a depth of about 1 inch. Set the venison on the vegetables and roast for about 1½ hours, basting occasionally with the pan juices.

Venison is usually served slightly pink, so roast it longer for well-done meat. Transfer the venison to a heated serving dish. Turn the oven off and return the meat to it to rest, with the door open.

To finish the sauce, strain the roasting juices into a measuring cup and skim off the excess fat. Add enough marinade to make 1½ cups. Heat this stock in a saucepan. Bring to the boil and add the cream, whisking briskly. Reduce the heat and simmer the sauce, stirring frequently, for about 5 minutes. Add the lemon juice and correct the seasoning to taste.

Pour the sauce over the venison and garnish the dish with pear halves filled with lingonberry or cranberry sauce. The pears may be warm or cold.


Suckling pig is the traditional Christmas roast for the Caribbean, Pacific, and Mediterranean islands and for much of southern and eastern Europe. In many places it is traditionally spit-roasted, and still is in those parts of the world where Christmas is celebrated in warm weather. Stuffings are as varied as the places it is eaten, from a simple flavoring of tamarind rind and banana leaves in the Philippines, to elaborate dressings of meat, fruit, and spices in the Caribbean. Cubans stuff suckling pigs with rice and beans and nuggets of guava paste, and, oddly, the Rumanians use a rum and olive oil basting liquid, a technique which would seem more appropriate to the West Indies.

Suckling pigs weigh from about 4 pounds to 12 pounds cleaned weight, and can be bought fresh or chilled. It is usually necessary to order them in advance; when shopping, allow ¾ of a pound to a pound per serving.

To truss a suckling pig, sew the stomach opening neatly after stuffing, or secure with skewers. Draw the back legs away from the body and tie with string; bring the front legs forward and tie. If oven space does not permit the pig to be roasted in this extended pose, fold the legs underneath it and secure with skewers or string. Wedge the mouth open with a piece of crumpled foil which will be replaced after cooking with an apple, orange, or baked potato. Protect the snout and ears with foil for part of the cooking time. Rub the pig with salt and place it on a rack in a shallow roasting pan. Baste it frequently during cooking. If it is necessary to protect its skin with foil, make the covering very loose and remove for the last half hour of roasting so that the skin will be crisp.

The meat is cooked when the juices run clear. Test with a skewer inserted into the thigh.

## TIMETABLE FOR ROASTING SUCKLING PIG (AVERAGE ONLY)

| WEIGHT OF PIG (including stuffing) | OVEN TEMPERATURE 400°F |
|---|---|
| 4 pounds | 1½–1¾ hours |
| 6 pounds | 2¼–2½ hours |
| 8 pounds | 2¾–3 hours |
| 10 pounds | 3¼–3½ hours |
| 12 pounds | 3¾–4 hours |
| 14 pounds | 4¼–4½ hours |

Roast suckling pig is one of Spain's gastronomic triumphs and this recipe from the Basque country makes an impressive party dish.

## LECHONA ASADA VASCA
### Roast Suckling Pig

[SPAIN]                                          TO SERVE 8 TO 10

*1 8-pound suckling pig*
*Salt*
*Olive oil*

### FOR THE STUFFING

*2 cups fresh white bread*
*    crumbs*
*2 tablespoons milk*
*4 medium onions, chopped*
*    fine*
*½ pound ground pork*
*½ pound ground veal*
*1 liver of suckling pig,*
*    chopped fine*
*2 tablespoons chopped*
*    parsley*

*1 teaspoon dried thyme*
*1 teaspoon dried rosemary*
*½ cup dry sherry*
*¼ cup brandy*
*2 eggs, beaten*
*1 teaspoon salt*
*Black pepper, freshly*
*    ground, to taste*
*6 eggs, hard-boiled and*
*    sliced*

FOR THE GARNISH

*1 red eating apple*

Wash the pig, pat it dry, and rub it inside and out with salt.

To prepare the stuffing, put the bread crumbs in a large bowl and moisten them with the milk. Add the onions to the bowl with the ground pork, veal, and the liver. Add the herbs, sherry, brandy, and eggs. Season with salt and pepper and mix the ingredients together thoroughly.

Line the inside of the pig with the slices of egg, then pack it with the stuffing. Truss, brush with olive oil, and roast as directed on page 74. Baste with the pan juices and additional olive oil if needed.

Serve the pig on a large dish with a shiny red apple in its mouth, and a thin gravy made from the skimmed pan juices. Whole roasted red and green peppers and dark-green watercress are often used as further garnish.

Caribbean islanders enjoy highly flavored food, as this recipe for suckling pig shows. "Seasoning up" is a term used in the English-speaking islands for the marinade used to flavor the animal before it is stuffed.

## ROAST SUCKLING PIG

[TRINIDAD]                                    TO SERVE 10 TO 14

*1 10–12 pound suckling pig*

FOR THE MARINADE

| | |
|---|---|
| 2 medium onions, chopped fine | ¼ cup cane, or malt vinegar |
| 2 cloves garlic, crushed | ¼ cup dark rum |
| 4 scallions, minced | 2 teaspoons salt |
| 1 bunch celery leaves, minced | 2 tablespoons soy sauce |
| | 2 teaspoons cayenne pepper |

FOR THE STUFFING

| | |
|---|---|
| ¼ cup butter | 2 medium tomatoes, peeled |
| 2 medium onions, chopped | and chopped coarse |
| fine | 1 small red chili pepper*, |
| 2 cloves garlic, minced | chopped fine |
| 8 cups fresh white bread | 2 tablespoons capers |
| crumbs | 1 teaspoon thyme |
| ½ cup milk | 1½ teaspoons salt |
| 20 green olives, pitted and | Black pepper, freshly |
| chopped coarse | ground, to taste |
| ½ cup seedless raisins | |

TO BASTE

Reserved marinade
½ cup peanut oil

To prepare the marinade, mix all the ingredients together well in a small bowl.

Wash the suckling pig and pat it dry. Paint it inside and out with the marinade and leave it to stand at room temperature for about 2 hours.

To make the stuffing, melt the butter in a small pot and sauté the onions and garlic gently until tender but not brown. Transfer them to a large mixing bowl. Moisten the bread crumbs with milk and add to the onions. Add the olives, raisins, tomatoes, chili pepper, capers, thyme, salt, and a generous sprinkling of freshly ground pepper. Mix the ingredients well together.

Scrape the marinade off the pig and reserve it. Stuff the pig loosely with the filling and sew or skewer the opening. Truss and roast as directed on page 74. Baste with the reserved marinade and peanut oil combined.

---

* When handling chilies it is a good idea to wear rubber gloves, as the volatile oils in their flesh and seeds can irritate the skin. Be careful not to rub your eyes and, if not wearing gloves, wash your hands thoroughly in soap and water after working with them. For most recipes, unless otherwise stated, the stalks and seeds of chilies should be removed and the flesh torn into small pieces.

## ROAST SUCKLING PIG

{JAMAICA}                                    TO SERVE 10 TO 14

*1 10–12 pound suckling pig*

### FOR THE STUFFING

*¼ cup butter*
*1 large onion, chopped*
   *fine*
*1 clove garlic, minced*
*8 cups fresh white bread*
   *crumbs*
*1 cup seedless raisins,*
   *chopped coarse*

*1 red chili pepper\*, chopped*
   *fine*
*1 tablespoon powdered*
   *ginger*
*Grated rind of 1 lime*
*3 tablespoons Tabasco*
   *sauce*
*1 teaspoon salt*

### TO BASTE

*Olive oil*

Melt the butter in a small saucepan and sauté the onion and garlic until soft but not brown. Transfer them to a large mixing bowl and add the bread crumbs, raisins, chili pepper, and the ginger. Add the grated lime rind and mix the ingredients thoroughly. Sprinkle the mixture with the Tabasco sauce and the salt, and mix again.

Stuff the pig loosely with this filling. Truss and roast as directed on page 74. Baste with pan juices and olive oil.

Paw paw applesauce (see page 233) and/or creole sauce (see page 228) may be served with either of the previous two recipes.

Roast loin of pork is a popular Christmas roast in Scandinavia, and the following Danish recipe is especially simple and delicious. For this roast do not let the butcher remove the skin. Ask him to chine the joint for easy carving, and to score the skin deeply at ½-inch intervals.

\* For preparation of chilies, see note on page 76.

## STEGT SVINEKAM
### Roast Loin of Pork

{DENMARK}                                                    TO SERVE 8

> 1 6-pound loin of pork
> ¼ cup drippings or butter
> Salt
> 6 cloves
> 12 small bay leaves

Preheat oven to 450°F. Place the pork loin skin side down in a roasting pan. Pour in boiling water to a depth of about 1 inch and place the pan in the very hot oven for 15 minutes.

Take the pork from the oven, reduce the heat to 350°F, and pour off the stock, reserving it for basting. Dry the roasting pan and smear it with drippings or butter. Rub the pork well with salt. Push the cloves and bay leaves into the cuts in the skin and roast the pork skin side up on a rack. Baste every 30 minutes with about 2 tablespoons of reserved stock.

Roasted apple halves filled with red currant jelly, sugar-browned potatoes (see page 117), and red cabbage (see page 126) are the usual accompaniments for this roast.

Roasted spareribs are a specialty of the Swedish *smörgåsbord* table which is at its most magnificent over the Christmas season.

## UGNSTEKET REVBENSSPJÄLL
### Roasted Spareribs

{SWEDEN}                                              TO SERVE 4 TO 6

> 5 pounds pork spareribs,      ¼ teaspoon powdered
>    bones cracked                 ginger or powdered
> 1½ tablespoons salt             mustard
> ½ teaspoon ground white      1 cup canned prune juice
>    pepper

Preheat oven to 400°F. Trim and wipe the meat. Mix together the salt, pepper, and ginger or mustard and rub the mixture onto the meat. Lay the spareribs on a rack in a shallow roasting pan and place in the 400°F oven for 15 minutes. Reduce the heat to 350°F and baste the spareribs with the prune juice. Continue roasting for 1 hour, basting occasionally, or until the meat is tender.

Cut the spareribs into pieces and arrange them on a warmed serving dish. Skim the pan juices and serve them separately. Applesauce and cooked prunes are the usual accompaniments.

Baked hams appear on festive occasions wherever pigs are reared. Their variety, once rich beyond belief, is now diminishing as commercial products take the place of old and cherished curing arts practiced in farm and cottage kitchens. Finland's sauna-smoked hams; England's York and Bradenham hams; Ireland's Limerick hams; America's Virginia, Smithfield, and Kentucky hams; France's *jambon de Paris;* Germany's Mainz and Westphalian hams; Czechoslovakia's Prague hams; Spain's Asturias hams—all are distinctively flavored and justly famous.

The best hams are made from the hind leg of a pig and may be dry-cured, pickled, smoked, or simply dried. Unsmoked hams are usually described as "green." Hams are sometimes baked in a crust—which is later discarded—to prevent them from drying out. More usually, though, they are boiled or parboiled, then baked with a decorative glaze or pastry case to be eaten hot or cold.

Buy a whole ham ready-cooked or boil an uncooked ham at home. To prepare an uncooked ham, soak it in cold water for 24 hours, then simmer in a mixture of white wine or cider, water, and herbs (choose your favorites). Allow 25 minutes per pound cooking time. Never try to hurry the cooking by fast boiling, which will dry out the ham. Simmer it gently, covered, and cool it in its own stock.

## PROSCIUTTO IN CROSTA
### Ham in Pastry

[ITALY]                                          TO SERVE 8 TO 10

> *1 6-pound boiled ham (see above)*
> *1 pound prepared puff pastry (see page 209)*

Preheat oven to 425°F. Remove the skin and fat from the boiled ham. Roll the puff pastry about ¼ inch thick. Place the ham, top side down, in the center of the pastry, and wrap the pastry over it, sealing the edges firmly. Set the covered ham seam side down on a damp baking pan and decorate the top with pastry leaves or flowers fashioned from the trimmings. Bake for about 35 minutes.

Serve the ham warm or cold. A white sauce is served separately with warm ham, and very sweet candied fruits in a heavy syrup flavored faintly with mustard, *mostardi di frutta,* invariably garnish this dish.

To bake an uncooked ham, first simmer it for 15 minutes to the pound, then wrap it in foil and bake it in the center of a preheated moderate oven, 350°F, for 10 minutes per pound. Half an hour before cooking is completed, turn up the oven to 425°F and take the ham from the oven. Remove the foil and peel off the skin.

To finish the ham, score the fat with a diamond pattern of intersecting diagonal cuts, sprinkle the fat generously with brown sugar and pat it well in. Decorate with whole cloves pushed into the fat at the corners of the diamonds. Return the ham to the oven and bake for a further 30 minutes to set the glaze.

Decorations can be varied to include halved glacé cherries or apricots, pineapple rings, and slices of any glacéed fruit. These should also be patted with sugar or painted with honey before the final baking. Alternative glazes may be made with honey, marmalade, corn or maple syrup.

Serve glazed ham hot or cold. Spiced peaches or pears cooked in red wine go well with hot or cold ham, and cooked prunes are usually served in Scandinavia.

Smoked leg of lamb called *hangikjöt,* boiled or braised and served with a white sauce flavored with nutmeg, peas, and mashed potatoes, is a national specialty much enjoyed at Christmas in Iceland. Roast baby lambs are eaten in Spain and in Sardinia, but the one country that really goes to town on lamb at Christmas is, of course, New Zealand. The festive crown roast and a boned, stuffed leg, known as "colonial goose," are two favorite Christmas recipes.

The cut of lamb used for crown roasts is called rack in the United States, best end of neck in England, fair end in Ireland, *côtes* or *côtelettes premières* in France. It is made by joining together two or three of these joints, each consisting of 5, 6, or 7 chops. Allow at least 2 chops per serving when ordering a prepared crown roast from the butcher, or making one at home by sewing the joints together after removing the chine bones and trimming the chop-bones. A crown may be roasted with or without stuffing. In either case the exposed bones should be protected from charring with individual foil hats. These are replaced for serving with paper frills or small glazed onions.

## CROWN ROAST OF LAMB WITH RAISIN AND NUT STUFFING

{NEW ZEALAND}                                          TO SERVE 6

> *1 12-chop crown roast*
> *¼ cup butter or beef drippings*

### FOR THE STUFFING

| | |
|---|---|
| *¼ cup butter* | *¼ teaspoon dried thyme* |
| *1 medium onion, chopped* | *¼ teaspoon dried rosemary* |
| *fine* | *¼ teaspoon dried tarragon* |
| *1 clove garlic, minced* | *1 lemon* |
| *½ pound mushrooms,* | *½ teaspoon salt* |
| *chopped fine* | *Black pepper, freshly* |
| *4 cups fresh whole-wheat or* | *ground, to taste* |
| *white bread crumbs* | *1–2 eggs, beaten* |
| *1 cup seedless raisins* | |
| *½ cup shelled walnuts,* | |
| *broken into pieces* | |

### FOR THE GRAVY

| | |
|---|---|
| *Pan juices* | *1 tablespoon red currant* |
| *1 cup chicken stock, or* | *jelly* |
| *mixture chicken stock* | *Salt to taste* |
| *and white wine* | *Black pepper, freshly* |
| *1 teaspoon cornstarch* | *ground, to taste* |

To make the stuffing, melt the butter in a small saucepan and sauté the onion and garlic until soft and slightly browned. Add the mushrooms and cook gently, covered, until the mushrooms have released their liquid.

Transfer the mixture to a large mixing bowl. Add the bread crumbs, raisins, walnuts, thyme, rosemary, and tarragon. Grate the rind of the lemon over the bowl and season the mixture with salt and freshly ground pepper. Toss the ingredients together thoroughly before adding as much egg as you need to moisten the mixture. This stuffing should be fairly loose.

Pile the stuffing into the crown. Weigh the roast and calculate the cooking time at 30 minutes to the pound.

Preheat oven to 375°F. Melt the butter or drippings in a shallow roasting pan and set the crown in it. Roast for the first 10 minutes at 375°F, then reduce the temperature to 350°F for the remainder of the cooking time.

When the roast is ready, put it on a warmed serving dish and return it to the oven, switched off and with the door open. Let it rest while making the gravy. Skim the pan juices and add chicken stock, or mixture of stock and white wine. Thicken the gravy with the cornstarch mixed with small amount cold water, and sweeten it with the red currant jelly. Check the seasoning and adjust to taste.

Serve the crown roast with a pitcher of gravy, more red currant jelly, fresh peas, and boiled new potatoes.

## COLONIAL GOOSE
### Stuffed Leg of Lamb

[NEW ZEALAND]                                                    TO SERVE 6

*1 4-pound leg of lamb, boned*
*2 tablespoons butter*

### FOR THE STUFFING

*⅔ cup dried apricots,*
*  chopped coarse*
*3 cups fresh white or*
*  whole-wheat bread*
*  crumbs*
*¼ cup butter*
*1 tablespoon clear honey*

*1 small onion, chopped*
*  fine*
*¼ teaspoon dried thyme*
*½ teaspoon salt*
*Black pepper, freshly*
*  ground, to taste*
*1 egg, beaten*

## FOR THE MARINADE

*2 large carrots, scraped and
    chopped fine
1 large onion, chopped fine
1 bay leaf, crumbled
2 tablespoons chopped
    parsley*

*¼ teaspoon salt
Black pepper, freshly
    ground, to taste
1 cup dry red wine*

## FOR THE GRAVY

*Pan juices
1 cup chicken stock or white wine*

Ask the butcher to bone the leg or prepare it at home. Lay the meat, fat side down, on a wooden board. With a sharp, pointed knife, work the meat away from the bone at the top of the leg, down to the first joint. Now cut along the line of the bone from the opposite end of the leg. Work the flesh away from the bone, being careful not to puncture the skin in any other place. Sever the bone from all the flesh and ligaments and draw it out. Lay the meat out flat, making occasional shallow cuts until the piece is approximately the same thickness over its entire surface.

To make the stuffing, put the apricots in a mixing bowl with the bread crumbs. Melt the ¼ cup of butter and the honey together in a small saucepan. Add the onion and cook over low heat until soft but not brown. Add the cooked onion, butter, and honey to the apricots along with the thyme, salt, and a generous sprinkling of freshly ground pepper. Toss the mixture to blend the ingredients, then bind it with the beaten egg.

Spread the stuffing in the middle of the boned lamb, and fold the meat into a neat parcel which will cook evenly. Sew the roast firmly with a needle and strong thread. Set aside.

For the marinade, put the carrots and onion in a bowl large enough to hold the stuffed lamb, and add the bay leaf, parsley, salt, pepper, and wine. Stir the marinade and add the meat. Leave the lamb to marinate in a cool place for 6 to 12 hours, or longer in the refrigerator, turning it from time to time.

To roast the lamb, preheat the oven to 350°F. Pat the lamb dry and set it in a shallow, generously buttered roasting pan. Spread the rest of the butter on the meat and roast it for about 35 minutes per pound, basting occasionally with the pan juices.

Rest the "colonial goose" on a warmed serving dish in the oven, switched off and with the door open. Skim the fat from the pan juices and make a thin gravy by adding chicken stock or white wine. Serve the gravy separately and remove the trussing threads from the meat before carving.

Fresh peas and new potatoes, boiled and buttered, are the traditional accompaniments to "colonial goose." Any of the garnishes served with goose or turkey go very well with this roast.

A majestic roast of beef, hot for the main Christmas meal or cold for a buffet table, is another popular seasonal choice.

Only prime cuts of well-hung beef will make a perfect roast, crusty brown on the outside and pale pink at the center. Look for dark red meat, succulent and flecked with a light marbling of fat, and with creamy white fat on the outside.

The cooking times suggested here are for good-quality beef. If you are quite certain that your roast comes from a prize-winning animal, reduce the cooking time a little.

### TIMETABLE FOR ROASTING BEEF (AVERAGE ONLY)

| CUT | TEMPERATURE 425°F          325°F | DEGREE OF DONENESS |
|---|---|---|
| Filet (whole) | 8–10 minutes per pound | very rare |
| | 14 minutes per pound | medium rare |
| | 21–22 minutes per pound | well-done |
| Rib roast (2 ribs, about 5 pounds) | First 15 minutes, then 16 minutes per pound | rare |
| | First 15 minutes, then 25 minutes per pound | medium |
| | First 15 minutes, then 32 minutes per pound | well-done |
| Rib roast (4 ribs, about 11 pounds) | First 15 minutes, then 15 minutes per pound | rare |
| | First 15 minutes, then 20 minutes per pound | medium |
| | First 15 minutes, then 36 minutes per pound | well-done |
| Sirloin (boned and rolled) | First 15 minutes, then 15 minutes per pound | rare |
| | First 15 minutes, then 27 minutes per pound | medium |
| | First 15 minutes, then 37 minutes per pound | well-done |

Filet steak, roasted in one piece and weighing 4–6 pounds, makes surprisingly economical use of this expensive cut because shrinkage is minimal. Allow 4–6 ounces, uncooked weight, per serving. Bard the meat with fine strips of pork fat, or seal in the juices by browning the roast very quickly in hot beef drippings on top of the stove before roasting. Fold about 6 inches of the thin end of the meat back on itself and tie the roast in several places so that it is the same diameter throughout. A classic *béarnaise* sauce makes a wonderful accompaniment to this succulent meat, which may be served either in steak-sized chunks or thick slices.

For rib roasts, allow 12–16 ounces per serving, and for boned, rolled sirloin, 6–8 ounces per person, uncooked weights.

## ROAST BEEF AND YORKSHIRE PUDDING
[ENGLAND]                                     TO SERVE 6 TO 8

> *1 5–6 pound rib roast*
> *¼ cup beef drippings or butter*
> *Salt*
> *Black pepper*

**FOR THE PUDDING**

> *1 cup flour*
> *¼ teaspoon salt*
> *2 large eggs*
> *5 ounces milk*

Preheat oven to 425°F. Coat the meat with drippings or butter and season generously with salt and pepper. Put the beef on a rack over a roasting pan and brown it at 425°F for 15 minutes. Lower the heat to 325°F and roast the meat, basting occasionally, using the timing chart on page 84.

To make the Yorkshire pudding, sift the flour and salt into a mixing bowl and make a hollow in the center. Mix the eggs with a little of the milk, add to the flour, and stir to make a smooth paste. Gradually beat in the rest of the milk and leave the batter to stand for at least an hour before baking it.

About 40 minutes before the beef is ready, pour the batter into the roasting pan under the beef. The pudding will be ready when the beef is done, and richly flavored with its juices.

If lighter Yorkshire pudding is preferred, make individual puddings. Divide ¼ cup (4 tablespoons) beef drippings among 6 or 8 small baking pans or muffin tins, and heat the prepared tins in the oven toward the end of the roasting time. As soon as the meat is out of the oven, pour the batter into the tins and bake for 15 minutes on a high shelf. Leave the meat in a warm place to settle before carving.

Hot horseradish relish, as it comes from the bottle or toned down with heavy cream, or English mustard are served with roast beef. Roast potatoes and any green vegetable are good accompaniments. Buttered baby beets are excellent, too.

A Christmas barbecue? Well yes, in a word, or rather words—*pachamancha, hangi,* and *lova.* These are the pit barbecues of the southern hemisphere and they are surprisingly alike at opposite sides of the globe. *Pachamancha* is the main celebration meal in the country districts on the coast and in the mountains of Peru. Pork, whole baby lamb, chickens, and sweet and ordinary potatoes are wrapped in banana leaves and cooked in pits on heated stones. The stones are first warmed by fires, and when the flames have died the pits are lined with leaves, the food piled in and covered with more leaves, and earth from the pit digging heaped on top. Two or three hours later the food is dug out and morsels of tender meat and poultry distributed among the participants.

Baby lambs are also cooked in the New Zealand *hangi,* a Maori pit barbecue adopted by everyone and found now in urban backyards, on beaches, and in the country. Foil has taken the place of leaves for wrapping the food but the principle is much the same. Baby lambs stuffed with *kumara* (sweet potato) and pumpkin are a *hangi* specialty.

Huge family parties gather to make the Fijian *lova.* Braided coconut fronds protect the pork, chickens, fish, potatoes, and other vegetables from the heated river stones. Heart-shaped *taro* leaves enclose parcels of corned beef mixed with onion, chili, and coconut cream called *palusami.* Heaps of breadfruit and banana leaves topped with earth hold in the heat and smoke. *Kava,* the ceremonial drink of Fiji, is consumed in great quantities. Offering beer is regarded as sophisticated.

Another kind of barbecue is also made for Christmas by the Spanish-Indian creoles of Peru. *Antichuchos*—skewers of bull's heart marinated in vinegar, onion, herbs, and chili—and *papa rellena* (see page 115) are eaten with lots of music.

# COLD CUTS

Brawn became Christmas fare in England in Tudor times, although it had been made for feasts since the Middle Ages. It retains its popularity as a Christmas dish in Sweden and Hungary, but is not so often seen now in England.

The most spectacular brawn was the boar's head, a royal dish made from the head and shoulders of a wild boar, boned, stuffed, and reassembled with a decorative grimace. Queen Victoria's guests were still being offered the real thing in 1888. A photograph of her Christmas sideboard shows one made with a boar taken from Windsor Great Park. Beside it is a brawn presented by Queen's College, Oxford, and a 312-pound baron of beef.

As wild boars ran out, mere pigs got the boar's-head treatment and still appear, complete with macaroni tusks, on ceremonial occasions. One of Queen Victoria's chefs, Charles Elmé Francatelli, left the following instructions for making a boar's head out of a domestic pig.

"Procure the head of a bacon hog, (for this purpose, the head must be cut off before the pig is scalded, and the bristles singed off with a lighted straw; by this means, it will have all the appearance of a wild boar's head.) which must be cut off deep into the shoulders; bone it carefully, beginning under the throat, then spread the head out on a large earthenware dish, and rub it with the following ingredients:—Six pounds of salt, four ounces of saltpetre, six ounces of moist sugar, cloves, mace, half an ounce of juniper berries, four cloves of garlic, six bay leaves, a handful of thyme, marjoram and basil.

When the head has been well rubbed with these, pour about a quart of port wine lees over it, and keep in a cool place for a fortnight; observing that it must be turned over in its brine every day during that period.

"When about to dress the head, take it out of the brine and wash it thoroughly in cold water; then absorb all the exterior moisture from it with a clean cloth, and spread it out upon the table. Next, pare off all the uneven pieces from the cheeks, etc., cut these into long narrow fillets, and put them with the tongue, fat bacon and truffles, prepared as directed for the galatine; then line the inside of the head with a layer of forcemeat (the same kind as used for galatines), about an inch thick, and lay thereon the fillets of tongue, bacon, truffles, and here and there some pistachio kernels (the skin of which must be removed by scalding); cover these with a layer of forcemeat, and then repeat the rows of tongue, etc. When the head is sufficiently garnished to fill it out in its shape, it should be sewn up with a small trussing needle and twine, so as thoroughly to secure the stuffing. The head must then be wrapped up in a strong cloth, previously well spread with butter, and sewn up in this, so as to preserve its original form: it should next be put into a large oval braising pan, with any carcases of game (especially of grouse, from its congenial flavour) or any trimmings of meat there may be to hand, and also four cowheels, or six calves' feet; then moisten with a copious wine *mirepoix,* in sufficient quantity to cover the surface of the head. Set the brazier on the stove fire; as soon as it boils up, skim it thoroughly, then remove it to a slow fire (covered with the lid containing live embers), that the head may continue to simmer or boil very gently, for about 5 hours. As soon as it appears to be nearly done, remove the brazier from the fire, and when the heat of the broth has somewhat subsided, let the head be taken upon a large dish. If it appears to have shrunk considerably in the wrapper, this must be carefully tightened, so as to preserve its shape; it should then be put back into its braise, there to remain, until the whole head has become set firm by cooling.

"The head must next be taken out of the braise or stock, and put in the oven, upon a deep baking dish, for a few minutes, just to melt the jelly which may adhere to the wrapper. It must then be taken out quickly, and the wrapper carefully removed, after which, glaze the head with some dark-coloured glaze; place it on its dish, ornament it with aspic jelly and serve.

"Forcemeat for galatine: Chop up one pound of white veal, with the same quantity of fat bacon, and season with chopped mushrooms, parsley, nutmeg, pepper, salt and aromatic seasoning. When these are chopped quite fine, pound the whole in a mortar, with the yolks of 3 eggs, and remove the forcemeat into a basin.

"Peel one pound of truffles and cut up a boiled red tongue, and about one pound of fat bacon or boiled calf's udder, into narrow fillets, about a quarter of an inch square."

It was customary to place a red apple in the jaws, and sometimes the boar's head was crowned with a wreath of bay, holly, or laurel.

A modern Swedish recipe for a brawn is made with pork and veal and set with gelatin.

## FLÄSK-OCH KALVSYLTA
### Jellied Pork and Veal

[SWEDEN]                                   TO SERVE 10 TO 12

| | |
|---|---|
| 2 pounds lean pork | 1 medium onion, chopped |
| 2 pounds shank of veal |   coarse |
| 2 tablespoons salt | 1 medium carrot, scraped |
| 15 white peppercorns, |   and chopped coarse |
|   crushed | White pepper, to taste |
| 10 allspice berries, | 2 tablespoons white wine |
|   crushed |   vinegar |
| 3 bay leaves, crushed | ½ package gelatin |
| 5 cloves | |

Put the pork and veal into a large pot, cover them with cold water, and bring to the boil. Drain the meat and repeat the process. When the fresh water comes to the boil, skim the surface and add the salt, pepper, allspice, bay leaves, cloves, and the onion and carrot. Reduce the heat, cover, and simmer for 1½ to 2 hours, or until the meat is tender.

Remove the meat, and when it is cool enough to handle, cut it into small cubes and set aside.

Return the veal bones to the stock and cook them for another ½ hour. Strain the stock and return about 4 cups to the pot with the meat and cook for another 10 minutes. Add more white pepper to taste, and the vinegar. Soak the gelatin in ½ cup of stock taken from the pot, and when it is soft, add to the meat. Stir until the gelatin has dissolved completely.

Rinse 1 or more molds with cold water, fill with the meat and stock, and leave to set in a cool place. Unmold onto a serving dish and cut into slices. Pickled beets are served with jellied pork and veal.

Spiced beef, a medieval recipe for preserving the meat, is still made on the east coast of the United States, in Ireland, and in northern England. Usually it is served cold, but in Ireland, where it is a traditional Christmas meat, it is sometimes eaten hot. The Irish cookery writer Theodora Fitzgibbon gives this recipe in *The Food of the Western World.*

"Lean cuts such as brisket, rump, round, or tailend should be used. For a 6 lb joint, 3 bay leaves, 1 teaspoon cloves, 2 chopped shallots, 1 teaspoon each mace and allspice, ½ teaspoon crushed peppercorns, 3 tablespoons brown sugar, and chopped thyme and rosemary are all well mixed in a mortar. Then 1 lb coarse salt and 1 teaspoon saltpetre are added and mixed well in. This mixture is rubbed all over the meat, which is then laid on a bed of the same mixture. The meat is left for 2 days, more of the spiced mixture already in the bowl being rubbed in each day. Then 2 tablespoons treacle [molasses] is poured over and rubbed with the spiced salt mixture, into the joint. The meat is left for a week, being turned and rubbed each day. At the end of this time, it is tied up, covered with water, and simmered very gently with root vegetables for 5–6 hours. Then it is pressed between 2 dishes and weighted."

# CASSEROLES, ETC.

The casseroles, pot roasts, ragouts, and sundry stews made for Christmas are hearty, warming recipes—forgiving dishes to be kept warm for latecomers, heated up for unexpected guests, and left unattended for hours at a time while everyone has a party.

*Christmas colombo* from Martinique is usually made with pork. The curry mixture, *poudre de colombo,* brought to the Caribbean in the middle of the last century by migrant Hindu workers, is a mild one. Most of the tropical fruits and vegetables for this bright, golden dish can be found, fresh or canned, in markets and specialty food stores.

## CHRISTMAS COLOMBO

[MARTINIQUE]                                    FOR 6 TO 8

### FOR THE POUDRE DE COLOMBO

1/4 teaspoon turmeric
1 teaspoon ground coriander
    seeds
1 teaspoon ground mustard
    seeds

3 cloves garlic, chopped
    coarse
2 fresh red chili peppers,*
    seeded and chopped
    coarse

* See note page 76 on preparing fresh chilies.

## FOR THE CASSEROLE

3 pounds pork
4 tablespoons peanut or
  coconut oil
2 medium onions, chopped
2 cloves garlic, minced
1 tablespoon tamarind pulp
1 green mango, peeled and
  chopped coarse
¾ pound West Indian
  pumpkin
1 large green papaya
  (optional)
1 large eggplant
1 chayote, peeled and sliced

1 pound taro or white
  tropical yam, peeled
  and sliced
½ cup dry white wine or
  coconut milk
½ cup chicken stock
1–2 fresh hot peppers,
  seeded and chopped
  fine
Salt to taste
1 teaspoon lime juice
2 tablespoons dry Madeira
  or rhum vieux

To make the *poudre de colombo,* put the turmeric, coriander, and mustard in a small bowl or mortar. Add the garlic and the peppers. Pound these ingredients to a paste.

Cut the pork into large cubes. Heat the oil in a heavy frying pan over high heat and brown the pork lightly in several batches. Transfer the meat to a large, heavy casserole.

Sauté the onions in the oil remaining in the pan over low heat. Add the garlic and the *poudre de colombo.* Fry together for a few minutes, stirring occasionally, then transfer the onion mixture to the casserole.

Add to the casserole the tamarind pulp, mango, pumpkin, papaya, eggplant, chayote, and taro. Pour in the wine or coconut milk and chicken stock, and add 1 or more hot peppers. Bring slowly to the boil on top of the stove, reduce the heat, cover, and simmer very gently until both the meat and vegetables are tender, about 3 hours. Stir occasionally during cooking and add more stock if the stew becomes too dry.

Just before serving, add salt to taste, and stir in the lime juice and Madeira or *rhum vieux.* Plain boiled rice is the usual accompaniment to this substantial stew, which freezes well, too.

A pot roast of boned loin of pork stuffed with prunes and apples and cooked in a wine and cream sauce is another pork dish served in Denmark and Sweden. In Cyprus, *afelia,* pork cooked in red wine and handfuls of crushed coriander seeds, is invariably served on the day after Christmas, a day for visiting friends and eating erratic, leisurely meals. *Afelia* can be made in advance, left waiting, and reheated. It usually is.

## *AFELIA*
### *Pork and Coriander Casserole*

{CYPRUS}                                          TO SERVE 12 TO 16

*6 pounds lean pork*

**FOR THE MARINADE**

*½ pound fatty bacon*
*1 teaspoon salt*
*Black pepper, freshly ground, to taste*
*4 cups dry red wine*

**FOR THE CASSEROLE**

*¼ cup pork drippings or lard*
*½ cup coriander seeds, crushed*
*Salt to taste*
*Pepper to taste*

Cut the pork into 1-inch cubes. Put the meat in a deep bowl. Cut the bacon into small dice and add to the bowl with the salt and freshly ground pepper. Pour on the wine and leave the pork in a cool place to marinate for at least 24 hours. Marinating the pork for up to a week is not unusual and results in a flavor said in Cyprus to resemble wild boar.

Preheat oven to 300°F. Lift the meat from the marinade and pat it dry. Take out the bacon dice and pat dry also. Melt the drippings or lard in a heavy frying pan and fry the pork, the bacon from the marinade, and the coriander seeds in small batches until well browned. Transfer the meat, seeds, and pan juices to a deep casserole with a well-fitting lid.

Pour in the marinade, adjust the seasoning, and cook for about 3½ hours, or until the meat is tender. Skim off any excess fat before serving with boiled rice or potatoes.

Stuffed cabbage is a dish which brings tears of nostalgia to the eyes of expatriate Hungarians, Bulgarians, and Transylvanians. Variations on the theme of pork, bacon, smoked sausage, and cabbage in a rich sauce of sour cream and paprika are apparently limitless. It is served with bread dumplings or boiled potatoes, or both, and made well in advance for lunch on Christmas day. As the Hungarian explains: "Only the cabbage is good reheated, not friendship or love."

## TOLTOTT KAPOSZTA
### Stuffed Cabbage

{HUNGARY}                                        TO SERVE 8

### FOR THE CABBAGE ROLLS

| | |
|---|---|
| 8 large fresh white cabbage leaves | 1 egg, beaten |
| 1/4 pound bacon | 1 tablespoon paprika |
| 1 small onion, chopped fine | 1/2 teaspoon salt |
| 1 pound lean pork, ground | Black pepper, freshly ground, to taste |
| 1 cup cooked white rice | |

### FOR THE CASSEROLE

| | |
|---|---|
| 3 tablespoons pork drippings or lard | Black pepper to taste |
| 1 pound pork belly | 1 tablespoon flour |
| 1 small onion, chopped fine | 1 cup stock |
| 2 tablespoons paprika | 1 cup sour cream |
| 5 cups sauerkraut | 1 pound smoked sausage |
| Salt to taste | 8 pork chops |

To make the cabbage rolls, blanch the cabbage leaves in boiling water for about 5 minutes. They should be flexible but not too tender. Drain and set them aside.

Chop the bacon into fine dice and cook it in a heavy frying pan over low heat until the fat runs. Add the onion and cook together until the onion is soft, but not brown. Raise the heat and add the ground pork. Stir it for a minute or two with the bacon and onion. Transfer the mixture to a bowl and add the cooked rice, egg, paprika, salt, and a generous sprinkling of freshly ground pepper. Mix together thoroughly.

Divide the pork among the cabbage leaves and roll them up from the stalk end, tucking in the sides to make neat parcels. Lay the rolls seam side down on a plate and set aside.

To prepare the casserole, melt 2 tablespoons of the pork drippings or lard in a large, heavy casserole. Cut the pork belly into 16 pieces and fry gently until the fat in the meat begins to run. Take out the pork and set aside. Add the onion to the casserole and fry gently until soft but not brown. Take the casserole off the heat and stir in the paprika. When it is thoroughly blended, add the drained sauerkraut, reserved fried pork, salt, and pepper. Set aside.

Melt the remaining tablespoon of pork drippings or lard in a small saucepan and stir in the flour. Cook the *roux* for a minute, then gradually add the stock, stirring constantly. Cook the sauce for another 2 minutes before stirring in the sour cream.

Pour half the sour cream sauce into the casserole and mix it well with the sauerkraut and pork. Arrange the cabbage rolls on top of the sauerkraut and cover them with the rest of the sour cream sauce. Return the casserole to the stove and bring slowly to the boil. Lower the heat, cover tightly, and simmer gently for about 1½ hours.

To finish the casserole, cut the smoked sausage into 8 pieces. Grill or fry the sausage and pork chops until tender. Arrange them on top of the cabbage rolls and serve very hot.

More sour cream may be added to the casserole at the end of the cooking time. Dill and caraway seeds are often used in this dish.


In Polish homes the substantial winter casserole is *bigos,* a hunters' stew of venison, beef, pork, and smoked sausage cooked slowly on a bed of sauerkraut with dried mushrooms, onions, apples, and tomatoes in a rich wine gravy. On New Year's Eve *bigos* is washed down with vodka. Danish housewives make *kraseragout,* a ragout of goose giblets and onions seasoned with a hint of curry powder and paprika. Madeira or sherry are added toward the end of the cooking time.

*Cassoulet,* one of the triumphs of French country cooking, is a peasant dish so good that gourmets make long detours to sample a recommended one. Like the chef's stockpot, a fine restaurant's *cassoulet* is a living thing, topped up and added to, always the same and always subtly different. Save the drippings and leftover pieces of Christmas goose for this recipe. Turkey, duck, ham—all find their way to new life through the *cassoulet* pot.

## CASSOULET
### Poultry and Beans

[FRANCE]                                                    TO SERVE 8

4 cups white kidney or navy
    beans
½ pound fat bacon,
    chopped coarse
2 large onions, chopped
    fine
5 cloves garlic, minced
2 large tomatoes, peeled
    and chopped fine
1 tablespoon chopped
    parsley
½ teaspoon dried thyme
¼ teaspoon dried sage
5 cups beef or chicken
    stock

Salt to taste
Black pepper, freshly
    ground, to taste
1 clove garlic
1½–2 pounds cooked
    goose, duck, turkey, or
    chicken, cut into large
    pieces
1 pound fresh coarse pork
    sausages
½ cup goose drippings, or
    other drippings
2 cups fresh white bread
    crumbs

Soak the beans overnight. Next day bring them to the boil in at least double their volume of fresh water and cook them, covered, until just tender, about 2½ hours. Cook the beans gently so that most remain whole. Drain and reserve.

Cook the bacon slowly in a heavy pot until the fat begins to run. Add the onions, garlic, and tomatoes. When the onions are soft but not browned, add the herbs and stock. Season to taste with salt and freshly ground pepper. Cover and simmer for about ½ hour.

Preheat oven to 300°F. To assemble the dish, cut the clove of garlic and rub over the inside of a deep casserole. Put the goose or other poultry in the bottom of the pot with the sausages and the drippings. Spread the beans over the meat and pour in the stock. Bring the *cassoulet* slowly to the boil on top of the stove, then spread the crumbs over the top and finish cooking, uncovered, for about 1½ hours, or until most of the stock has been absorbed and the bread crumbs have formed a crust over the beans.

Serve the *cassoulet* just as it is, in bowls or deep soup plates.

*Guajolote con molé poblano*, turkey with a chili and chocolate sauce, is Mexico's most celebrated and celebrative dish. As is the way with such successful combinations of ingredients, the number of recipes to choose from is great. Authenticity is claimed for a recipe given in a pamphlet sold by the Convent of Santa Rosa in Puebla where the dish is said to have been invented in the eighteenth century for a visiting bishop. Its proportions are heroic compared with the timid versions usually given, but the quantities of chilies called for—2 pounds mulato chilies, and 2½ pounds each of pasilla and ancho chilies—are quite unobtainable for most cooks and make a truly enormous quantity of sauce.

Cans of this complicated concoction are widely available in specialty food shops. In Mexico, where all kinds of chilies are sold from heaped market stalls and packaged in supermarkets, city dwellers can buy freshly ground chili blends—dark, dry pastes—from bins labeled with the names of the dishes they are to be used for. A good shop will have several *molé poblano* pastes to choose from and you will be asked whether you would like a hot or a sweet mixture. The recipe which follows produces a sauce which is pungent and has heat without hellfire.

## GUAJOLOTE CON MOLÉ POBLANO
### Turkey with Chili Sauce

[MEXICO]                                      TO SERVE 10 TO 12

*1 8–9 pound turkey*
*½ cup butter or lard*

**FOR THE SAUCE**

*6 ancho chilies*
*6 mulato chilies*
*4 pasilla chilies*
*1¼ cups sesame seeds*
*½ cup lard*
*1 pound tomatoes, peeled and chopped coarse*
*1 cup blanched almonds, chopped coarse*
*4 tablespoons seedless raisins, chopped coarse*
*6 cloves garlic, minced*
*1 teaspoon powdered aniseed*
*1 teaspoon powdered cinnamon*
*½ teaspoon powdered cloves*
*Black pepper to taste*
*1 fried tortilla, or 1 slice white bread*
*1–2 cups turkey or chicken stock*
*Salt to taste*
*1 ounce unsweetened cooking chocolate*

First prepare the chilies.* Remove the stalks and seeds and tear the flesh into small pieces. Cover chilies with boiling water and leave them to soak for at least an hour and preferably overnight.

Put the turkey into a large, heavy pot and cover with cold water. Bring to the boil, skim the stock, cover, and simmer for about 1 hour.

Preheat the oven to 400°F. Take the turkey out of the pot, strain and reserve the stock. Pat the bird dry, spread it with butter or lard, and set it in a generously greased roasting pan. Roast for 1 hour or more until turkey is well-browned and the meat cooked through. Test with a sharp skewer inserted into the thickest part of the leg, near the body. The juices should run clear. The skin should be rather hard and brittle.

To make the sauce, toast the sesame seeds until golden in a heavy frying pan over high heat, shaking the pan occasionally. Drain the chilies.

Melt the lard in a large, heavy pot and fry together the chilies, tomatoes, almonds, raisins, sesame seeds, and garlic. Use low heat and sauté the mixture gently until the chilies and garlic are soft.

Purée the mixture in an electric blender, or put it through a mechanical food mill using the finest mesh disk.

Transfer the purée to a large, wide pot and add the spices and fried tortilla or bread, broken into small pieces. Add sufficient reserved stock to make a thin sauce, and stir the mixture over low heat until it thickens. Add salt to taste and the chocolate. Stir until the chocolate melts.

Transfer the turkey to a heated serving dish and pour the sauce over it.

Note: It is more usual now to cut the parboiled turkey into serving pieces and sauté it than to roast it whole.


Puerto Rico's chicken and rice stew, *asopao de pollo,* is made for the main Christmas meal. The mixture of chicken, sweet peppers, and rice is not an unusual one; it is the addition of cheese and olives which gives this dish its individual character.

* For preparation of chilies, see note on page 76.

## ASOPAO DE POLLO
### Chicken and Rice Stew

{PUERTO RICO}                    TO SERVE 4 TO 6

2 cloves garlic
1 teaspoon salt
½ teaspoon oregano
1 2½–3 pound chicken
3 tablespoons lard
1 medium onion, chopped
1 medium green bell
    pepper, seeded and
    chopped
2 ounces cooked ham,
    chopped fine
2 medium tomatoes, peeled
    and chopped
1½ cups long-grain white
    rice

Black pepper, freshly
    ground, to taste
6¼ cups chicken stock
¾ cup green peas
1 tablespoon capers
20 pimento-stuffed green
    olives
1 cup Parmesan cheese,
    freshly grated
2 medium red bell peppers
6 or more asparagus tips,
    cooked

Peel the garlic and crush it with the salt and oregano. Cut the chicken into 6 or 8 pieces and rub the seasoned garlic into them. Melt the lard in a heavy casserole or Dutch oven and sauté the chicken until golden. Lift out the chicken and set aside.

Fry the onion and green pepper together in the fat remaining in the pan until the onion is soft but not brown. Add the ham and the tomatoes, stir the mixture, and return the chicken to the casserole. Cover and cook over low heat for about ½ hour, or until the chicken is tender. Lift out the chicken and set it aside to cool.

Add to the casserole the rice, lots of freshly ground pepper, and the chicken stock. Cover and cook for a further 20 minutes, or until the rice is tender.

Cut the cooked chicken into bite-sized chunks, discarding the bones. Return it to the casserole with the peas, capers, olives, and cheese. Stir all these together, then lay strips of red pepper and the asparagus tips on top of the stew. Cover and cook for a few minutes more, until the chicken is hot and the red pepper is tender but still crisp.

Serve asopao de pollo in bowls or soup plates.

Hospitality in the Philippines is a legendary generosity. A Filipino will save for a fiesta the way an American will save for a trip. Fiesta foods are much the same for Christmas as for other major festivals and they involve days, and often nights, of preparation. Everyone helps; cooking the feast is part of the party. After midnight mass on Christmas Eve there are presents and sometimes a savory snack. The main meal, an exotic spread of hot and cold foods, is eaten before church. *Arroz a la Cataläna,* a pilaf of chicken, pork, shrimp, and clams; *pollo relleno,* a boned fowl stuffed with pork, ham, eggs, cheese, and pickles, steamed and served hot; *paella;* roast suckling pig; and huge bowls of plain and fried rice and salads are just some of the fiesta dishes. *Callos con garbanzos,* tripe with chick-peas, is another, and demonstrates once again the influence of Spain on Filipino cuisine. *Chorizos de Bilbao* are Spanish sausages made from beef and pork seasoned with garlic and hot red pepper.

## CALLOS CON GARBANZOS
### Tripe with Chick-Peas

[PHILIPPINES]                                      TO SERVE 6 TO 8

*2 pounds tripe*
*1 1-pound cow heel or*
   *shank of veal*
*4 tablespoons olive oil*
*6 cloves garlic, minced*
*1 large onion, chopped fine*
*3 tablespoons tomato paste*
*2 chorizos de Bilbao (hot*
   *Spanish sausage), cut*
   *into 1-inch slices*

*1 medium red bell pepper,*
   *seeded and chopped*
*20 green olives*
*2 cups chick-peas, cooked*
*Salt to taste*
*Black pepper, freshly*
   *ground, to taste*

Thoroughly clean the tripe and cow heel. Put them into a large pot with just enough water to cover. Bring slowly to the boil, cover tightly, and simmer over low heat until very tender. This will usually take about 3 hours, but the cooking time can vary according to the type of tripe used. Drain and cool the meat. Skim the stock of fat and reduce it to about 2 cups by fast boiling. Cut the tripe into strips about 1 inch by ½ inch. Take the meat off the cow heel and cut it into pieces of approximately the same size.

Heat the oil in a casserole or Dutch oven and sauté the garlic and onion until golden. Add the reduced stock, tomato paste, sausages, and the red pepper. Cook, covered, over low heat for about 10 minutes or until the pepper is tender. Add the tripe, cow heel, olives, and chick-peas. Season to taste with salt and freshly ground pepper. Bring the mixture to the boil and simmer for a further 5 minutes before serving very hot.

*L'estouffat de boeuf* is one of the traditional dishes served in Gascony on Christmas Eve. It is in this region of southwest France that Armagnac is made, hence its lavish use. Ask the butcher to tie the meat into a thick, sausage-shaped roll. Long, slow cooking is the secret of this magnificent dish.

## L'ESTOUFFAT DE BOEUF
### Slow-Cooked Beef

{FRANCE}                                              TO SERVE 6

*¾ pound fresh pork rind*          *1 large onion, peeled and*
*3 pounds top round of beef*            *quartered*
*Salt to taste*                    *2 small carrots, scraped*
*Black pepper, freshly*            *½ cup Armagnac or brandy*
*   ground, to taste*             *2 cups dry red wine*
*4 shallots, peeled*

Preheat oven to 325°F. Put the fresh pork rind into an oval casserole which will hold the meat without too much space around it. Season the beef with salt and freshly ground pepper, and lay it on the pork rind. Arrange the shallots, onion, and carrots around the meat and add the Armagnac or brandy and the wine. The liquid should just cover the meat. Cover, using kitchen foil to make a good seal if necessary, and put the casserole in the preheated oven. After 1 hour reduce the oven heat to 275°F and continue cooking for about 6 hours.

   To finish, skim the fat from the casserole and cut the pork rind, which is usually eaten with the meat, into serving pieces. Carve the beef into thick slices and lay them on a warmed serving dish. Pour on the gravy with its pork rind and vegetables. Serve with plenty of creamed potatoes.

# SAVORY PIES

Savory pies is a loose description of the offerings in this chapter. It covers everything from *juustipiirakkaa,* the little rye-crust cheese pies served with broth in Finland, to the banquet-sized Christmas pies of old England, by way of the fiesta *tamales* of Central and South America, and Caribbean and African specialties cooked in a similar fashion. These are splendid recipes for hot or cold buffet parties.

> Little Jack Horner sat in a corner
> Eating a Christmas pie.
> He put in his thumb
> And pulled out a plum
> And said "What a good boy am I."

The plum Jack Horner of the nursery rhyme found was not the fruit, though it could be seen as a fruit of his labor. Jack Horner was steward to the last Abbot of Glastonbury. He was entrusted with delivering a Christmas pie from the abbot to Henry VIII in London. During the journey he looked under the pie crust and found the deeds to several manor houses in the county of Somerset. He helped himself to the papers of the Manor of Mells, which remained in the Horner family for some years afterward.

The great English Christmas pies were truly majestic constructions. For the best of them a coffin of strong pastry—which was not intended to be eaten—enclosed, say, a goose stuffed with a chicken, stuffed with a pheasant, stuffed with a partridge, stuffed with a pigeon. All the birds were boned, encased in strong paste, and the gaps filled with pieces of game, forcemeat, herbs, and hard-boiled eggs. After baking, highly flavored stock was poured in to fill every nook and cranny, and when it had set to a jelly, melted butter was used to seal the pie. Effectively, this made a terrine which would keep for some time and which allowed the pies, the most famous of which were made in Yorkshire, to be sent as gifts all over the country in the days before fast trains.

Pies of this type were first made in the Middle Ages when a plain flour-and-water crust was wrapped around meat to prevent its drying out during baking. This method of baking or roasting meat is still used occasionally, especially for cured hams, but the pastry now is usually made to be eaten.

Pies raised with a hot-water crust are quite easy to make. The process is not a quick one, but the results are spectacular and delicious—so much crisper and tastier than bought pies that the effort is more than repaid. Once baked they keep fresh in a refrigerator for about a week, but the pastry loses its special crunch. Ideally these pies should be baked no more than a day before they are to be eaten; however, freezing pies as soon as they are finished allows them to be made well in advance. Thaw them at room temperature for 12 to 24 hours, depending on size. Although aspics do sometimes lose their set when thawed, I have not found this to be so with raised pies.

## RAISED GAME PIE

{ENGLAND}                                                    TO SERVE 8

### FOR THE FILLING

2 pounds pheasant, grouse,
    partridge, or hare
½ cup port wine
Salt to taste
Black pepper, freshly
    ground, to taste
¾ pound lean pork
½ pound bacon

1 medium onion
½ teaspoon dried sage
1 tablespoon chopped
    parsley
Grated rind of ½ lemon
½ pound fresh pork
    sausage meat

## FOR THE JELLIED STOCK

| | |
|---|---|
| *2 pounds veal bones, chopped* | *1 medium carrot, scraped and chopped coarse* |
| *Game carcasses (from game above)* | *2 bay leaves* |
| *1 medium onion* | *6 black peppercorns, crushed* |

## FOR THE PASTRY

| | |
|---|---|
| *4 cups flour* | *1 cup lard, or half lard* |
| *1 teaspoon salt* | *and half butter* |
| *1 egg yolk* | |

## TO GLAZE

*1 egg, beaten*

First prepare the ingredients for the filling. Cut the meat off the game and reserve the carcasses for the stock. Slice the meat into slivers about 2 inches long by ¼ inch wide and thick. Marinate these in the port with a little salt and black pepper, and set aside.

Put the game meat trimmings, lean pork, bacon, and onion through the coarse blade of a grinder and mix the ground meats in a bowl with the sage and parsley. Season with salt, plenty of freshly ground pepper, and the lemon rind. Mix well and set aside.

Roll teaspoonfuls of the sausage meat into balls and set aside.

To make the stock, put the veal bones and game carcasses into a large pot with the onion and carrot. Cover with cold water and bring to the boil. Skim the stock, add the bay leaves and peppercorns, cover, and simmer for 2½ hours. Strain the stock through a fine sieve lined with cheesecloth and discard the bones. Reduce the stock to about 1¼ cups by fast boiling. Set aside to cool.

To make the pastry, sift the flour and salt into a warmed mixing bowl. Make a well in the flour, drop in the egg yolk and cover it over with flour. Heat the lard, or lard and butter with ¾ cup water in a small saucepan, and when the fat has melted, bring to the boil. Pour immediately over the flour and stir vigorously with a wooden spoon until the mixture is cool enough to handle.

Turn out the dough onto a lightly floured board and knead it until it is soft and pliable. Rest the dough, covered, in a warm place for about 20 minutes.

Preheat oven to 450°F. To assemble the pie, lightly grease an oval or rectangular spring form pan, 2-quart capacity, or line a 7-inch loose-bottomed cake pan with foil. Pat dry the strips of marinated game.

Roll out two-thirds of the pastry into a piece large enough to line the pan. Fold the pastry in half and lower it carefully into the mold. Unfold it and ease it smoothly and evenly into the base and up the sides of the mold. Press the dough well into the junction of the base and sides, and into any indentations on a fancy mold. Ideally, the lining should be about ¼ inch thick. If it is too thin the pie will suffer a structural failure, and if it is too thick there will be a layer of cooked but soggy dough between the meat and the crust.

Put half the ground pork and bacon mixture in the bottom of the lined pan. Cover with slivers of game, arranged lengthwise and interspersed with the sausagemeat balls. Top with the remaining pork and bacon. Press the mixture in lightly and mold the top into a dome shape. Dampen the top edge of the pastry with the beaten egg. Roll the remaining dough to a thickness of about ¼ inch, lift it over a rolling pin, and lay it gently on top of the pie. Press the lid on firmly and trim the pastry with a sharp knife. Decorate the edge and insure a tight seal by pressing firmly with the back of a fork. Cut a 1-inch cross through the pastry in the center of the lid and fold back the four points to make a good opening for escaping steam. Reroll the pastry trimmings and cut decorative flowers or leaves. Stick them to the pie lid with beaten egg glaze, then paint all the exposed pastry with the glaze.

Set the pie on a baking sheet and bake in preheated oven for 20 minutes to set the pastry. Reduce the heat to 325°F, cover the pie loosely with foil, and bake for 2½ hours. Remove the foil and bake for an additional ½ hour. Leave the pie in its mold until almost cool.

Remove the mold and when the pie is nearly cold, pour into it as much of the cool liquid stock as it will accept. Pour slowly through a small funnel or icing nozzle.

Leave the pie in a cool place for several hours before serving. The jelly will set and fill the gaps between the pastry and the meat, which will have shrunk during baking.

Serve the pie cold, cut into slices or wedges.

With so much work involved, it is well worth doubling or tripling the quantities to make several pies in one session.

For a classic pork pie of the same size, fill with 2¾ pounds of fresh pork from the leg or shoulder. The meat should have a moderate amount of fat. Cut it into ¼-inch dice and mix with 1 teaspoon salt, ½ teaspoon black pepper, and 1 leaf of sage, chopped very fine. Season the stock with marjoram, sage, thyme, and bay leaves.

Queen Victoria's chef, Francatelli, explains how to raise a pie without a mold in his instructions for a capon pie with truffles. His own recipe for hot-water crust is too hard and cardboard-like for modern tastes, so quadruple the pastry recipe for game pie if you are ambitious enough to construct his magnificent pie for a large party.

"First, bone a capon, spread it out on the table, and season the inside with prepared spices and a little salt; then spread a layer of forcemeat of fat livers, and place upon this, in alternate rows, some square fillets or strips of fat bacon, tongue, and truffles; cover these with a layer of the forcemeat, repeat the strips of bacon, then fold both sides of the skin over each other, so as to give the capon a plump appearance, and set it aside on a dish.

"Next, pare off the sinewy skin from the mouse piece, or inner part of a leg of veal, *daube* it with seasoned lardons of fat bacon, then place this, and an equal quantity of dressed ham, with the capon.

"Prepare 4 lbs of hot water paste; take two-thirds of this, mold it into a round ball on the slab with the palm of the hand, and then roll it out in the form of a band, about two feet long and six inches wide; trim the edges, and pare the ends square, taking care to cut them in a slanting direction; wet them with a paste brush dipped in water with a little flour, and wrap them over one another neatly and firmly, so as to show the join as little as possible. Next roll out half the remainder of the paste, either in a circular or oval form, about a quarter of an inch thick, to the size the pie is intended to be made; place this, with buttered paper under it, on a baking sheet, wet it round the edge with a paste brush dipped in water, and stick a narrow band of the paste, about half an inch high, all round it, to within an inch of the edge. The wall or crust of the pie is to be raised up round this, and by pressing on it with the tips of the fingers, it should be made to adhere effectually to the foundation. Then, by pressing the upper part of the pie with the fingers and thumbs of both hands, it will acquire a more elegant appearance, somewhat resembling the curved lip of a vase. The base must be spread out in proportion to the top, by pressing on it with the thumb. The bottom and sides of the pie should now be lined with a coating of forcemeat of fat livers, or, if preferred, with veal and fat bacon, in equal proportions, well-seasoned, chopped fine and pounded. Next place in the veal and ham, previously cut up in thick slices and well seasoned, and fill up the cavity with some of the forcemeat. Then add the capon and cover it over, and round, with the remainder of the forcemeat, placing some truffles in with it, and cover the whole with thin layers of fat bacon. Roll out the remainder of the paste, and after wetting this, and the pie round the edges, use it to cover in the pie, pressing the edges tightly with the fingers and thumb, in order to make them adhere closely together. Trim the edge neatly and pinch it round with the pastry pincers. The pie should then be egged over, and decorated, for which latter purpose a similar kind of paste must be used, being first rolled out thin, then cut out in the form of leaves, half moons, rings, etc., and arranged according to the designs required: or, if preferred, a moulding raised from decorating boards with some of the paste, may be used instead.

"The pie must be placed in the oven, and baked for about 4 hours, and when done, should be withdrawn, and about a pint of strongly reduced consommé (made from the carcasses of the capons, two calves feet and the usual seasoning), should be introduced within it through a funnel. It must then be kept in a cold place until wanted for use; when the cover should be carefully removed without breaking it, and after the top of the pie has been decorated with some bright aspic jelly, it may be put on again and sent to table.

"Note: For making pies of turkeys, fowls, pheasants, grouse, partridges etc., follow the above directions."

Malta's party pie is *timpana* and, despite its solidity, it often precedes roast turkey on the Christmas table.

## TIMPANA
### Macaroni Pie

[MALTA]                                            TO SERVE 6 TO 8

| | |
|---|---|
| 1 large onion, chopped fine | 1/2 pound chicken livers, |
| 4 tablespoons butter or oil | quartered |
| 1/2 pound lean pork, ground | 1 pound elbow macaroni |
| 1/2 pound beef, ground | 4 eggs, beaten |
| 1/2 teaspoon salt | 1/4 cup grated Parmesan |
| Black pepper, freshly | cheese |
| ground, to taste | 1 pound prepared puff |
| 3 tablespoons tomato paste | pastry (see page 209) |
| 1 1/4 cups beef or chicken | or flaky pastry |
| stock | |

Fry the onion in 3 tablespoons of the butter or oil in a large pot until golden. Add the ground meats, salt, and a generous sprinkling of freshly ground pepper. Sauté gently for about 15 minutes, then add the tomato paste and stock. Simmer, partially covered, for 1 to 1½ hours.

Preheat the oven to 350°F. Melt the remaining tablespoon of butter in a small pot and sauté the chicken livers until just firm. Set aside.

Boil the macaroni in plenty of salted water until barely tender. As soon as it is done rinse it in cold water and drain.

Mix the macaroni with the meat and tomato mixture. Add the eggs and the grated cheese. Check the seasoning and adjust to taste.

Roll out three-quarters of the pastry and lay it on a lipped pie plate. Spread half the meat and macaroni mixture over the base, top with fried chicken livers, and finish with the remainder of the meat and macaroni. Roll out the remaining pastry and lay it over the pie. Seal the edge by pinching it with your fingers, or pressing firmly with the back of a fork. Slash the lid with two small diagonal cuts to let the steam escape.

Bake the *timpana* for 1 to 1½ hours. A wide, flat pie will cook more quickly than a deep one. When the pie is cooked leave it to stand for about 15 minutes in a turned-off oven. This makes it easier to cut into neat slices or wedges. Serve hot or warm.

Canada also has a double-crust Christmas pie called *tourtière* or *pâté de Noël*, filled with chopped pork and veal or chicken, and seasoned with plenty of onion and allspice.

The Filipino fish pastries, *pastelitos de pescado*, are a simple fiesta dish which translates well into canapés. Use any cooked white fish for these pastries.

## PASTELITOS DE PESCADO
### Fish Pastries

{PHILIPPINES}                              TO MAKE 20 TO 24 PIECES

FOR THE PASTRY

| | |
|---|---|
| 4 cups cake or all-purpose flour | 1 teaspoon salt |
| | ¾ cup butter |
| 1 teaspoon sugar | 4 egg yolks, beaten |

FOR THE FILLING

2 tablespoons butter

1 medium onion, chopped
  fine

2 medium tomatoes, peeled,
  seeded, and chopped
  fine

2 cups cooked fish, flaked

¼ pound frankfurters,
  chopped fine

¼ cup grated American or
  Cheddar cheese

Salt to taste

Black pepper, freshly
  ground, to taste

TO GLAZE

2 egg yolks, beaten

To make the pastry, sift the flour, sugar, and salt together into a mixing bowl. Dice the butter into the bowl and work it lightly into the flour with your fingertips or a pastry blender. When the mixture has the texture of fine bread crumbs, mix in the egg yolks. Sprinkle the mixture with just enough cold water to bring the dough together. Gather the dough into a ball and rest it in the refrigerator.

To make the filling, melt the butter in a large frying pan and sauté the onion and tomatoes together until the onion softens. Add the flaked fish, the frankfurters, and the cheese. Season the mixture to taste with salt and freshly ground pepper, and cook the ingredients together for 3 minutes more.

Preheat oven to 400°F. Roll the pastry dough into a large rectangle about ⅛ inch thick. Divide in two and trim the pieces to matching size. Cover one piece of pastry with the filling, spread in an even layer, and top with the second piece of pastry. Run the rolling pin lightly over the top. Cut the filled pastry into neat rectangles and arrange them on a greased and floured baking sheet. Brush each piece with beaten egg yolk and bake for about 20 minutes or until the pastry is golden brown. Serve hot or cold.

# JUUSTIPIIRAKKAA
### Cheese Piirakkaa

[FINLAND]                                                              TO MAKE 24

**FOR THE CRUST**

½ teaspoon salt                          ¾ cup all-purpose flour
1 tablespoon melted butter               ¾ cup rye flour
  or oil

**FOR THE FILLING**

2 cups grated Cheddar or Gruyère cheese
2 tablespoons flour

**TO BASTE**

¼ cup hot milk
1 tablespoon melted butter

Preheat oven to 450°F. To make the pastry, mix ½ cup water with the salt and shortening in a bowl and beat in the white flour to make a smooth paste. Add the rye flour and stir until well blended, then turn the dough out onto a floured board and knead it until smooth. Pat the dough out with your hands into a sausage shape 1 inch in diameter, and cut it into 24 pieces. Roll each piece of dough into a thin circle 3 to 4 inches in diameter.

To make the filling, simply mix the grated cheese with the flour.

Place about 2 tablespoons of filling on each piece of pastry and spread it to within ½ inch of the edge of each circle. Fold two sides of the pastry toward the center, leaving a ½ inch band of filling exposed in the middle. Crimp the edges of the now oval pastries and arrange the *piirakkaa* on a greased sheet. Bake for about 15 minutes, or until the pastries are lightly browned. Mix the milk and butter, and brush twice during baking with the mixture, and again as soon as they are out of the oven.

Serve the *piirakkaa* with soup. They should be brought to the table hot, covered with a napkin to soften the rye crust a little. If they are to be eaten cold, wrap them in foil while still hot to prevent the pastry from hardening too much.

*Tamales* have been the fiesta food of Mexican Indians since the Aztec priests first made them as offerings to the gods. In the wake of the Spanish explorers came missionaries, and the place of *tamales* as a sacred food was transferred to the Christian festivals. Mexican *tamales* vary from region to region, as well as with the skill of the cook. The most celebrated are made from blue Mexican corn shortened with lard.

*Tamales* are akin to stuffed pasta, inasmuch as morsels of meat and vegetables in a well-seasoned sauce are enclosed in cooked dough. But there the similarity ends. *Tamale* fillings are usually highly spiced with chili and they are always cooked in individual wrappers by steaming.

The main difficulty facing Mexicans far from home is the dough itself. In the old days, dried corn was soaked in a mixture of water and wood ash, a lye in other words, and cooked, then scraped for hours on a slab of volcanic rock. Now cornmeal flour called *masa harina* does away with the back-breaking work, but its availability is very limited outside Central America and large cities in North America. (Mexican embassies always know if there is any to be bought locally.) *Masa harina* is an off-white flour and has a distinctive taste which comes from treating the corn with lye. Fine yellow cornmeal, however, is widely available and makes a nutty-flavored dough often served in the Yucatan.

Corn shucks, or husks, the proper wrappers for *tamales* in many parts of Mexico, and banana leaves, used in the Yucatan, are seldom obtainable either. However baking parchment and aluminum foil are less colorful substitutes which work well. Cut them into rectangles 9 inches by 4 inches.

Pork and turkey, in addition to the chicken in the following recipe, are traditional *tamale* fillings at fiesta time, and any leftover turkey with chili and chocolate sauce, *guajolote con molé poblano* (see page 97), may, of course, be used instead of the chicken and sauce given in the following recipe.

## TAMALES DE POLLO
### Chicken Tamales

{MEXICO}                                          TO MAKE 24

24 corn husks
5 tablespoons lard
2 cups instant masa harina
    or cornmeal flour
1½ teaspoons baking
    powder

½ teaspoon salt
1½ cups hot chicken stock
    or water

FOR THE FILLING

> *¾ pound cooked chicken, diced fine*
> *6 tablespoons Chimolé (Mexican chili sauce) (see page 229)*

Soak the corn husks in hot water for about ½ hour to soften them, then pat dry.

Cream the lard in a large bowl until very light and fluffy. Sift together the *masa harina,* baking powder, and salt. Gradually beat the flour mixture into the lard a little at a time. When all the flour has been incorporated add the hot stock a little at a time, beating constantly, to form a soft dough.

To prepare the filling, combine the cooked chicken with the sauce.

To assemble the *tamales,* put a rounded tablespoonful of the dough in the middle of each corn husk, parchment, or foil wrapper and spread it into a rectangle which extends almost the full width, but only about 3 inches along the length. Put a rounded tablespoon of filling on the center of each piece of dough. Fold one long side of the wrapper just past the center of the filling, then fold in the opposite side to make an overlapping center seam. Turn the ends in over the seam, overlapping them just enough to tuck into each other.

To cook the *tamales,* lay them, seam side down, in a fish kettle, steamer, or colander, in as many layers as necessary. Steam them, tightly covered, over boiling water for about 1 hour, or until the dough is cooked.

Serve *tamales* very hot, piled on a heated serving dish, in their wrappers.

*Nacatamales* are still the traditional Christmas Eve feast in rural Nicaragua where they are eaten very hot with *tortillas* and black coffee after "cock Mass" at midnight. Banana leaves are the correct wrappers for *nacatamales* and each, at the size of a thick paperback book, is a meal in itself. The dough is the same as for Mexican tamales and a typical filling would consist of chunks of pork and bacon combined with cooked rice and potato, slices of onion, bell pepper, tomato, olives, raisins, and a spoonful of garlic and tomato sauce, all topped with a sprig of mint. About 4 hours' steaming is needed for *nacatamales,* which are often prepared in advance and reheated so that all the flavors are well blended.

The cornmeal dough for Ecuador's *tamales navidenos* is enriched with eggs, sugar, and fresh cottage cheese, and these small, chicken-filled confections are steamed in *achira* leaves. They are a traditional second course of the main Christmas meal, eaten after soup and before roast turkey. Improvising a substitute for the local cooking pot, the *tamalera,* presents no problems, but only *achira* leaves will do for the wrappers. Without the taste and color they impart to the food, say Ecuadorian cooks, there are no *tamales navidenos.*

Maybe it says more of national characteristics than of differing cuisines that Nigerians see the replacement of leaves with kitchen foil as progress and happily use it for their festive dish *moyin-moyin.* A Nigerian cook uses foil if she can afford it and positively enjoys improvisation. Black-eyed peas are the basis of the dough for *moyin-moyin,* and fillings vary greatly with the whim of the cook and what is available in the market.

## MOYIN-MOYIN
### Bean-Dough Parcels

[NIGERIA]                                                    TO MAKE 18

| | |
|---|---|
| 18 foil wrappers | 1 tablespoon chili powder |
| 3 cups black-eyed peas | Salt to taste |
| 1 cup palm oil or vegetable oil | Pepper to taste |
| 2 small onions, chopped fine | ¾ pound cooked pork sausage, kidney, or liver, diced |
| 4 medium tomatoes, peeled and chopped fine | |

To make the foil wrappers, cut kitchen foil into rectangles about 12 inches by 4½ inches. Make each piece into a bag about 3 inches by 6 inches by folding the strips in half and turning the edges over three times on either side.

Break up the black-eyed peas in a coffee grinder to pieces the size of chopped nuts for a dessert topping. When broken, put into a bowl and cover them with cold water. After 5 minutes skim off the skins and eyes which have floated to the surface, drain the residue, and pick out any remaining pieces of skin. Put the skinned peas in an electric blender or liquidizer and blend them to a smooth paste with sufficient water to produce the consistency of very thick cream. Set aside.

Heat the oil in a heavy pot and fry the onions and tomatoes until the onions are golden. Add the chili powder and stir. Now combine the black-eyed pea and onion mixtures, add the seasonings to taste, and stir them thoroughly until well blended.

To assemble the *moyin-moyin,* put a tablespoonful of the pea and onion mixture into each bag, followed by a portion of the meat and another tablespoonful of peas. Turn over the tops of the bags three times to make a good seal, but allow plenty of room for the mixture to swell.

Stand the packages upright in a fish kettle or steamer, or in a colander over a pot, and steam them, tightly covered, over boiling water for about 45 minutes. The contents are fully cooked when the bean dough has a solid consistency throughout. Uncooked centers are damp like under-cooked cake.

Serve *moyin-moyin* in their wrappers on a warmed dish. *Jollof* rice (see page 128) is the usual accompaniment. Desserts and fruit are seldom served at mealtimes in Nigeria but are eaten as snacks. Drinking with meals is not customary either, but at Christmas beer, mineral water, or the powerful local gin are offered after Christmas dinner.

Stuffed banana leaves are also festive fare in Puerto Rico where the dough is made of grated and mashed plantains. A typical filling for *pasteles criollos* includes a fried mixture of beef and pork with capers, raisins, olives, and onions. These, too, are steamed for about an hour.

The meatballs made for Sweden's Christmas *smörgåsbord* are walnut-sized or even smaller. Peru's Christmas meatballs, called *papa rellena,* "stuffed potatoes," are indeed potato-sized. Each is a meal in itself. They are a hit with children who think it fun to find a meatball inside a golden jacket of fried potato.

# PAPA RELLENA
## Stuffed Potatoes

{PERU}                                                    TO SERVE 6

*3 pounds potatoes*                    *Salt to taste*
*2 tablespoons butter*                 *Black pepper, freshly*
*1 large onion, chopped fine*              *ground, to taste*
*1 clove garlic, minced*               *2 eggs, beaten*
*1½ pounds pork or beef,*              *½ cup flour*
    *ground*                          *½ cup lard*
*3 hard-boiled eggs, chopped*
    *fine*

Peel the potatoes and boil them in salted water until quite tender. Drain, mash them very thoroughly, and set aside.

Melt the butter in a large, heavy frying pan. Add the onion, garlic, and the pork or beef. Sauté them together over low heat until the meat is cooked through and slightly browned. Transfer to a bowl and add the hard-boiled eggs. Season the mixture to taste with salt and freshly ground pepper.

Form the meat mixture into 6 balls. Divide the mashed potato into 6 portions and cover each meatball with an even layer of potato. Roll the potato-covered balls in beaten egg and then in flour. Melt the lard and carefully fry the balls over low heat, turning them gently until they are crisp and golden all over.

The first time I tried this recipe I was sure the meatballs would fall apart or their potato jackets disintegrate in the frying pan. Surprisingly, they did not. Herbs may, of course, be added to the meat, although the original recipe does not list any.

# VEGETABLES AND SALADS

Vegetables are just about the last consideration when Christmas menus are being planned, often because their choice is determined—like the words of the popular song "love and marriage, love and marriage, go together like a horse and carriage"—by the selection of the bird or roast. Roast goose calls for caramelized potatoes and red cabbage in Denmark, and distinctive casseroles of puréed potatoes, turnips, or carrots are more or less mandatory with the baked Christmas hams of Finland. New Zealanders' choice of new potatoes and peas with the sweet new season's lamb might appear equally conservative but for their delightful custom of gathering the vegetables fresh from the garden on Christmas morning. With buttered asparagus or corn on the cob to begin the meal, weeks of skillful gardening are invested in bringing them all to the Christmas table at their peak.

Roast potatoes and boiled brussels sprouts turn up beside the Englishman's turkey with a regularity which would be less monotonous if either vegetable were generally more skillfully cooked. So, as well as particular Christmas dishes, this chapter includes some general guidance on cooking a few everyday vegetables, plus some recipes which are especially useful because they can be prepared in advance.

First let's deal with roast potatoes. The raw materials should be baking potatoes and fresh fat or oil. Peel the potatoes, cut them into chunks of approximately equal size, and parboil them in salted water for 5 minutes. Drain and dry them, then put them in a roasting pan with hot fat or drippings and roast near the top of a very hot 425°F oven for about 40 minutes. If the potatoes are turned over half through their cooking and served as soon as they are ready, this method produces roast potatoes which are crisp outside and creamy smooth inside. It works very well if you happen to be roasting meat or poultry at such a high temperature.

To accompany slow-roasted meat, using an oven temperature of about 350°F, put the parboiled potatoes in the roasting pan with the meat for the last hour of its cooking time. While this second method will certainly produce very tasty potatoes, there is no guarantee they will be crisp, as juices from the meat or poultry will soak into them.

So if, like me, you favor slow-roasted meat and crisp roast potatoes, and do not have two ovens, try the pan method. Boil even-sized chunks of old potato in salted water until they are tender but not falling apart. Drain the potatoes well. In a pot on top of the stove heat enough fresh vegetable oil to cover the potatoes. When the oil is really hot (about 375°F is ideal, or when a cube of day-old bread will brown in 40 to 50 seconds) drop in the cooked potatoes and fry them over fairly high heat until they are crisp and golden. Lift them from the pan, drain them on kitchen paper, and serve immediately.

I particularly like peanut oil for frying, but corn oil or blended vegetable oils are fine. Olive oil is too distinctively flavored for this job. Lard or drippings can also be used for pan-roasting potatoes.

## BRUNEDE KARTOFLER
### Sugar-Browned Potatoes

[DENMARK]                                         TO SERVE 4 TO 6

> 2 pounds small new potatoes
> ¼ cup sugar
> ¼ cup sweet butter

Wash the potatoes and cook them in their skins in boiling salted water until they are tender but not falling apart. Drain them, and when they are cool enough to handle, peel off the skins with a pointed knife.

Put the sugar in a heavy frying pan and melt it over low heat. Stir the sugar occasionally until it is a deep golden color and gives off a rich caramel smell. Be careful not to let it turn too dark or it will have a bitter, burned taste. Add the butter and mix it thoroughly with the caramel.

Add the potatoes to the caramel and cook them over very low heat, jiggling the pan until each potato has a glossy brown coat.

Some recipes recommend rinsing the potatoes in cold water just before caramelizing to make them take on an even coating. A more reliable tip is to have patience and cook the potatoes very gently.

Heap the caramelized potatoes on a warmed serving dish and serve immediately, or use them to garnish roast pork, duck, goose, or baked ham.

If you use canned new potatoes for this recipe, try to find a variety packed in salt water with no added flavoring, and dry them thoroughly before caramelizing.

Finland's special potato casserole must have originated with one of those happy accidents that sometimes happen in the kitchen. Its originality is due to a "malting" process during which starch in the potato mixture turns into a simple sugar. In modern kitchens this chemistry takes place in a very slow oven. But it is not hard to imagine a farmer's wife of long ago leaving a dish of mashed potato near her big wood-burning stove while she busied herself with Christmas breadmaking, and discovering that the potato had turned yellow, sweet, and unexpectedly delicious. Its taste is reminiscent of chestnuts.

## IMELLETTYPERUNASOSELAATIKKO
### Potato Casserole

{FINLAND}                                              TO SERVE 6 TO 8

| | |
|---|---|
| 3–4 pounds baking potatoes | 4 tablespoons dark corn syrup (optional) |
| Milk | Butter |
| ¼ cup flour | Salt to taste |

Peel the potatoes, boil them in salted water until tender, drain and mash them thoroughly. Beat the mashed potato, adding a little milk if it is too stiff to work, and mix in the flour, blending it thoroughly. Add the syrup if you are using it.

Preheat oven to 225°F. Butter a heavy casserole, one which has a well-fitting lid. Put the potato mixture into the dish, cover it tightly, and bake in the very slow oven for 5 hours. Check the mixture from time to time, adding a little milk if it appears too dry. This very slow cooking will make the potato slightly yellow, and very soft and sweet.

To finish the dish, add salt to taste and beat the mixture smooth. Dot the top of the purée with butter. Raise oven temperature to 375°F and bake dish, uncovered, for about 20 minutes or until browned on top. Serve the potato casserole piping hot with baked or boiled ham.

## JANSSONS FRESTELSE
### Jansson's Temptation

[SWEDEN]                                                    TO SERVE 4 TO 8

> 4 pounds baking potatoes
> 1 pound onions
> 12 anchovy fillets
> 1½ cups light cream
> 2 tablespoons butter

Preheat oven to 400°F. Peel the potatoes and grate them coarsely. Peel the onions and slice them into thin rings. Chop the anchovy fillets into small pieces.

Butter a gratin or oven-to-table baking dish and cover the bottom with a layer of grated potato. Cover with a layer of onion rings and anchovies and another layer of potato. The number of layers will depend on the size of the dish, and the top layer should be potato. Pour on half the cream and dot the dish with the rest of the butter. Bake for 20 minutes. Now pour on the remaining cream and bake for another 30 minutes, or until the potatoes are tender.

Serve Jansson's Temptation straight from the oven as a first course or supper dish, or as a hot buffet dish with some of the cold Scandinavian herring specialties (see pages 35–37).

Another unusual potato-based dish comes from South America and mixes whole boiled potatoes with a cheese and chili sauce. Although garnished as a salad, it is served hot, or at least warm, and makes an interestingly different accompaniment to almost any cold meat or poultry.

# PAPAS A LA HUANCAINA
## Potatoes Huancaina Fashion

{PERU}                                          TO SERVE 6 TO 8

3 tablespoons lemon juice
1 dried hot red chili,
    preferably bontaka,
    seeded and chopped
    fine
Black pepper, freshly
    ground, to taste
1 large onion, sliced into
    thin rings
8 medium potatoes
6 ounces cheese, queso
    blanco or mozzarella

5 ounces heavy cream
1 teaspoon ground turmeric
2 fresh red or green chilies*
Salt to taste
¼ cup olive oil
4 eggs, hard-boiled and
    quartered
8 black olives
1 head lettuce, preferably
    iceberg

Pour the lemon juice into a bowl and add the dried chili with a generous sprinkling of freshly ground pepper. Add the onion rings to the lemon juice, stir into the marinade, cover the bowl and set it aside.

Peel the potatoes and cook them whole in boiling salted water until they are tender, but not falling to pieces.

While the potatoes are cooking, make the sauce. Crumble or coarse-grate the cheese and combine it with the cream, turmeric, 1 of the fresh chilies, seeded and chopped fine, salt and pepper. Use a blender or beat by hand until the mixture is smooth and creamy.

Heat the olive oil over moderate heat in a heavy frying pan. Pour in the sauce, reduce the heat, and, stirring constantly, cook it for 5 to 8 minutes, or until it thickens.

To assemble the dish, drain the potatoes and arrange them on a warmed serving dish. Pour the sauce over them. Drain the onion rings and scatter them over the dish. Garnish with the remaining fresh chili, seeded and cut into tiny slivers, the hard-boiled eggs, black olives, and the shredded heart of a crisp lettuce.


Another warming winter dish which makes magic of potatoes and cheese is the alpine favorite, *gratin Savoyard*. This version, rich, creamy, and tantalizingly flavored with garlic, is the one served by Jacques

* For preparation of chilies, see note on page 76.

Dandel of *Jacques Bar* in Val d'Isère to skiers ravenous and ruddy from days spent hurtling down the mountains of the Haute Savoie.

## GRATIN SAVOYARD
### Savoyard Potatoes

{FRANCE}                                              TO SERVE 6 TO 8

| | |
|---|---|
| *1 clove garlic, peeled* | *2½ cups milk, or a mixture* |
| *3 pounds baking potatoes,* | *of milk and light* |
| *peeled and sliced thin* | *cream* |
| *Salt to taste* | *1 egg yolk* |
| *Black pepper, freshly* | *2 ounces cheese, Beaufort or* |
| *ground, to taste* | *Gruyère type, grated fine* |
| *Nutmeg to taste* | *2 tablespoons butter* |

Preheat oven to 350°F. Rub a gratin or shallow oven-to-table dish with the clove of garlic and arrange a layer of overlapping potato slices in the base. Season the potatoes with salt, freshly ground pepper, and grated nutmeg. Continue layering the potatoes and seasoning until all the slices are used up.

Mix the milk, or milk and cream, and egg yolk together and pour enough into the dish to come up to the level of the top layer of potatoes. You may need more or less milk according to the size of the dish. Sprinkle the cheese over the potatoes and dot the top with butter. Bake uncovered for about 2 hours, or until the potatoes are tender and all the milk has been absorbed. It is almost impossible to overcook this dish, which will also keep warm for hours with occasional additions of milk to prevent it drying out.

Serve *gratin Savoyard* with plain roasts, cold meat, or poultry. Leftovers are almost unheard of, but this dish does reheat well. If you are preparing it in advance, omit the cheese and cook the potatoes through; then reheat with the cheese topping.

Variations on the same theme are numerous and go under many names. Try stock, wine, and cream in differing proportions as the cooking liquid. Tuck onion rings, pieces of ham, or grated cheese between the layers of potato. Use lots of garlic, or none at all.

In Puerto Rico where the Day of the Kings, Epiphany, on January 6th is the principal feast day of the Christmas season, baked yams accompany stuffed banana leaves and chicken on tables laden with festive delicacies to sustain long hours of dancing and singing.

## BATATAS
### Baked Yams

[PUERTO RICO]                                    TO SERVE 6 TO 8

| | |
|---|---|
| *3 pounds yams* | *½ cup butter* |
| *Salt to taste* | *1 cup milk* |
| *Black pepper, freshly ground, to taste* | |

Preheat oven to 375°F. Peel the yams and cut them into slices about ⅛ inch thick. Season the sliced yams with salt and freshly ground pepper. Butter a gratin or shallow baking dish and arrange the slices of yam in overlapping layers, dotting each layer with small pieces of butter. Pour in the milk and bake the dish, uncovered, for about 1½ hours, or until the yams are tender.

Cooking times for yams can vary greatly according to the type and maturity of the root. It is easier to keep the dish warm after it is cooked through than to risk spoiling trickier recipes while waiting for the yams.

Tiny new potatoes, whole chestnuts, and baby onions tossed together in a butter glaze make a good-looking combination to serve with roast turkey, and offering them all in one dish saves time while serving, especially at big family gatherings. Cold turkey is fine, but not for Christmas dinner.

## GLAZED POTATOES, CHESTNUTS, AND ONIONS
[UNITED STATES]                                  TO SERVE 8 TO 10

| | |
|---|---|
| *2 pounds fresh chestnuts* | *½ cup butter* |
| *4 cups turkey or chicken stock, or salted water* | *2 tablespoons superfine granulated sugar* |
| *2 pounds new potatoes* | |
| *2 pounds small white onions* | |

Using a small, sharp knife, slit the skin on the rounded side of each chestnut. Drop the chestnuts into rapidly boiling salted water and boil them vigorously for 10 minutes. Drain, and when they are cool enough to handle, peel off the skins, being careful to keep the chestnuts whole.

In a heavy pot, heat the stock or salted water to boiling, drop in the peeled chestnuts, and simmer them gently for about 20 minutes or until they are just tender. Drain and keep warm.

Cook the new potatoes in briskly boiling salted water until they are tender, about 15 minutes. Drain, and as soon as they are cool enough to handle, peel off the skins. Keep warm.

Peel the onions. Heat the butter in a large, heavy frying pan over low heat. Add the onions and sugar and cook, covered, shaking the pan frequently, until the onions are tender, about 20 minutes. Lift out the onions, leaving behind as much of the cooking liquid as possible, and combine them with the potatoes and chestnuts.

Turn up the heat under the frying pan and reduce the liquid by fast boiling to a syrupy glaze. Pour it over the vegetables and turn them in it gently until all are glistening.

Serve immediately.

Another classic Finnish casserole is *lanttulaatikko,* a purée of turnips with cream. It is an essential Christmas dish which makes a real treat of the often-scorned yellow turnip. Rutabagas are the variety chosen by Finnish cooks, but any yellow winter turnip works well as long as it is not too woody.

## LANTTULAATIKKO
### Rutabaga Casserole

[FINLAND]                                        TO SERVE 6 TO 8

| | |
|---|---|
| 4 pounds rutabagas or Swedish turnips, peeled and cut into large dice | ¼ cup light cream Salt to taste Nutmeg to taste |
| ¼ cup dry white bread crumbs | 2 eggs, beaten 3 tablespoons butter |

Cook the rutabagas, or turnips, in boiling salted water until tender, between 25 to 40 minutes depending on the type and age of turnips available. Drain and mash thoroughly. Preheat oven to 350°F. Soften the bread crumbs in the cream, combine with the turnips, and season well with salt and nutmeg. Mix in the eggs.

Turn the mixture into a well-buttered casserole or soufflé dish large enough to allow room for it to rise a little, dot the top with butter, and bake for about 1 hour or until lightly browned on top.

Almost as good, but less festive-looking, is a purée of well-drained boiled turnips beaten with a generous lump of butter and plenty of freshly ground black pepper.

Young white turnips are the kind to choose for the next recipe, a sharply flavored combination of turnips and oranges which is particularly good with rich meats like pork and goose.

## TURNIPS WITH ORANGES

[ENGLAND] TO SERVE 4 TO 6

12 young white turnips  
2 medium oranges  
Salt to taste  

¼ cup butter  
Black pepper, freshly ground, to taste

Peel the turnips carefully to retain their attractive shape. Grate fine the rind of 1 orange and reserve it. Squeeze the juice from both oranges. Put the whole turnips and the orange juice into a pot, add a little salt, and simmer, covered, over low heat for about 25 minutes, or until the turnips are tender. Drain and discard the cooking liquid.

Put the turnips in one layer in a well-buttered oven-to-table dish. Dot each turnip with butter and sprinkle with the grated orange peel and freshly ground pepper.

Put the dish under a hot broiler for a minute or two to melt the butter and crisp the orange peel.

Serve immediately.

Parsnips, like turnips, are a neglected vegetable and seldom appear on restaurant menus, although their place in country cooking wherever they are grown is long established. Their distinctive sweet taste and mealy texture go well with Christmas meats and poultry. Peeled and parboiled parsnips can be roasted with the meat or braised with butter or drippings. Boiled parsnips are very good puréed with cream and black pepper, and mixed purées of parsnips with potatoes, carrots, or turnips are inexpensively delicious. Parsnip fritters look more festive if there is time for last-minute frying.

## PARSNIP FRITTERS

[UNITED STATES]                                          TO SERVE 4

| | |
|---|---|
| 1 pound parsnips | 2 tablespoons milk |
| 2 tablespoons butter | 3 tablespoons flour |
| Salt to taste | 2 tablespoons drippings or |
| Black pepper to taste | butter |

Peel the parsnips, cut into roughly equal-sized chunks, and boil, covered, in salted water for about 30 minutes or until they are tender. Drain and mash them thoroughly, or rub through a coarse sieve. Add butter, season generously with salt and pepper, and add milk. Mix together until well blended. Shape the parsnip mixture into 8 small patties and coat each piece with flour.

Melt the drippings or butter in a heavy frying pan and fry the fritters slowly over low heat, turning them once, until they are golden brown and crisp on the outside.

Lift them gently from the pan, drain on paper towels, and serve immediately. The parsnips will absorb a lot of fat, which makes these fritters a rich accompaniment to lean meats like turkey and chicken.

Whole baby beets are at their best served hot with lots of melted butter and freshly ground black pepper. They go well with roast game and roast beef. Fresh, precooked, and even bottled beets (provided there is no vinegar in the recipe) are all suitable for reheating in butter. Fresh uncooked beets should be boiled whole, in their skins, for about 1 hour, or until they are tender. Leave the tapering roots on the beets until after they are boiled or their color will bleed away in the water. When they are cool enough to handle, rub off the skins and trim away the roots and stalks. Reheat them in butter on top of the stove, shaking the pot from time to time to stop them from sticking.

Braised red cabbage is a firmly established accompaniment to the roast Christmas goose of Denmark, where, no doubt, its festive color as well as its seasonal availability have contributed to the tradition.

## RØDKAAL
### Braised Red Cabbage

[DENMARK]                                              TO SERVE 6

2 pounds fresh red cabbage
1/4 cup butter
2 1/4 tablespoons superfine
    granulated sugar
1 teaspoon salt
6 tablespoons white wine
    vinegar

4 tablespoons red currant
    jelly
1 small eating apple, peeled
    and grated

Preheat oven to 325 °F. Remove any damaged or floppy outer leaves from the cabbage and quarter it. Cut away the tough central stalk and slice the cabbage fine.

Combine the butter, sugar, salt, and vinegar with 6 tablespoons water in a heavy casserole and bring to the boil on top of the stove. Toss in the shredded cabbage and bring to the boil again, stirring to make sure that all the cabbage is coated with the cooking liquid. Cover the casserole tightly and bake in preheated oven for about 2 hours. Check occasionally to make sure the cabbage is not drying out, and add a little water if necessary.

Add the red currant jelly and the apple, and return the casserole to the oven for another 10 minutes.

Braised red cabbage reheats well. It is often prepared a day or two in advance to improve the sweet-sour taste.

A less sweet and more subtly flavored version of oven-braised red cabbage omits the vinegar and red currant jelly, and uses pork belly, juniper berries, and dry white wine to flavor the dish. Variations of the recipe, with or without the apple, are popular throughout northeast Europe.

Still with the cabbage family, we come to Brussels sprouts. Commercially frozen sprouts are better than limp "fresh" sprouts from the grocer or supermarket. If you can buy or pick good, fresh brussels sprouts, strip off the outer leaves and cut away the tough stalks. Drop them into boiling salted water and cook briskly until they are still a little crisp inside, or just tender right through if you prefer. Rinse them quickly in cold water. Melt a generous lump of butter in the pan you cooked them in, and turn the cooked sprouts in the melted butter. Serve them quickly in a heated dish with a liberal sprinkling of freshly ground black pepper .

If you are using frozen sprouts, follow the instructions on the package. Overcooking is the most usual reason for soggy, yellowish sprouts and they do not take kindly to being kept warm.

Big, creamy butter beans are traditionally served with roast goose or pork in parts of northern England.

## BAKED BUTTER BEANS

[ENGLAND]                                    TO SERVE 4 TO 6

*1 pound butter beans,
    cooked or canned*
*6 tablespoons butter*
*1 medium onion, chopped
    fine*
*2 medium tomatoes, peeled,
    seeded, and chopped*
*2 stalks celery, chopped fine*
*1 sprig fresh parsley,
    chopped fine*

*Pinch of thyme, fresh or
    dried*
*Pinch of rosemary, fresh or
    dried*
*Salt to taste*
*Black pepper, freshly
    ground, to taste*

Preheat oven to 350°F. Drain the canned beans and rinse in cold running water.

Melt two-thirds of the butter in a pot over medium heat. Add the onion, tomatoes, and celery and sauté them together until just soft. Stir in the parsley, the thyme, and rosemary. Season the mixture generously with salt and freshly ground pepper, and stir in the beans.

Butter an oven-to-table dish and turn the beans into it. Dot the beans with the remaining butter and bake for about 20 minutes.

Serve hot, directly from the baking dish.

*Jollof* rice and *moyin-moyin* (see page 113) are Nigeria's favorite festive dishes and they are made for all kinds of celebrations, including Christmas. At its simplest, *jollof* rice is no more than brown rice colored red and flavored with chili and tomato. But that is seen as poor fare for a feast, and meat is added "to make it a little bit fascinating" as an enthusiastic Nigerian cook put it. Pieces of bacon, chicken, and kidney, simmered in stock and then fried in oil, are the most popular additions. Herbs, too, such as thyme and bay leaf, are added according to taste and availability. The finished dish is dry, rather like an Indian pilaf, with each grain of rice separate and any fried meat added at the last moment.

## JOLLOF RICE

[NIGERIA]                                          TO SERVE 6 TO 8

*½ cup peanut or other*          *¼ cup tomato paste*
*    vegetable oil*              *6 cups meat or chicken*
*6 medium onions, chopped*       *    stock*
*    coarse*                     *3 cups brown rice*
*4 hot Nigerian peppers or*      *Salt to taste*
*    fresh red chilies\*,*
*    seeded and chopped*
*    fine*

Put the oil in a large pot with a tightly fitting lid, and heat it over low heat. Sauté the onions, the peppers or chilies, and the tomato paste gently together. When the onions have softened a little, add the stock and simmer the mixture for about 10 minutes.

Wash the rice and add it to the cooking liquid. Stir to blend the ingredients well, and season to taste with salt. Bring the rice to the boil, lower the heat to a simmer, close the lid firmly and cook gently for about 35 minutes, or until the rice is tender. All the liquid should have been absorbed and each grain should be separate. The exact cooking time varies greatly according to the variety of brown rice used. If the rice becomes too dry before it is fully cooked, add water by sprinkling it, a little at a time, into the pot.

Serve *jollof* rice piled on a warmed dish or bowl. Fry bite-sized pieces of cooked meat or poultry and heap them on top of the rice.

\* For preparation of chilies, see note on page 76.

In the farmhouses of Cumberland and Northumberland, savoury pudding has been made for generations as an accompaniment to roast goose or pork. Prunes or raisins can also be included in the dish, which must have been a welcome winter warmer for men coming in from a night's lambing on the snow-covered hills of the border country. The oatmeal in this recipe is a pointer to the area's affinity with Scotland.

## SAVOURY PUDDING

[ENGLAND]                                    TO SERVE 8 TO 10

*1 cup fine oatmeal (not oat flakes or rolled oats)*
*2⅔ cups fresh bread crumbs*
*2½–2¾ cups milk*
*2 large eggs*
*¾ cup flour*
*4 ounces suet, shredded or grated*

*1 tablespoon fresh chopped sage, thyme, and parsley, mixed; or dried, crumbled and mixed*
*Pepper to taste*
*Salt to taste*
*3 medium onions, chopped*

Preheat oven to 375°F. Put the oatmeal and bread crumbs into a large bowl. Heat 2½ cups of the milk to the boiling point and pour it into the bowl. Let the mixture stand for about 10 minutes, then beat in the eggs.

In another bowl, mix the flour with the suet, herbs, pepper, and salt. Add the onions to this mixture.

Now combine the oatmeal and flour mixtures and beat well. Add a little more milk if the pudding is too stiff to beat.

Turn the mixture into a well-buttered cake tin or soufflé dish and bake for about 1 hour.

Serve savoury pudding hot in thick slices or wedges with roast goose or pork.

The Scottish roots of the next recipe, for the Christmas specialty of Barbados, *jug jug,* are well-documented—which is just as well, because it would take a detective of some gastronomic distinction to divine such a metamorphosis. Folklore has it that *jug jug* started life as an attempt by Scots exiled to Barbados in the seventeenth century to recreate the haggis of their homeland. This would have been for the celebration of Hogmanay, or New Year's Eve, of course, but somewhere down the centuries *jug jug* has become a Christmas specialty and is served as an accompaniment to ham or roast chicken.

Pigeon peas are an important ingredient of this odd delicacy and go by many names. Jamaicans call them *gungo, gunga,* or *goon-goo* peas. In Trinidad they are known, among other names, as *arhar dahl,* and in the Spanish-speaking islands as *gandules.* In one of London's leading health-food shops recently I saw them labeled *sprouting beans.* They are sold dried or in cans. To prepare dried pigeon peas, soak them overnight and boil them the next day in fresh, salted water for about 15 minutes.

## JUG JUG
### A Caribbean Haggis

{BARBADOS}                  TO SERVE 8 TO 10

| | |
|---|---|
| ¼ *pound lean pork* | *Pinch of thyme* |
| ¼ *pound corned beef* | *2 scallions, chopped* |
| *1 pound cooked pigeon* | *2 ounces ground millet* |
|   *peas* | *Salt to taste* |
| *2 medium onions, chopped* | *Black pepper, freshly* |
|   *coarse* |   *ground, to taste* |
| *1 sprig parsley* | *3 tablespoons sweet butter* |
| *3 stalks celery, with leaves,* | |
|   *chopped coarse* | |

Put the pork into a heavy pot, add enough water to cover it, and bring the liquid slowly to the boil. Reduce the heat and simmer, covered, for about 40 minutes. Chop the corned beef into large cubes and add it to the pork. Simmer the meats for another 20 minutes before adding the pigeon peas. Cook them together for a minute or two, then strain the mixture, reserving the stock, and set aside.

Return the stock to the pot and add the onions, parsley, celery, thyme, scallions, and the millet. Season the mixture to taste with salt and freshly ground pepper, and bring to the boil. Lower the heat, and cook, stirring constantly, for about 15 minutes.

Put the meat and pea mixture through a grinder and add it to the millet mixture. Cook them gently together for another 25 minutes, by which time the *jug jug* should be fairly dry and stiff.

Add 1 tablespoon of the butter and mix it in thoroughly before heaping the *jug jug* on a warmed serving dish. Spread it with the rest of the butter and serve it, like a vegetable, with a large spoon.

The tart flavor of cooking apples is a popular contrast with rich Christmas roasts, and many stuffing recipes include them. The Danes traditionally serve the apples with roast goose or duck, as a garnish appreciated by the eye as well as the stomach.

## AEBLER MED SVEDSKER
### Apples with Port and Prunes

[DENMARK]                                                        TO SERVE 8

16 prunes
1⅓ cups superfine granulated sugar
1 cup port wine
8 cooking apples

Marinate the prunes in an ovenproof dish with 1 tablespoon of the sugar and the port wine for 6 hours or overnight. Preheat oven to 350°F, and bake the prunes uncovered in the marinade for about half an hour, or until the prunes are plump and tender but not falling apart.

Peel the apples carefully to preserve their shape and cut each one in half vertically. Neatly hollow out the cores. Heat 4 cups water with the rest of the sugar in a large, preferably shallow pot, and boil the syrup for a minute or two before adding the apples. Simmer the apples gently for about 10 minutes, or until they are tender but not breaking up.

Heat oven to 400°F. Drain the apples and the prunes. (The syrup and the port marinade can be boiled down together for a really good fresh fruit-salad dressing.)

Place a prune in the hollow of each apple and arrange the apples on a generously buttered baking dish. Cover the dish with foil and bake in the hot oven for 10 minutes. Serve immediately arranged around the roast.

Salads are usually associated with summer, so it is a surprise to find that the strongest traditions for Christmas salads are found north of the equator and call for winter vegetables. In Naples the eel or carp of Christmas eve is accompanied by this delicious cauliflower salad.

## INSALATA DI RINFORZ
### Cauliflower Salad

{ITALY}                                    TO SERVE 4 TO 6

| | |
|---|---|
| *1 large cauliflower* | *1 teaspoon prepared* |
| *2 cloves garlic* | *mustard* |
| *18 black olives* | *Salt to taste* |
| *1 tablespoon capers* | *Pepper, freshly ground, to* |
| *¼ cup olive oil* | *taste* |
| *1 tablespoon lemon juice* | |
| *1 teaspoon superfine* | |
| *granulated sugar* | |

Cut off the green leaves and tough central stalk of the cauliflower and break the head into florets. Bring a large pot of salted water to the boil and drop the florets into it. Cook the cauliflower until it is just tender, but still has a bite of crispness, and drain it.

Rub the serving bowl or dish with a cut clove of garlic. Put the cooked cauliflower into the bowl and sprinkle it with olives and capers.

To make the dressing, blend or shake together the olive oil, lemon juice, sugar, mustard, salt, freshly ground pepper, and pressed or finely chopped garlic to taste. Pour it over the cauliflower and mix well.

If chopped or crushed garlic in any salad dressing is too much of a good thing, use oil flavored subtly with garlic instead. Soak 3 bruised cloves of garlic in about a cup of olive oil. Keep the oil in a covered jar for several days, then discard the garlic and use the oil for salad dressings.

A good winter salad from Poland (where it is called Greek Salad) calls for parsley root, which is often very difficult to find. Grated parsnip or celeriac are suitable substitutes in this sweet-sour salad.

## SAŁADKA GRECKA
### Greek Salad

{POLAND}                                        TO SERVE 6

| | |
|---|---|
| *4 tablespoons vegetable oil* | *4 tablespoons tomato paste* |
| *2 large carrots, scraped and* | *Salt to taste* |
| *grated coarse* | *Sugar to taste* |
| *1 medium parsley root,* | *Lemon juice to taste* |
| *scraped and grated* | *Black pepper, coarsely* |
| *coarse* | *ground, to taste* |
| *1 large onion, chopped fine* | *Paprika to taste* |

Heat the oil in a heavy pot over medium heat. Drop in the carrots, parsley root, and onion and fry them quickly for about 2 minutes. Add the tomato paste and about 4 tablespoons of water, lower the heat, and cook the vegetables, uncovered, for about 10 minutes, or until they are tender. Season to taste with salt, sugar, lemon juice, pepper, and paprika.

Arrange the salad on a dish and serve it very cold. Its sweet-sour taste goes well with the cold herring dishes on pages 35–39.

Beet salads are popular throughout Scandinavia. They invariably turn out pink, which makes them an eye-catching choice for any buffet table.

## PUNAJUURISALAATTI
### Beet Salad

{FINLAND}                                           TO SERVE 6 TO 8

2 medium potatoes, peeled                  2 medium tart apples,
2 medium carrots, scraped                      peeled, cored, and
1 pound cooked fresh                            diced
    beets*, peeled                          1 small onion, grated coarse
                                            2 medium dill pickles, diced

**FOR THE DRESSING**

1 cup heavy cream                          Salt to taste
2 tablespoons lemon juice                  White pepper, freshly
2 teaspoons beet juice                         ground, to taste
    (optional)                             Sugar to taste

**FOR THE GARNISH**

1 head iceberg lettuce

Cook the potatoes in boiling salted water until they are tender but not breaking up. Cook the carrots in boiling salted water until they are tender. Cut the cooked vegetables, including the beets, into neat dice.

To make the dressing, whip the cream until it is thick but not stiff.

* For preparation of beets, see page 125.

Add the lemon juice and beet juice and season it to taste with salt, freshly ground pepper, and sugar.

Combine the dressing with the diced vegetables, apples, onion, and pickles and pile the mixture into a bowl lined with crisp lettuce leaves.

Red cabbage and apple salad sharpened with horseradish is a Swedish specialty. It makes an interesting change from the ubiquitous coleslaw. Use one of the bottled varieties of horseradish if fresh grated horseradish is not obtainable.

## RODKÅLSSALLAD
### Red Cabbage Salad

{SWEDEN}                                    TO SERVE 4 TO 6

*1 cup unsweetened         1 pound fresh red cabbage,*
*     applesauce                 shredded fine*
*1 ounce fresh grated      Salt to taste*
*     horseradish           Pepper to taste*

Blend the applesauce with the horseradish and combine with the shredded cabbage; season with salt and freshly ground pepper. Chill for about 3 hours before serving.

A mixture of diced celery, avocado, walnuts, and black olives is one of the salads served with roast turkey in Chile.

# PUDDINGS

The puddings of Christmas are many, varied, and, with a few exceptions, wonderfully rich. The most splendid of them all is England's Christmas or plum pudding. Who invented it and when? Historians of the kitchen do not all agree, so let us start with the entry on plum pudding given by Theodora FitzGibbon in *The Food of the Western World,* her astoundingly comprehensive and thoroughly readable encyclopedia of European and North American food.

"Its innovation at the English court was the occasion for one of the presentations with which William the Conqueror frequently favoured members of his domestic staff, in this case Robert Argyllon, who received a manor at Addington in Surrey. He received it, according to the *Cook's Oracle* (fourth edition, 1822), "by the service of making one mess in an earthen pot in the kitchen of our Lord the King, on the day of his coronation*, called De la Groute, i.e., a kind of Plum porridge or Water gruel with plums in it. This dish is still served up at the Royal Table, at Coronations†, by the Lord of the said Manor of Addington.' The present-day Christmas pudding evolves from the substitution of prunes, and later still dried fruits, for plums, with the addition of spices, eggs, etc."

* William the Conqueror was crowned on Christmas Day 1066.
† It was last served at the coronation of George IV in 1820.

The likeliest explanation for how the sloppy eleventh-century concoction evolved into the rich pudding we know now is given by F. Marian McNeill in *The Scot's Kitchen.* In a lengthy footnote she writes:

"From the earliest times, our Celtic forefathers celebrated the winter solstice and the return of the fructifying sun from the farthest point in its circuit with a ceremonial cutting of the mistletoe, the bringing in of evergreens, and the supping of a festive gruel which was the symbol of the inexhaustible Cauldron of Keridwen—a sort of Celtic cornucopia—and the portent of future abundance. In the Highlands, this gruel has always been a special kind of sowans*; in the Lowlands, they used more commonly a rich brose†, known as the Yule Brose. In the Middle Ages (and long after), when sugar, spices, and dried fruits were increasingly imported from foreign lands, the more prosperous classes celebrated the festival with plum pottage or porridge.

"In the early years of the eighteenth century, plum porridge mysteriously solidified into plum pudding. Nobody knows just how, when, or where it happened. Possibly in some household the porridge was accidentally allowed to boil dry, but was removed before it got burned, and the participants decided that it tasted better that way—and the idea caught on."

So far, we have English and Scots claims for the invention of Christmas pudding, but the matter does not, of course, rest there. The French, not having the temerity to claim such a celebrated institution for their own, but ever-jealous of their reputation in the kitchen, go one better by entertaining the notion that Christmas pudding is *Greek.*

The Greek claim is a long story, beautifully told by Elizabeth David in *Spices, Salt and Aromatics in the English Kitchen* under the title "The Christmas Pudding Is Mediterranean Food."

"A white cube of a house, two box-like rooms and a nice large kitchen. No bath. No plumbing. A well and a fig tree outside the front door and five yards away the Aegean. On the horizon a half circle of the islands of Andros, Tinos, Seriphos. In the village, about three dozen houses, two churches (one Orthodox, one Roman Catholic), one provision shop. Down on the shore one shack of a tavern, and in the village street a more important one,

* Sowans is a floury substance extracted from bran or husks of oats soaked in water, allowed to ferment slightly, and prepared by boiling.
† Brose is a dish made by pouring boiling water or milk on oatmeal or oat-cake. It is most usually seasoned with salt and pepper, but may have other flavorings.

stacked with barrels and furnished with stout wooden tables. Christo, the owner of this second tavern, was one of the grandees of the village. He operated, in addition to the tavern, a small market garden, and sold his produce in the island's capital seven miles away. He also had a brother-in-law, called Yannaki. Yannaki was that stock Greek village character, the traveller come home after experiencing glamorous doings and glorious events in far-off places. True to type, he spoke a little Anglo-American and, more uncommonly, a little French; he was always on hand to help out if foreigners came to the village. He seemed a kind and cheerful man, rich too; at any rate, he owned a spare donkey and was prepared to lend me this animal, along with a boy to talk to it, so that I could ride into the town when I needed to stock up with fresh supplies of beans and oil, bottled wine, cheese, dried fruit, and boxes of the delicious Turkish Delight which was—still is— a speciality of the island.

"Before long it transpired that the greatest favour I could bestow upon Yannaki in return for the loan of his transport would be some tomato soup in tins and perhaps also a jar or two of English 'picklies'.

"Handing over to one of the brothers who owned the hotel and the Turkish Delight factory in the capital a bundle of drachmae which would have kept me in wine and cheese for a month, I got in return four tins, vintage, of the required soup. Of English piccalilli, which I took it was what Yannaki meant by picklies, there was no sign nor sniff, and very relieved I was. Many more such exotic luxuries, and it would be cheaper for me to leave my seashore village for Athens and a suite at the Grande-Bretagne.

"The tomato soup gave Yannaki and Christo and their families a great deal of pleasure. It was the real thing, no mistaking it. In return I was offered baskets of eggs, lemons, oranges, freshly dug vegetables and salads, glass after glass of wine in the tavern. And, then, next time the picklies? I *was* English wasn't I? Then I should certainly be able to produce these delicacies.

"For days I scanned the horizon for sight of an English yacht. I could, in my turn, have bartered fresh vegetables and fruit for the jars of mustard pickles which I knew must grace the table of any English *lordos* grand enough to be roaming the Aegean seas. It was late in the season. That way no yacht came.

"Anybody who has experience of the stubborn determination, courteous but quite unrelenting, of an Aegean islander when he has made up his mind about something will understand why, in the end, I was obliged to set to and make those confounded pickles myself.

"Into the town then for mustard, vinegar, spices. Long mornings I spent cutting up cauliflowers and onions, carrots and cucumbers. Afternoons, I squatted in my kitchen fanning the charcoal fires into a blaze brisk enough to boil the brew. The jars, the only ones I could find, which I had bought to pack the stuff in were of one oke capacity, three pounds, near enough. Also they were of rough earthenware, unglazed, and exceptionally porous. Before I could even give the filled jars away they were half empty again, the liquid all soaked up by that sponge-like clay. Every one had to be replenished with a fresh batch of pickle. To me the mixture seemed fairly odd, but with my village friends it was successful enough. In fact, on the barter system, I could have lived for nothing so long as I was prepared to dedicate my life to pickle-making. Before long, though, it was getting on for December, and references to 'Xmas pudding' began to crop up in the tavern talk. By now I had learned a little more about these kindly village tyrants. If Christmas pudding they wanted, Christmas pudding I should have to give them. But not, so help me, made on the improvised happy-go-lucky system I'd used for the mustard pickles. Once more into the town (I never could stay five seconds on a horse or a mule or even a bicycle, but by that time I had at least found out how to sit on a donkey and get the animal moving over stony paths and up and down steep hills) to telegraph home for a recipe. When it arrived, it turned out to be one of those which calls for a pound of almost everything you can think of, which was lucky. Simply by multiplying each by three it was all turned into okes. A large-scale Christmas party was now simmering, so there wouldn't, I thought, be an oke too much.

"Now, all those with their fine talk of the glories of Old English fare, have they ever actually made Christmas pudding, in large quantities, by Old English methods? Have they for instance ever tried cleaning and skinning, flouring, shredding, chopping beef-kidney suet straight off the hoof? Have they ever stoned bunch after bunch of raisins hardly yet dry on the stalk and each one as sticky as a piece of warm toffee? And how long do they think it takes to bash up three pounds of breadcrumbs without an oven in which they could first dry the loaves? Come to that, what would they make of an attempt to boil, and to keep on the boil for nine to ten hours on two charcoal fires let into holes in the wall, some dozen large

puddings? Well, I had nothing much else to do in those days and
quite enjoyed all the work, but I'd certainly never let myself in for
such an undertaking again. Nor, indeed, would I again attempt to
explain the principles of a hay-box and the reasons for making one
to peasants of whose language I had such a scanty knowledge and
who are in any case notoriously unreceptive to the idea of having hot
food, or for that matter hot water or hot coffee, hotter than tepid.

"All things considered, my puddings turned out quite nicely.
The ones which emerged from the hay-box were at just about the
right temperature—luke-warm. They were sweet and dark and rich.
My village friends were not as enthusiastic as they had been about
the mustard pickles. What with so many of the company having
participated in the construction of the hay-box, my assurances that
the raisins and the currants grown and dried there on the spot in the
Greek sun were richer and more juicy than the artificially dried
hygienically treated and much-travelled variety we got at home,
my observations on the incomparable island-made candied citron
and orange peel (that was fun to cut up too) given me by the
neighbours, and the memorable scent of violets and brilliantine
given to the puddings by Athenian brandy, a certain amount of the
English mystery had disappeared from our great national festive
dish.

"That *le plum-pudding n'est pas Anglais* was a startling discovery made by a French chef, Phileas Gilbert, round about the turn
of the century. No, not English indeed. In this case le plum-pudding
had been almost Greek. What I wished I'd known at the time was
the rest of Gilbert's story. It seems that with a passing nod to a
Breton concoction called *le far* 'obviously the ancestor of the English
pudding', and earlier French historian, Bourdeau by name, unable
or perhaps unwilling to claim plum pudding for France, says that
it is precisely described by Athenaeus in a report of the wedding
feast of Caranus, an Argive prince. The pudding was called *strepte,*
and in origin was entirely Greek."

History aside, the traditions surrounding Christmas pudding are as
rich as the stuff itself. First there is the sprig of holly on top—to keep
away witches, as some authorities would have it, and the silver coins or
charms inside—for luck. There is the mixing ceremony when every
member of the family takes a turn or two with the wooden spoon on
Stir up Sunday (the Sunday which falls closest to St. Andrew's Day in

November), and the serving ritual of taking it to the table with blue flames of burning brandy licking over it.

In Cornwall, where Christmas puddings are given as presents, the worth of the gift is judged by the weight of the pudding and the amount of fruit packed into it. This is one way of looking at a good pudding, but there are others. For one of my grandmothers the best Christmas pudding was the blackest Christmas pudding she could make. Some people like them heavy, others light. The one point on which almost everybody agrees is that Christmas pudding should be as fruity as possible.

A fine, homemade Christmas pudding puts commercially made varieties to shame. It takes a fair amount of time but no great amount of skill to make one, and the following tips apply to all the recipes. Dried fruit should always be of the best quality you can find. Whole candied caps of orange, lemon, and citron peel usually have a much better flavor than the mixed peel sold in small dice. The easiest way to prepare either type for those recipes including peel is to put it through a grinder, using the coarse blade.

Many recipes use dark beer, such as Guinness, instead of milk or brandy. Any bitterness in the taste of the beer is more than offset by the sweetness of the fruit, and some cooks insist that beer brings out the flavor of the fruit better than spirits.

Long steaming helps to make Christmas pudding dark and the second steaming will make it darker than the first. It is important not to let water get into the puddings while they are steaming. Fill the pudding basins to within 1 inch of the rim, and cover them with buttered wax paper and kitchen foil. Cut circles of paper and foil and about 1 inch wider all around than the diameter of the basins. Lay the foil on top of the paper and put both on together, then press the overlap down the sides of the basins so that the foil holds the paper in place while both are tied on firmly with string.

To store the puddings after the first steaming, allow them to cool, then remove the buttered paper and foil and re-cover the basins with fresh paper, not buttered this time.

Before steaming the puddings a second time (for serving) cover them the same way as for the initial cooking.

To steam the puddings, place the basins in one or more large pots with tightly fitting lids and pour in boiling water until it comes about one-third of the way up the sides of the basins. Bring the water back to the boil over high heat, then clamp on the lid and reduce the heat until the water is bubbling gently. Be careful not to let the pot boil dry, and bring up the water level with boiling water as required.

To serve the puddings, turn them out onto heated serving plates and pour about 2 tablespoons of heated brandy over each. Light the warm brandy immediately.

Plum Pudding Sauce (see page 235), Hard Sauce (see page 236), wine sauces or custards, or cream are the traditional accompaniments to serve with Christmas pudding.

Christmas puddings mature and improve in flavor if stored in a cool, dry place for several months. Adding extra brandy after the first steaming, when the puddings are completely cold, and again before they are reheated on Christmas Day, is an optional refinement. I recommend it.

My idea of a perfect Christmas pudding is one that is dark-colored, light-textured, and fragrant with fruit, spice, and brandy. The following recipe, dating from around 1700, combines these virtues. The quantities listed make two large puddings, each big enough to serve ten to twelve people. If you halve the ingredients to make one large or two small puddings there is no need to vary the cooking times.

## CHRISTMAS PUDDING

[ENGLAND, CIRCA 1700]                    TO SERVE 20 TO 24

2 cups dried currants
2¼ cups seedless raisins
1½ cups sultana raisins
1 lemon
2 cups suet, shredded
6 cups fresh white bread
    crumbs
½ cup blanched almonds,
    chopped fine

1 teaspoon grated nutmeg
¾ cup dark brown sugar
4 large eggs
¾ cup brandy, or brandy
    and rum combined
5 ounces milk

Put the dried fruit into a large mixing bowl. Using the finest blade, grate the peel of the lemon over the fruit. Add the suet, bread crumbs, almonds, nutmeg, and sugar and mix ingredients thoroughly.

In a separate bowl beat together the eggs, brandy, or brandy and rum, and the milk, and stir the liquid into the fruit mixture. Mix well.

Let the mixture, which is a fairly dry one, stand in a cool place for about 12 hours before dividing it between 2 or more buttered pudding basins. Cover the basins with buttered wax paper and foil and steam the puddings for 6 hours (see page 140).

On Christmas Day steam the puddings for at least another 2 hours before serving.

The next recipe makes a pudding which is lighter in color than the last. King George I was known as the "Pudding King"—a comment on both his taste for the food of his homeland and the English prejudice on the subject of German food—and this is the recipe served to him on his first Christmas in England in 1714.

## KING GEORGE I's CHRISTMAS PUDDING

{ENGLAND}                                        TO SERVE 25 TO 30

1 1/4 cups pitted prunes,
   chopped
1 1/2 cups seedless raisins
1 1/2 cups sultana raisins
1 1/4 cups dried currants
1/2 cup pitted dates,
   chopped
1 cup glacé cherries, chopped
1/2 pound mixed candied
   fruit peel, chopped
   or grated coarse
2 cups self-rising flour
3 cups suet, shredded
5 cups fresh whole wheat
   bread crumbs

1 1/2 cups light brown sugar
1 teaspoon mixed spice
   (commercially
   packaged; or cloves,
   cinnamon, and
   nutmeg)
1 teaspoon salt
1/2 nutmeg
6 large eggs
5 ounces milk
1 tablespoon lemon juice
5 ounces brandy

In a large bowl mix together the prunes, raisins, sultana raisins, currants, dates, cherries, and fruit peel. Add the flour and mix it with the fruit, using your hands. Add the suet, bread crumbs, sugar, mixed spice, and salt. Grate the half nutmeg into the bowl and mix the dry ingredients together thoroughly.

In a separate bowl beat together the eggs, milk, lemon juice, and brandy. Pour this mixture into the dry ingredients and stir until well blended.

Leave the pudding mixture to stand in a cool place for about 12 hours before dividing it between 2 or more buttered pudding basins. Cover the basins with buttered wax paper and foil and steam the puddings for about 6 hours (see page 140).

On Christmas Day steam the puddings for at least another 2 hours before serving.

The plum pudding recipe used by Charles Elmé Francatelli, chef to Queen Victoria, is more heavily spiced. It also makes a more solid pudding. This recipe calls for only one boiling, so the pudding is not a dark one.

## QUEEN VICTORIA'S PLUM PUDDING

[ENGLAND]                                    TO SERVE 16 TO 20

2¼ cups seedless raisins
2 cups dried currants
½ pound mixed candied
    orange, lemon, and
    citron peel, chopped
    or ground
5 cups beef suet, shredded
4 cups flour, sifted
2 cups dark brown sugar

2 tablespoons ground
    cinnamon, cloves, and
    nutmeg, mixed
½ teaspoon salt
2 lemons
4 large eggs
1 scant pint milk
½ cup brandy

Put the raisins, currants, and fruit peel into a large mixing bowl with the suet, flour, sugar, spices, and salt. Grate the rind of the 2 lemons over the bowl and mix the ingredients together thoroughly.

In a separate bowl beat the eggs with the milk and brandy. Pour this mixture into the dried fruit mixture and stir until all is well blended.

Leave the pudding mixture to stand in a cool place for about 12 hours before turning it into 1 large or 2 or more, smaller pudding basins. Cover with buttered wax paper and foil and steam for 4½ hours (see page 140).

Francatelli's serving instructions are: "dish it up with a German custard sauce over it."

A New Zealand version of Christmas pudding uses sago and butter instead of flour and suet to make a light-colored and textured pudding. This recipe, too, calls for only one steaming.

"Soak 4 tablespoons of sago overnight in one cup of sweet* milk. Add to this I breakfast cup of freshly grated white breadcrumbs; 1 tea cup currants; 1 tea cup sultanas; ½ tea cup brown sugar; ½ teaspoon baking soda; pinch of salt; 1 tablespoon melted butter. Stir well. Place in buttered basin and steam three hours. Serve with brandy butter and whipped cream."

The expense of making traditional plum puddings for large family gatherings no doubt accounts for the great number of recipes which include quite large quantities of root vegetables to stretch more costly ingredients. Eliza Acton's *Modern Cookery For Private Families,* first published in 1845, and a classic of the English kitchen, gives a good one. Her style is so clear and so evocative I would not presume to standardize it—except to suggest steaming the pudding in the manner described on page 140.

"Mix well together one pound of smoothly-mashed potatoes, half a pound of carrots boiled quite tender, and beaten to a paste, one pound of flour, one of currants, and one of raisins (full weight after they are stoned), three-quarters of a pound of sugar, eight ounces of suet, one nutmeg, and quarter of a teaspoonful of salt. Put the pudding into a well-floured cloth, tie it up very closely, and boil it for four hours. The correspondent to whom we are indebted for this receipt says, that the cost of the ingredients does not exceed half a crown, and that the pudding is of sufficient size for a party of sixteen persons. We can vouch for its excellence, but as it is rather apt to break when turned out of the cloth, a couple of eggs would perhaps improve it. It is excellent cold. Sweetmeats, brandy, and spices can be added at pleasure.

"Mashed potatoes, 1 lb; carrots, 8 oz; flour, 1 lb; suet, ½ lb; sugar, ¾ lb; currants and raisins, 1 lb each; nutmeg, 1; little salt; 4 hours."

"The Author's Christmas Pudding," as Miss Action titles her own recipe, includes apple and makes enough for six people.

"To three ounces of flour, and the same weight of fine, lightly-grated bread-crumbs, add six of beef kidney-suet, chopped small, six

* i.e., not sour

of raisins, weighted after they are stoned, six of well-cleaned currants, four ounces of minced apples, five of sugar, two of candied orange-rind, half a teaspoonful of nutmeg, mixed with pounded mace, a very little salt, a small glass of brandy, and three whole eggs. Mix and beat these ingredients well together, tie them tightly in a thickly-floured cloth, and boil them for three hours and a half. We can recommend this as a remarkably light small rich pudding; it may be served with German wine, or punch sauce.

"Flour, 3 oz; bread-crumbs, 3 oz; suet, stone raisins, and currants, each 6 oz; minced apples, 4 oz; sugar, 5 oz; candied peel, 2 oz; spice, ½ teaspoonful; salt, few grains; brandy, small wine-glassful; eggs, 3; 3½ hours."

Leftover Christmas pudding can be sliced and fried in butter, or sprinkled with sugar and served with whipped cream or Hard Sauce (see page 236. Another delicious way of serving it is Miss Acton's "The Elegant Economist's Pudding." Again, she speaks for herself.

"Butter thickly a plain mould or basin, and line it entirely with slices of cold plum or raisin pudding, cut so as to join closely and neatly together; fill it quite with a good custard; lay, first a buttered paper, and then a floured cloth over it, tie them securely, and boil the pudding gently for an hour; let it stand for ten minutes after it is taken up before it is turned out of the mould. This is a more tasteful mode of serving the remains of a plum-pudding than the usual one of broiling them in slices, or converting them into fritters. The German sauce, well milled or frothed, is generally much relished with sweet boiled puddings, and adds greatly to their good appearance; but common wine or punch sauce, may be sent to table with the above quite as appropriately.

"Mould or basin holding 1½ pint, lined with thin slices of plum pudding; ¾ pint new milk boiled gently 5 minutes with grain of salt; 5 bitter almonds, bruised; sugar in lumps, 2½ oz; thin rind of ½ lemon, strained and mixed directly with 4 large well-beaten eggs; poured into mould while just warm: boiled gently 1 hour."

You can use aluminum foil over the buttered paper instead of the floured cloth.

New Zealanders are much attached to English Christmas traditions but Christmas pudding can be just too much when the festivities come at the height of summer. This New Zealand recipe for a rich ice cream bombe is probably just as fattening as the traditional plum pudding, but at least it is cold and needs no last-minute attention or precious space on the stove on Christmas Day.

## CHRISTMAS ICE CREAM

[NEW ZEALAND]                                    TO SERVE 10 TO 12

| | |
|---|---|
| 1½ cups fine shortbread cookie crumbs | 1¼ cups mincemeat |
| 5 tablespoons melted butter | 2½ cups vanilla ice cream |
| 1 pint heavy cream | 1½ cups glacé cherries |
| 1 tablespoon brandy | ⅓ cup blanched almonds, chopped coarse |
| ½ teaspoon vanilla extract | ½ teaspoon almond extract |

Butter a 3-pint bombe mold or bowl. Combine the shortbread crumbs with the melted butter and line the mold with this mixture, pressing it evenly around the sides. Chill until this crust is firm.

Whip the cream and stir in the brandy and vanilla extract. Combine the cream with the mincemeat. Spoon this mixture into the lined mold, spreading it around the sides in an even layer and leaving a deep hollow in the center for the ice cream. Freeze until the mincemeat and cream mixture is firm.

Soften the ice cream slightly. Stir in the cherries, whole or chopped, the nuts, and the almond extract. Pack this mixture into the mold and smooth it over evenly. Cover and freeze for at least 12 hours.

Unmold the bombe straight from the freezer. Dip the mold *briefly* in hot water and turn the bombe out onto a flat plate. Return it to the main compartment of the refrigerator for about an hour before serving.


Port wine jelly was a smart pudding to serve at festive gatherings in the nineteenth century. Expense is no doubt one reason it is so seldom made now. Set in an elaborate mold it looks lovely and tastes even better. Serve it on its own, or with whipped cream and tiny almond cookies. You could even go wild and decorate it with gold leaf (from art supply stores) as was the custom for jellies served at fifteenth-century feasts.

Only half the wine is subjected to heat, so the flavor of the jelly is superb and so is its effect. This is not a jelly to serve to children.

## PORT WINE JELLY

{ENGLAND}                                    TO SERVE 4 TO 6

| | |
|---|---|
| 3 packages unflavored gelatin | ⅔ cup superfine granulated sugar |
| 2½ cups port wine (red, not tawny) | ¼ teaspoon grated nutmeg |
| 2 teaspoons lemon juice | ¼ teaspoon powdered cinnamon |

Soak the gelatin in one-quarter of the port and the 2 teaspoons of lemon juice for a few minutes. When it has softened, add one-quarter more of the port, the sugar, and the spices, and bring the mixture almost but not quite to the boil, stirring constantly. When the gelatin has completely dissolved, strain the mixture through a fine sieve, or better still, through a sieve lined with cheesecloth. Allow the jelly to cool completely before adding the rest of the port.

Pour the jelly into a dampened mold and leave it to set in the refrigerator or in a cool place.

To unmold the jelly, dip the mold *briefly* in hot water, and turn it out onto a flat plate.

Another heady pudding is the delicious and quickly made eighteenth-century trifle called a whim-wham. Trifle is a traditional Boxing Day and Christmas party pudding in England.

## WHIM-WHAM

{ENGLAND}                                    TO SERVE 6

| | |
|---|---|
| 2 tablespoons butter | 2 oranges |
| 1 scant cup blanched almonds | ½ generous cup sweet sherry |
| 1 tablespoon superfine granulated sugar | ½ cup brandy |
| 18 ladyfingers, broken into halves | 1 scant pint heavy cream |

Melt the butter in a heavy frying pan and fry the almonds over medium heat until golden. Sprinkle them with the sugar and shake the pan over low heat until the sugar melts. Spread the almonds on a lightly greased plate to cool. The sugar and butter will harden to form a brittle caramel coating.

An hour or two before serving, put the ladyfingers into a large serving bowl. Squeeze the juice from the oranges, mix it with the sherry and brandy, and pour into the bowl. (The alcohol evaporates and the ladyfingers become soggy if the liquid is added too long before serving.)

Just before serving, whip the cream until it holds a peak. Pour it over the ladyfingers, which should have absorbed all the liquid. Sprinkle the top with toffee-coated almonds and serve at once.

## OLD-FASHIONED TRIFLE

[SCOTLAND]                                    TO SERVE 8 TO 10

2 eggs
2 egg yolks
2 tablespoons superfine
    granulated sugar
1 teaspoon cornstarch
2½ cups milk
½ vanilla bean
8 ladyfingers or ¼ pound
    stale sponge cake
½ cup strawberry jam

¼ pound macaroons or
    ratafias (see page
    219, crumbled
¾ cup sweet sherry, or
    sherry and brandy
    mixed
1 scant pint heavy cream,
    whipped
3 tablespoons flaked
    almonds

Mix together in a bowl the eggs, extra yolks, sugar, and cornstarch. Heat the milk and vanilla bean slowly together until almost at the boiling point. Take off the heat, remove the vanilla, and pour the milk over the egg mixture, stirring briskly. Cook the custard very gently, stirring constantly, until it has thickened. (Egg custard burns easily, so it may be cooked in a double boiler or in a bowl over a pot of hot water. The water should be kept just simmering.) Cover and cool the custard.

Spread the ladyfingers, split in half, or the pieces of stale sponge cake, with the jam, and arrange them in the bottom of the serving bowl. Sprinkle them with the crumbled macaroons or ratafias, and the sherry, or sherry and brandy mixed. Spoon the cold custard into the bowl and cover it with the whipped cream.

Toast the almond flakes until they are golden, and when they are cool, sprinkle them over the trifle.

There are endless variations on the trifle theme. The essential ingredients are a good egg custard and plenty of lightly whipped cream. The jam can be strawberry, apricot, or cherry, or use the fruits themselves. Sherry almost always plays a part in a trifle, but any of the fruit-flavored liqueurs can be used, diluted with sherry, or fruit syrup, or juice. The top of the trifle may be left plain, or piped and decorated with glacé fruits, small ratafias, or crystallized flowers.

Poppy seeds lend their distinctive flavor to two Christmas specialties of eastern Europe. Lithuania's traditional Christmas Eve dish is a fermented oatmeal porridge served with a sauce made by boiling crushed poppy seeds and chopped almonds with milk and sugar. *Mak,* an unusual poppy seed pudding from Poland, is just one of a selection of desserts made for the Christmas meal.

## MAK
### *Poppy Seed Dessert*

[POLAND]                                          TO SERVE 8 TO 10

| | |
|---|---|
| *1 pound poppy seeds* | *½ scant cup blanched* |
| *4 tablespoons sweet butter* | *    almonds, chopped fine* |
| *1¼ cups sugar* | *2 tablespoons sultana raisins* |
| *⅓ cup candied orange peel,* | *3 tablespoons honey* |
| *    chopped fine* | *½ teaspoon almond extract* |
| *⅓ cup candied lemon peel,* | *½ teaspoon vanilla extract* |
| *    chopped fine* | *2 egg whites, beaten stiff* |

FOR THE DECORATION

*5 blanched almonds, slivered*

Wash the poppy seeds, put them into a pot, and cover them with boiling water. Cook them, covered, for about 30 minutes, or until you can squash the seeds between your finger and thumb. Strain the cooked poppy seeds through a very fine sieve or cloth.

Crush the drained poppy seeds in a food mill or with a pestle and mortar. The paste will take on a whitish tinge.

Melt the butter in a shallow, heavy-bottomed pan and fry the paste together with the sugar, the candied orange and lemon peel, the almonds, and the sultana raisins. Stir in the honey and continue frying the mixture very gently for about 10 minutes, stirring constantly. Remove from the heat, and when the mixture has cooled to lukewarm stir in the almond and vanilla extracts. Last, fold in the beaten egg whites.

Turn the *mak* into a serving dish and decorate it with slivers of blanched almond.

This is a very rich pudding, so serve it cold in small portions accompanied by thin, semisweet cookies.

Another choice for ending Poland's elaborate Christmas Eve feast is a refreshing cranberry pudding. Cornstarch or arrowroot can be substituted for potato flour as a thickener for this simple dessert.

## KISIEL ZURAWINOWI
### Cranberry Dessert

{POLAND}                                      TO SERVE 4 TO 6

> *1 pound fresh cranberries*
> *½ cup granulated sugar*
> *¼ cup potato flour, or cornstarch*

Boil the cranberries briskly in 1¾ cups water until the skins burst.

Rub the cooked berries through a sieve. Return the purée to the cooking pot and add the sugar. Mix the potato flour with a little water and stir it into the purée. Bring the mixture to the boil, reduce the heat, and cook gently until it thickens.

Pour the thickened purée into a pretty bowl and serve it chilled with whipped cream.

A compote of stewed dried fruits—figs, prunes, apples, apricots, peaches, and pears—generously laced with gin or rum is another traditional choice offered for the dessert course in Poland. Allow the cooked fruit to cool before adding the spirits.

In Chile, sliced custard apples in an uncooked syrup of orange juice and confectioners' sugar are a popular seasonal choice.

A rich egg custard and semolina cream encased in delicate phyllo pastry and soaked in spiced syrup is a festive dessert served in Greek homes. Phyllo pastry is sold ready-made in specialty food stores where it often goes under the name strudel pastry.

## GALACTOBOURIKO
### Custard Pastry

{GREECE}                                        TO SERVE 12 TO 16

*12 sheets phyllo pastry*
*½ cup melted butter*

### FOR THE FILLING

*1 quart milk*                          *¼ cup butter*
*½ cup semolina*                        *5 large eggs*
*1 teaspoon cornstarch*                 *¼ teaspoon salt*
*1 piece, 1-inch-square, lemon*         *Vanilla extract to taste*
  *rind*                                *1 teaspoon powdered*
*1 cup sugar*                             *cinnamon*

### FOR THE SYRUP

*2 cups sugar*
*2 inches cinnamon stick*

Preheat oven to 375°F. To make the filling, in a heavy-bottomed pot heat the milk to just below the boiling point. Add the semolina, cornstarch, and lemon rind and stir briskly over medium heat until the mixture thickens. Cool to lukewarm, then beat in ½ cup of the sugar and the ¼ cup butter.

In a separate bowl, beat the eggs with the remaining ½ cup sugar. Combine the egg and semolina mixtures, adding salt, vanilla extract, and cinnamon to taste.

Generously butter a baking pan 12 inches by 8 inches and at least 1¼ inches deep. Lay a sheet of phyllo pastry in the bottom, trimming it if necessary, and paint it with melted butter. Top with 5 more sheets of pastry, painting each with butter before adding the next. Pour in the filling and cover it with 6 more sheets of buttered phyllo. Score the top layers of pastry with a diamond pattern. Bake in preheated oven for about 1 hour.

To make the syrup, put the 2 cups sugar into a pot with 1½ cups water and the cinnamon stick. Heat gently until the sugar has dissolved, then boil briskly for about 5 minutes. Pour the syrup over the pastry while it is still warm from the oven.

Serve *galactobouriko* warm or cold. It keeps for over a week in the refrigerator.

Another very sweet pudding made for Christmas is *natillas piuranas* from Peru.

## NATILLAS PIURANAS
### Caramelized Milk Pudding

[PERU]                                                      TO SERVE 6 TO 8

*2 cups sweetened, condensed milk*
*2½ cups milk*
*½ teaspoon baking soda*
*1¼ cups dark brown sugar*

Put the condensed milk, fresh milk, and baking soda into a pot and bring them to the boil over high heat, stirring constantly. Set aside.

Combine the sugar with 3 tablespoons water in a large, heavy-bottomed pot and cook over low heat until the sugar dissolves. Pour in the hot milk mixture and cook over very low heat, stirring constantly, for about 1¼ hours. The mixture will become a thick, amber-colored pudding.

Pour the pudding into 1 large or several individual serving dishes. Eat it at room temperature or chilled.

A less sweet milk pudding is eaten at Christmas in the Philippines, where the festive version of *leche flan* includes small coins for luck.

## LECHE FLAN
*Caramel Custard*

{PHILIPPINES}                                         TO SERVE 4 TO 6

### FOR THE CUSTARD

>2 cups milk
>8 egg yolks
>1 cup superfine granulated sugar
>Grated rind of 1 lemon

### FOR THE CARAMEL

>1 cup brown sugar

Preheat oven to 275°F. Scald the milk. Beat egg yolks and superfine granulated sugar together, then gradually beat in the milk. Add the grated lemon rind and mix thoroughly. Set aside.

To make the caramel, dissolve the brown sugar in ¼ cup water in a small saucepan over low heat, then boil the syrup briskly until it caramelizes. Do not let the caramel become too dark or it will taste bitter. Pour the caramel into a shallow, well-buttered ovenproof dish.

Pour the custard over the caramel. Stand the custard dish in a larger baking tray, and pour water into the outer container until it comes about halfway up the sides of the custard dish. Bake in preheated oven for about 1 hour or until the custard has set.

Cool the custard before turning it out of the mold, caramel side up. Lucky coins wrapped in aluminum foil can be pressed into the cold custard before it is unmolded.

Norwegians have another festive pudding for holidays—*mølsgrot* and waffles. *Mølsgrot* is a caramel-colored paste made from milk and sugar boiled down to a third of its original volume, then cooked again with sour milk or buttermilk, cream, semolina, and eggs. A hint of ground cardamom also flavors the pudding.

Norway's national festive dessert, *eggedosis,* is served after church on Christmas day.

## EGGEDOSIS
### Egg Flip

[NORWAY]                                      TO SERVE 6 TO 8

*10 egg yolks*                        *6–8 ounces brandy or*
*1 egg white*                          *Madeira wine*
*⅔ cup superfine granulated*
*  sugar*

Beat the egg yolks and the white in a large bowl. Add 2 teaspoons water and the sugar and beat the mixture over a pan of hot, but not boiling, water until it is pale and fluffy.

Pour about 1 ounce brandy or Madeira wine into each of 6 to 8 large wine glasses and top with the warm egg mixture.

Serve immediately, with macaroons or meringues. If the alcohol is omitted from the recipe, a glass of Madeira should be served separately with this pudding.

The macaroons and meringues served with *eggedosis* have undoubtedly become customary because so many egg whites are needed to make them. So here are two more pudding recipes using lots of egg whites. Both have excellent Christmas credentials.

## PAVLOVA
### Soft Meringue

[AUSTRALIA]                                      TO SERVE 6

FOR THE MERINGUE

*2 egg whites*                        *2 cups superfine granulated*
*1 teaspoon white wine*              *  sugar*
*  vinegar*                           *1 teaspoon cornstarch*
*3 tablespoons hot water*            *½ teaspoon vanilla extract*

FOR THE DECORATION

> *1 ¼ cups heavy cream, whipped*
> *2 kiwi berries, fresh or canned*

Preheat oven to 250°F. Put all the meringue ingredients into a large bowl and beat them together until the mixture holds a firm peak (about 3 minutes with an electric beater).

Mark a circle about 8 inches in diameter on a piece of aluminum foil and anchor the foil to a heavy oven tray with dabs of fat. Pile the meringue onto the foil and spread it as evenly as possible within the circle. Bake in preheated oven for 1 ½ hours.

When the meringue is cool, transfer it to a flat serving plate. Mask the whole creation with whipped cream and decorate it with slices of peeled kiwi fruit. Serve well chilled.

*Salzburger nocherln* brings drama to the table with bright flames of rum dancing over a mountain-shaped hot soufflé. It is well worth the last-minute preparation which gives the diners time to recover their appetites.

## SALZBURGER NOCKERLN
### Salzburger Soufflé

**[AUSTRIA]**                                    TO SERVE 4 TO 6

> *1 tablespoon honey*                  *½ teaspoon vanilla extract*
> *2 tablespoons heavy cream*     *Grated rind of 1 orange*
> *8 egg whites*                              *Grated rind of 1 lemon*
> *½ cup sugar*                              *2 tablespoons flour*
> *4 egg yolks*                               *4 tablespoons rum*

Preheat oven to 400°F. Put the honey and cream in an 8-inch soufflé dish in the bottom of the hot oven while you make the soufflé.

In a large bowl, beat the egg whites until they hold a stiff peak. Slowly beat in the sugar, then continue beating until the sugar has dissolved.

In a smaller bowl, beat together the egg yolks and vanilla extract. Add the grated orange and lemon rind and stir gently.

Carefully fold the egg-yolk mixture into the meringue, then fold in the flour.

Take the soufflé dish from the oven and spoon the mixture over the melted honey and cream. Heap it up into a mountain shape. Return the dish to the middle shelf of the oven for about 20 minutes, or until the soufflé is firm and golden brown.

While it is in the oven, clear space at the dining-room table for the finalé. Warm the rum in a long-handled soup ladle, set it aflame, and pour the flaming liquid over the soufflé. Serve immediately.

Rice pullings, enriched with eggs, nuts, spice, and sometimes sherry, have an honored, if mobile place in Scandinavian Christmas meals. In Denmark *grød* is sometimes served before the meat course, and a portion set aside for the *julenisse,* the little gnome who guards the family and lives in a barn or attic. Sweden's *julgröt* has a single whole almond baked in a plain rice pudding and whoever finds it will be the next person to marry. General good luck for the following year is assured to the Finn who finds the whole almond in the traditional baked rice pudding.

## UNNI RIISIPUURO
### Baked Rice Pudding

{FINLAND}                                          TO SERVE 6 TO 8

| | |
|---|---|
| 1 cup long-grain white rice | ½ cup unblanched almonds, |
| 3 cups milk | sliced |
| ¼ cup melted butter | 1 teaspoon powdered |
| ½ cup sugar | cinnamon |
| 3 large eggs | 1 blanched almond |
| ½ teaspoon salt | |

Preheat oven to 350°F. Cook the rice, uncovered, in rapidly boiling water until it is tender but not mushy. Drain and rinse in cold water.

Beat together the milk, melted butter, sugar, eggs, and salt. Combine with the cooked rice and pour into a well-buttered 2-quart oven-to-table dish. Mix the unblanched almonds with the cinnamon and sprinkle over the pudding. Bake for about 1 hour or until the pudding is as firm as desired. Press the whole almond into the pudding and cover the hole.

Serve the pudding hot or chilled. Pass around a pitcher of light cream.

Butter and cinnamon top the baked rice pudding served before roast goose in Denmark, and one dessert version is enriched with cream instead of eggs. A spoonful of cherry liqueur, or a cold raspberry or cherry sauce, tops each portion.

## RIS À L'AMANDE
### Rice and Almond Pudding

[DENMARK]                                            TO SERVE 8 TO 10

3¾ cups milk
1 cup long-grain white rice
⅓ cup superfine granulated
    sugar
½ cup blanched almonds,
    chopped

½ cup sweet sherry
1 teaspoon vanilla extract
1 cup heavy cream

Put the milk into a large heavy-bottomed pot and bring it to the boil. Add the rice and sugar, lower the heat, and simmer the rice, uncovered, for about 25 minutes, or until it is tender but not mushy. Remove from the heat and when the rice is cool, stir in the almonds, sherry, and vanilla extract.

Beat the cream until it holds a peak and fold it into the rice mixture. Turn the pudding into a pretty bowl and chill well before serving.

A very different cold pudding based on rice is eaten in the Philippines where *malagkit,* Chinese glutinous rice, is made into coconut-coated dumplings called *palitao,* served with toasted sesame seeds and sugar. The rice is soaked overnight in double its volume of water, drained in cheesecloth, ground, and then boiled to form a dough. Small balls of the dough are flattened, poached in boiling water until they float to the surface, and rolled in grated coconut.

In Malta a hot chestnut "stew" flavored with chocolate and tangerine completes the Christmas meal.

## MBULJUTA
*Chestnut Pudding*

{MALTA}                                        TO SERVE 4 TO 6

*1 pound dried chestnuts\**
*2 tablespoons cocoa*
*1 cup superfine granulated sugar*
*Rind of 1 tangerine, grated fine*

Put the chestnuts in a bowl, cover them with cold water, and leave them to soak for at least 12 hours.

Skim the soaking liquid, strain the chestnuts and reserve the liquid. Pick any loose pieces of skin from the chestnuts.

Put the chestnuts and reserved liquid into a heavy-bottomed pot, bring to a boil and cook, covered, for about 30 minutes, or until the chestnuts are tender. Add the cocoa, sugar, and grated tangerine rind. Continue cooking, partially covered, for another 30 minutes, stirring frequently. By this time some of the chestnuts will be whole or in large pieces and some will have broken down to form a sauce.

Finally, check the flavor and add more cocoa or sugar to taste. Serve hot.

Drinks tinted a violent pink with pomegranate juice are one of Mexico's colorful fiesta customs. Corn husks, too, are dyed pink for the sweet *tamales* served at Christmas. To color the corn husks, add red food coloring to hot water and soak them for about half an hour. Pat them dry and grease the inside surface of the husks with lard or butter before assembling the *tamales*. Baking parchment or aluminum foil cut into sheets approximately 9 inches by 4 inches can be substituted for the corn husks in which the pieces of stuffed dough are wrapped for steaming. Use any mixture of candied or glacé fruits for the filling, the more different kinds the better.

\* Available in Italian and other specialty food shops.

## TAMALES DULCES
*Sweet Tamales*

{MEXICO}                                        TO MAKE 24

*24 prepared corn husks*

**FOR THE DOUGH**

5 tablespoons lard
1½ cups instant masa harina
   or cornmeal
1½ teaspoons baking
   powder
½ teaspoon salt

⅔ cup superfine granulated
   sugar
½ teaspoon powdered
   cinnamon
1¼ cups warm water

**FOR THE FILLING**

*2–3 cups chopped candied fruits*

In a large bowl, cream the lard until it is light and fluffy. Sift together the *masa harina,* baking powder, salt, sugar, and cinnamon. Gradually beat the flour mixture into the lard, a little at a time. When all the flour has been thoroughly absorbed, add the warm water, a little at a time, beating constantly to form a soft dough.

To assemble the *tamales,* divide the dough among the 24 wrappers, using about 1 tablespoonful of dough per wrapper. Spread the dough to a 4-inch by 3-inch rectangle. It should extend close to the long edge of the wrappers. Drop a heaping tablespoonful of the fruit filling into the center of the dough. Fold one long side of the wrapper a little more than halfway across the filling. Fold the second long side in the same way to make an overlapping center seam. Now turn the ends to the middle to cover the seam, overlapping them enough to tuck one end into the other. (If you are using aluminum foil wrappers, bring the long sides to the center and fold over together before turning the ends to the middle.)

Stack the *tamales,* seam side down, in a large steamer, fish kettle, or in a colander which fits over a large pot. Steam them, covered, over boiling water for about 1 hour. Bring up level with boiling water during cooking if necessary.

To serve, arrange the *tamales dulces* on a heated serving dish. Eat them piping hot.

For unexpected guests, Brazil's Christmas dessert is a quick and easy pudding to make. Coconut milk may be substituted for the port.

## RABANADAS
### French Toast

{BRAZIL}                                        TO SERVE 4

| | |
|---|---|
| 8 slices French bread | 2 eggs |
| 3 tablespoons superfine | ¼ cup butter |
| granulated sugar | 1 teaspoon powdered |
| ¾ cup port wine | cinnamon |

Arrange the bread slices on a plate. Mix 1 tablespoon of the sugar with the port and pour it over the bread. Beat the eggs on another plate and when the bread has soaked up the sweetened port, dip each slice carefully into beaten egg to coat both sides.

Melt the butter in a large skillet or frying pan and fry the soaked bread on both sides until golden brown and crisp on the outside.

Arrange the *rabanadas* on a warmed serving plate and sprinkle with the rest of the sugar mixed with the cinnamon. Serve hot.

# BREADS

Mystic significance of one sort or another has so long been attached to bread that it is no surprise to find customs of decidedly pagan origin well mixed with the baking of special Christmas breads. In the Shetland Islands oatcakes called Yule-brunies are still baked with a hole in the center and edges pinched into points, a relic of the ancient Scandinavian Yule which was a festival of sun worship. In other parts of Scotland oatcakes impressed with a cross and called Yule-bannocks are baked at daybreak on Christmas morning in honor of the Virgin's delivery. The Yule log, dragged home from the forest on Christmas Eve, and so big that it burns for several days, survives still in Britain, and, of course, cakes baked in Yule-log shapes are common to many countries. In Swedish homes another old custom still practiced today is the *Julhög,* a pyramid of different breads and biscuits set before each member of the family on Christmas morning.

Germany's festive breads have been a feast for the eyes as well as the stomach since medieval times. As well as sculptured breads there are the famous *Gedildbrote,* picture breads embossed with stars, wreaths, horses, deer, serpents, and many more intricate patterns in most of which ancient symbolic meanings can be traced to their use as offerings to the gods of long ago when bread took the place of the animals that poor folk could not afford to sacrifice. Similarly, braided loaves may once have stood for offerings of hair. Crescent-shaped moon breads were being baked long before the Turks threatened Vienna. St. Nicholas loaves and braided breads in the shape of stars are popular Christmas breads in Germany today, and many of the old shapes are still repeated in the wealth of cookies made at Christmas time.

When everyday bread was coarse stuff, festive baking called for lavish use of fine ingredients, and many Christmas breads are so rich in fruit, fat, and spices that they are almost cakes. These special breads and the traditions of baking them survive even in homes where breadmaking is no longer an essential skill.

Of the plain Christmas breads the Scandinavian rye loaves are the main survivors, and so outstandingly good that it is easy to see why they are still made each year. The first is Finland's potato rye, a moist dark bread with a chewy crust and superb flavor.

## PERUNALIMPPU
### Potato Rye Bread

[FINLAND]                                        TO MAKE 2 LOAVES

*1 package active dried yeast*       *½ cup dark corn syrup or*
*1 cup potato-cooking*                    *molasses*
*water*                                  *1–2 teaspoons salt*
*2 cups rye flour*                       *2 teaspoons caraway seeds*
*2 cups warm mashed*                     *3½–4 cups all-purpose*
*potatoes*                               *flour, sifted*

FOR THE GLAZE

*1 tablespoon sugar*
*1 tablespoon warm water*

Preheat oven to 225°F. Sprinkle the yeast on 1 cup of the water in which the potatoes have cooked. The potato water should be lukewarm, about 110°F. Sift half the rye flour into a fairly large bowl and stir in the dissolved yeast mixture. Blend well together and set aside in a warm place.

In another bowl, combine the warm mashed potatoes with the syrup or molasses, salt, and caraway seeds. Add the remaining rye flour, beat the mixture smooth, cover the bowl and set it in the very cool preheated oven for 1½ hours. The potato mixture will soften in the oven as starches in the potato convert to simple sugars in what the Finns call a "malting" process.

Combine the yeast and potato mixtures in a large mixing bowl and blend them well together. Gradually add the sifted white flour, beating after each addition to make a stiff dough. The exact amount will depend on the consistency of the potato. Rest the dough in the mixing bowl for about 15 minutes before turning it out onto a floured surface and kneading it until smooth. This dough does not develop the elasticity of conventional mixtures.

Put the dough into a lightly oiled mixing bowl, rolling it to grease the mixture on all sides, and cover with a damp cloth or greased plastic bag. Set the bowl in a warm place for about 1 hour or until the dough has doubled its bulk. Punch down and leave the dough to rise again until it has doubled a second time.

Divide the dough into two equal pieces and shape each piece into a ball. Place the balls well apart on a greased and floured baking sheet and leave them to rise in a warm place for about 25 minutes, or until they appear puffy but have not quite doubled in size.

Preheat oven to 375°F. Bake the potato rye bread for 40 to 45 minutes or until the loaves sound hollow when tapped on the bottom.

Cool the loaves on a wire rack, and while still warm from the oven brush the tops with a glaze of sugar dissolved in warm water.

For Finland's Christmas rye bread, *Joululimppu,* the loaves are shaped into dented, lopsided rounds.

## JOULULIMPPU
### Christmas Rye Bread

[FINLAND]                                          TO MAKE 2 LOAVES

*½ cup molasses*          *2 teaspoons salt*
*Boiling water*           *1 package active dried yeast*
*4 cups rye flour*        *4–5 cups all-purpose flour*

FOR THE GLAZE

*1 tablespoon molasses*
*1 tablespoon warm water*

Mix the molasses in a large bowl with 1½ cups boiling water. Stir in 1 cup of the rye flour, beat well, and set the mixture aside for about ½ hour.

Now beat in another cup of rye flour and 1½ cups of boiling water. Set aside for about 1 hour.

Beat in ½ cup more boiling water and cool the mixture until luke-warm, then add the salt.

Sprinkle the yeast on ¼ cup warm water, about 110°F, and whisk well. When it has completely dissolved, stir into the molasses and rye flour mixture. Gradually add the remaining rye flour and the white flour, beating in each addition thoroughly, until a stiff dough is formed. Rest the dough for 15 minutes before turning it out onto a floured surface and kneading it until smooth.

Put the dough into a lightly oiled mixing bowl, rolling it to grease the mixture on all sides, and cover with a damp cloth or greased plastic bag. Leave it to rise in a warm place for about 1 hour, or until it has doubled in bulk.

Turn out onto a lightly floured surface and divide the dough into two pieces of equal size. Shape each piece into a ball and pull it gently into a peak on one side. Arrange the loaves well apart on a greased baking sheet. Using your thumb, punch the peaks down into the loaves, and leave them in a warm place to rise again until puffy, but not quite doubled in size.

Bake *Joululimppu* in a preheated moderately hot oven, 375°F, for about 50 minutes or until the loaves sound hollow when tapped on the bottom.

Cool the loaves on a wire rack, and while they are still warm from the oven, brush the tops with a glaze of molasses dissolved in warm water.


Yule-bannocks, the dry Scottish oatcakes exported all over the world, are baked on a thick, round iron griddle or girdle with a high, half-hoop handle. Oatcakes may also be baked on the large, smooth hot plates fitted to some electric stoves or on a pancake griddle. For the method, ancient and modern, I quote F. Marian McNeill writing in *The Scot's Kitchen*.

"Four special implements are used for baking oat cakes—the *spurtle*, or porridge-stick, for stirring the mixture; a notched *bannock-stick*, or rolling-pin, which leaves a criss-cross pattern on the upper side; the *spathe,* a heart-shaped implement with a long handle, made of iron, used for transferring the cakes from board to girdle; and the *banna-rack,* or toaster.

"If a quantity is to be made, the dough should be rather soft, as it stiffens whilst lying about to be made up. The best results are obtained by mixing enough for one round or bannock at a time using the quantities given below), the next bannock being prepared while the last is on the girdle.

"Put into a bowl four ounces of oatmeal, a pinch of baking-soda and a pinch of salt. Melt a teaspoonful of fat (bacon or poultry fat or butter or dripping; goose fat is excellent). Make a well in the centre of the oatmeal and add the melted fat with just enough hot water to make a stiff dough. Rub plenty of meal on to the baking-board; turn out the mixture and form into a smooth ball; knead with gradually spreading knuckles, working as quickly as possible, and roll out as thinly as possible—say an eighth of an inch. The process is not quite easy to one unfamiliar with the work, owing to the thickness of the dough and the tendency of the edges to break. The dough must be kept from sticking by constant rubbing over on both sides with dry meal, and the edges must be kept as even as possible by pinching with the thumb and forefinger. Invert a plate 5–7 inches in diameter on the dough and cut neatly into a round. Give a final rub with meal to make the cakes white. They may be left whole (bannocks) or cut into quarters (farls). Place on a moderately hot girdle over a clear fire, smooth side uppermost, and bake steadily till the cakes curl up at the edge. Remove them carefully, rub a little oatmeal over them, and toast the smooth side slightly before a bright smokeless fire. (Toasting-stones with an incised pattern to permit the sweating of the cakes were formerly used on the open hearth. An attachable iron toaster was used on the ordinary coal range.) Place for a few minutes in a warm place, e.g., a moderate oven. Keep buried in oatmeal in the girnel or meal chest; or failing these, in a tin. They are improved being heated shortly before they are served, unless they are freshly baked. The girdle should be put on to heat before the dough is mixed. To test the heat, sprinkle a little flour over it. If it browns at once the girdle is too hot; if it takes a few seconds to brown it will do. For scones and bannocks, sprinkle the girdle with flour, unless they are themselves sufficiently floury to prevent sticking. The girdle should never be washed, but should be cleaned when hot by being rubbed with coarse salt, and then dusted with a clean cloth."

What the Scots call tea breads, the Scandinavians call coffee breads, and they are baked in large quantities for the Christmas tables of Sweden and Finland. They are offered to visitors throughout the holiday and served with fresh coffee. Coffee breads are invariably eaten before more elaborate cookies and cakes, and may be baked in large, fancy loaves or small buns. There is a wealth of traditional shapes to choose from— braids, stars, twists, pinwheels, and many more with names like Christmas wagons, bishops' wigs, Lucia buns, Christmas pigs, golden chariots, and so on.

## SAFFRANSBROD
### Saffron Bread
[SWEDEN]                TO MAKE 2 LOAVES OR ABOUT 40 BUNS

*1 teaspoon saffron*                *1 cup melted butter*
*1 tablespoon brandy*               *8 cups flour, sifted*
*2½ cups milk*                      *1 cup superfine granulated*
*2 packages active dried yeast*         *sugar*
*¼ teaspoon salt*                   *1 cup seedless raisins*
*1 large egg*

**FOR THE GLAZE**

*1 egg, beaten*

Dry the saffron for about 5 minutes in a warm oven, 300°F, then dissolve it in the brandy. Heat the milk to lukewarm, about 110°F. Use ½ cup of the warm milk to dissolve the dried yeast. Sprinkle it over the milk, whisk well, and leave it for about 15 minutes.

In a large bowl mix the remaining warm milk with the saffron and brandy, salt, egg, melted butter, and 1 cup of the sifted flour. Add the yeast mixture, stirring constantly, and beat in the sugar, raisins, and remaining flour, a little at a time, until a firm dough is formed.

Put the dough in a lightly oiled bowl, rolling it to grease the mixture on all sides, and cover with a damp cloth or greased plastic bag. Leave it to rise in a warm place for about 2 hours or until doubled in bulk.

Turn out the dough onto a floured surface and knead it until smooth and elastic. The dough is now ready to shape.

To make two large braided loaves, divide the mixture into two equal pieces. Divide one piece into three equal pieces and roll them into three long strips. Braid the strips evenly, tucking the ends underneath, and carefully set the braid on a well-buttered baking sheet. Repeat with the second ball of dough. Set the loaves in a warm place to rise until the dough is puffy but not quite doubled in bulk. Brush the loaves with beaten egg glaze and sprinkle chopped almonds and sugar down the center of each braid. Preheat oven to 375°F and bake for 20 to 25 minutes or until the loaves are golden brown. Cool on a wire rack and serve warm.

To make saffron buns, roll small pieces of dough into "snakes" about 12 inches long. To make a simple S-shaped bun, coil the dough loosely from each end in opposite directions and put a raisin in the center of each curl. Two or three of these S-shaped pieces of dough may be set across each other to make larger, more ornate buns. Lay the buns well apart on a generously buttered baking sheet and leave them in a warm place to rise until the dough is puffy but not quite doubled in bulk. Preheat oven to 425°F, brush the buns with beaten egg glaze, and bake them for 10 to 12 minutes or until the buns are golden brown. Cool on a wire rack and serve warm.

Finland's coffee bread, *pulla,* is a moist, rich bread, eaten hot without butter. It is baked throughout the year, often for Sunday-morning callers, but at Christmas it is made into special shapes. Cardamom seeds, which on their own have an almost soapy taste, give *pulla* its distinctive flavor.

### *PULLA*
#### *Coffee Bread*

[FINLAND]                    TO MAKE 2 OR 3 LOAVES

*1 package active dried yeast*　*1 teaspoon powdered*
*½ cup warm water*　　　　*cardamom*
*2 cups milk*　　　　　　*4 eggs, beaten*
*1 cup superfine granulated*　*8–9 cups flour, sifted*
*　sugar*　　　　　　　*½ cup melted butter*
*1 teaspoon salt*

TO DECORATE

*1 egg, beaten*
*Glacé cherries or raisins*

Sprinkle the yeast on the ½ cup warm water in a large bowl. Whisk well and set aside in a warm place for about 15 minutes or until the yeast has completely dissolved. Scald the milk and cool it to lukewarm.

Add to the yeast mixture the milk, sugar, salt, cardamom, and eggs with 2 cups of the sifted flour. Beat to a smooth, thick batter. Gradually add 3 more cups of the flour, beating continuously to form a smooth, glossy dough. Beat in the melted butter, then add enough of the remaining flour to make a firm dough. Rest the dough, covered, for about 15 minutes before turning it out on a floured surface and kneading it until smooth and elastic.

Place the dough in a lightly oiled bowl, rolling it to grease the mixture on all sides, and cover with a damp cloth or greased plastic bag. Leave it to rise in a warm place for about 1 hour or until doubled in bulk. Punch down the dough, cover, and let it rise again until almost doubled in bulk. Chilling the dough at this stage will make it easier to form into fancy shapes.

To make two fancy Christmas cake loaves, *Joulukakut,* divide the dough into four equal pieces. Shape one piece into a flat, circular loaf about 12 inches in diameter, and place it on a lightly greased baking sheet. Divide the second piece of dough into three equal portions and roll each portion into a long, thin strand about 48 inches in length. Cut a 4-inch piece off each strand and reserve. Plait the strands into a braid and lay the braid in a circle on top of the loaf, about 1 inch inside the edge. Form the reserved short lengths into S-shaped curls and arrange them in a radial pattern from the center of the loaf. Make a second loaf with the remaining two pieces of dough. Set the loaves to rise in a warm place until they are puffy but not quite doubled in bulk. Preheat oven to 400°F, brush the loaves with beaten egg to glaze, decorate with cherries or raisins, and bake for 25 to 30 minutes or until golden brown. Do not overbake or the loaves will be too dry. Cool on a wire rack and serve warm.

To make three bishops' wig loaves, *papintukka,* divide the dough into nine equal pieces and roll each piece into a strand about 18 inches long. Fold the first strand in half and place it on a lightly greased baking sheet with the open end facing toward you. Curl the ends outward and upward into small coils. Place a second strand of dough on top and slightly above the first and curl its ends in the same way. Repeat with a third strand. The finished pattern will look like an inverted U with a row of three curls down each side. Repeat the pattern twice with the remaining six pieces of dough, and set the loaves to rise in a warm place until they are puffy but not quite doubled in bulk. Preheat oven to

400°F. Place half a glacé cherry or raisin on each curl and glaze the loaves with beaten egg. Bake for 20 to 25 minutes or until the loaves are golden brown. Cool on a wire rack and serve warm.

Germany's favorite Christmas fruit bread, *Dresdner stollen,* should be stored for at least 3 days after it is baked. It is a dry, cake-like bread which keeps well for several weeks and is often gift-wrapped in clear cellophane tied with a bow of red ribbon.

## WEIHNACHTS STOLLEN
### Christmas Bread

[GERMANY]                                                    TO MAKE 2 LOAVES

| | |
|---|---|
| 6 tablespoons rum | 1 cup superfine granulated |
| ½ cup seedless raisins | sugar |
| ½ scant cup dried currants | 6 cups flour |
| 1 scant cup candied orange, | 1 cup milk |
| lemon, and citron peel, | ½ teaspoon salt |
| chopped | ½ teaspoon almond extract |
| 1 cup glacé cherries, | 2 eggs |
| quartered | 1¼ cups sweet butter, |
| ¾ package active dried | softened |
| yeast | ¾ cup almonds, chopped |
| 3 tablespoons water, 110°F | ¼ cup confectioners' sugar |

Put the rum into a small bowl with the raisins, currants, candied peel, and glacé cherries. Set aside to soak.

Sprinkle the yeast on about 3 tablespoons of warm water, 110°F, mixed with 1 tablespoon of the sugar, whisk well, and set aside in a warm place until the yeast dissolves completely.

Drain the dried fruit, reserving the rum, and pat it dry. Toss the fruit in about 2 tablespoons of the flour and set it aside.

Dissolve ⅔ cup of the sugar with the milk and salt in a saucepan over very low heat. When the mixture is lukewarm remove from the heat and add the reserved rum, almond extract, and the yeast mixture.

Sift 5 cups of the flour into a mixing bowl and add the yeast mixture, stirring constantly. Beat the eggs until frothy and stir them into the dough, followed by about ⅔ cup butter. When the ingredients are thoroughly blended, turn out the dough onto a well-floured surface and knead it, sprinkling the dough with the remaining flour and kneading until it has all been incorporated. When the dough becomes smooth and elastic, press in the dried fruits and chopped almonds a handful at a time. Continue kneading lightly until these are well distributed in the dough. Place the dough in a lightly oiled bowl, rolling it to grease the mixture on all sides, and cover it with a damp cloth or greased plastic bag. Leave it to rise in a warm place for about 2 hours or until the dough doubles in bulk.

Punch down the dough, divide it in halves, and leave it to rest for about 10 minutes. On a lightly floured surface, roll out the dough into ½-inch-thick rectangles about 12 inches by 8 inches. Melt the remaining butter. Brush each strip generously with butter and sprinkle liberally with the remaining sugar. To shape the loaves, fold one long edge to the center; fold the opposite edge to overlap the center in a 1-inch seam. Press lightly to seal the edges and arrange the loaves, well apart, on a generously buttered baking sheet. Brush the dough with melted butter and set it aside to rise in a warm place until doubled in bulk.

Preheat oven to 375°F and bake the bread for about 45 minutes or until the loaves are golden brown. Cool on a wire rack. While still warm from the oven brush the loaves with the remaining melted butter and dust generously with confectioners' sugar. When completely cold, store the *stollen* in an airtight container and leave them to mature for at least 3 days before cutting.

*Christópsomo,* the Christmas bread of Greece, is flavored with chopped orange peel and the dough is rolled in sesame seeds before being formed into the shape of a cross and sprinkled with chopped almonds. Denmark's *Julekage* is flavored with cardamom like the Finnish *pulla.* The dough includes generous quantities of candied pineapple as well as the usual glacé cherries and candied citrus peel, and it is baked in a standard loaf tin. Austria's *stritzel* is the most elaborately braided of the Christmas loaves with a four-strand plait covered by a three-strand plait and topped with a two-strand twist. Nutmeg and cumin spice its well-egged dough. Norway's *Julekake* is even more richly filled, with spiced apples or dried fruit, candied peel and almond paste, and is often baked in fancy shapes. Tricorns, half moons, and figures of eight are three traditional forms which may well have their roots in pre-Christian festivities but are merrily continued today. This version, with an almond paste center, is best baked in a rectangular loaf pan.

# JULEKAKE
## Christmas Bread

½ package active dried yeast
½ cup water, 110°F
3½ tablespoons superfine
    granulated sugar
1 large egg
4 cups flour
¼ teaspoon salt
6 tablespoons butter

½ cup seedless raisins
½ cup dried currants
½ cup mixed candied peel,
    chopped
1 teaspoon powdered
    cardamom
6 ounces almond paste (see
    page 237

Sprinkle the yeast on about ½ cup warm water, 110°F, mixed with a teaspoon of the sugar. Whisk the mixture and set it in a warm place. When the yeast has completely dissolved, whisk in the egg and set the mixture aside.

Sift the flour, salt, and remaining sugar into a mixing bowl. Dice the butter into the bowl and, using your fingertips or a pastry blender, rub the fat lightly into the flour until the mixture resembles fine bread crumbs. Make a well in the center and pour in the yeast mixture. Sprinkle a little flour over the liquid, cover the bowl, and set it in a warm place for about ½ hour or until the yeast has bubbled through. Stir the flour gradually into the liquid. Turn out the dough onto a lightly floured surface and knead it lightly until it is smooth and elastic. Mix the dried and candied fruits with the cardamom and press them into the dough a handful at a time.

Put the dough in a lightly oiled bowl, rolling it to grease the mixture on all sides, and cover it with a damp cloth or greased plastic bag. Leave it to rise in a warm place for about 1 hour or until it doubles its bulk. Punch down, knead again lightly, and divide the dough into halves. Place the first half in a well-greased and floured loaf pan of about 1½ quart capacity. Roll the almond paste into a thick sausage about 1½ inches shorter than the length of the tin and lay it on the dough. Put the remaining dough on top of the almond paste and tuck it in lightly. Set the pan aside in a warm place until the dough is puffy but not quite doubled in bulk.

Preheat oven to 375°F and bake dough for 50 to 60 minutes. Cool on a wire rack. When completely cold, store the *Julekake* in an airtight container for at least 24 hours before slicing it.

# CAKES

Honey and dried fruits were the sweeteners used throughout Europe before cane sugar from the Caribbean plantations became an import which has grown steadily since the seventeenth century. Neolithic man knew the taste of honey and by the Bronze Age it had become more plentiful as greater areas of forest were cleared for grazing. The proverbial land flowing with milk and honey was no dream but a direct result of agriculture.

Oriental spices played an important role in Roman cooking, though honey was still the universal sweetener. Pliny said of cane sugar from India that it was "a kind of honey that collects in reeds," and added that its uses were only medicinal.

Raisins and currants and most of the spices we know today were lavishly employed by cooks to the medieval nobility. A form of gingerbread was already an established favorite in the thirteenth century when squares of the cake made in England were decorated with box leaves spiked with cloves. These decorations were sometimes gilded.

Travel played an important role in the growth of cakemaking. Traders and crusaders returned home to northern lands with recipes from the Far East and the Levant. Gradually, as the use of eggs and other raising agents was better understood and employed, cakes which had earlier been enriched breads evolved into the confections made today. Many of the cakes still made for Christmas are baked from recipes which have changed little for centuries. New kitchen equipment, and prepared and packaged ingredients, have taken much of the labor out of baking. But the rich spicy smells and tastes are just the same, and their enjoyment all the greater for a pinch of sentiment.

Honey cakes and gingerbreads, which are well-spiced, though not always with ginger, were among the first cakes to be made for Christmas celebrations. Some of the earliest were no more than dry white bread crumbs mixed with spice and honey to form a stiff paste which could be molded and decorated. Most of the recipes used today are simple ones, though the molds and decorations may be very elaborate. Germany's many types of *Lebkuchen* and *Pfefferkuchen* are among the most lavishly ornamented gingerbreads and are fashioned into iced pictures as well as houses, figures, and all kinds of fancy shapes. The Swiss, Dutch, Austrians, Danes, Norwegians, Finns, Swedes, Scots, and Silesians all make honey and spice cakes or cookies for Christmas, and now there must be more varieties of honey and ginger cakes made in America than anywhere else. As each new wave of immigrants brought its treasured recipes and patterns to the New World, the repertoire of American cooks grew to embrace them. Nowhere else in the world is there such a variety of *Süssgebäck,* or "sweet bakings," as the German language best catches it, at Christmastime.

Edinburgh gingerbread is a rich, moist cake which improves with keeping for a week or two in an airtight container. The mixture includes dates and walnuts and is traditionally baked in a square or rectangular pan.

## EDINBURGH GINGERBREAD

[SCOTLAND]                                         TO MAKE I CAKE

4 cups flour
1/4 teaspoon salt
1 1/2 teaspoons powdered
    ginger
1 1/2 teaspoons powdered
    cinnamon
1 1/2 teaspoons mixed spice
    (commercially
    packaged; or mixed
    cloves, cinnamon,
    ginger, and nutmeg)

1/2 teaspoon powdered cloves
1 cup pitted dates, chopped
    coarse
1 cup shelled walnuts,
    chopped coarse
1 cup butter
1 cup molasses
1 cup dark brown sugar
4 large eggs, beaten
1 teaspoon baking soda
1–2 tablespoons warm milk

Preheat oven to 350°F. Sift the flour, salt, and spices into a mixing bowl. Add the dates and walnuts to the flour.

In a small saucepan over low heat melt together the butter, molasses, and sugar. Pour this mixture gradually into the flour, stirring constantly. Add the eggs; dissolve the baking soda in a tablespoon of warm milk, and add to mixture. Stir the ingredients well with a wooden spoon so as not to mash the fruit, adding a little more warm milk if needed to make a mixture which will just drop from the spoon but is not too soft.

Spoon the mixture into a well-greased pan about 8 inches square and at least 2½ inches deep, lined with baking parchment. Spread the mixture evenly, and bake in preheated oven for 20 minutes. Then lower the heat to 300°F and continue baking for another 2 hours or until a skewer inserted in the center of the cake comes out clean. Cool the gingerbread on a wire rack, then strip off the paper and, when completely cold, store in an airtight container.

Sweden's ginger cake is a lighter mixture, often baked in a ring mold. It is not usually decorated.

## MJUK PEPPARKAKA
### Ginger Cake

[SWEDEN]                                    TO MAKE 1 CAKE

| | |
|---|---|
| ½ cup butter | 1 teaspoon powdered cloves |
| 1 cup superfine granulated | 1¾ cups cake or all-purpose |
| sugar | flour |
| 3 large eggs, beaten | 1 teaspoon baking soda |
| 1 teaspoon powdered ginger | ¾ cup sour cream |
| 1 teaspoon powdered | |
| cinnamon | |

Preheat oven to 325°F. Cream the butter in a large bowl, add the sugar, and beat the mixture until it is pale and very fluffy. Add the eggs a little at a time to the butter and sugar, beating vigorously.

Sift together the spices, flour, and baking soda, and fold half into the creamed mixture a little at a time. Fold in the sour cream, then incorporate the remaining dry ingredients.

Spoon the mixture into a ring mold, well-greased and dusted with dry bread crumbs. Bake the ginger cake for 50 to 60 minutes. Leave to cool in the pan for about 10 minutes, then turn out onto a wire rack. Store in an airtight container.

Oatmeal gives an interesting texture to *broonie,* a rough, solid gingerbread made for the New Year in the Orkney Islands.

*Nürnberger Lebkuchen* is another mixture made into small cakes which keep well in an airtight tin. They are made with 1 cup of granulated sugar and 4 egg whites beaten to a froth. Two cups of honey, 2⅔ cups of ground almonds, a tablespoon of mixed spice, and ½ cup of finely chopped candied peel are added with about 1½ cups flour. This mixture is spread thickly on wafers and dried for several hours before being baked and iced.

For a *Lebkuchen Häuschen,* the famous gingerbread house, a quite different recipe is used. It is for a cake which, if not eaten (and many such houses are brought out year after year), will dry out and keep from one season to the next. This kind of mixture is also used for other traditional fancy shapes. Lavish decoration is the rule for a *Lebkuchen Häuschen,* which is adorned with frosting, small cookies, and candy. If the cake is being made to last, be sure the decorations will too; choose candies and cookies that will not crumble or slowly dissolve when in contact with the air. Icing made with confectioners' sugar and egg white is very durable if kept dry.

For a 10-inch-high gingerbread house, bake three batches of the next recipe or triple the quantities given in the ingredients list. Cut the gingerbread as soon as it is baked with accurate cardboard or baking parchment patterns made according to the diagram. Store the cut pieces in an airtight container until they are to be assembled with icing cement. If a large jellyroll pan (about 18 inches by 12 inches) is not available, divide the mixture among smaller pans, calculating with the patterns the number of pieces needed.

# LEBKUCHEN HÄUSCHEN
*Gingerbread House*

[GERMANY]                                    MAKE 3 SEPARATE BATCHES

*6 cups flour*                              *1 cup honey*
*2½ teaspoons baking*                       *2⅔ cups superfine*
*    powder*                                *    granulated sugar*
*¼ teaspoon salt*                           *¼ cup butter*
*1 teaspoon powdered ginger*               *Juice and fine-grated rind*
*1 teaspoon powdered*                       *    of 1 lemon*
*    cinnamon*                              *1 large egg*
*1 teaspoon powdered cloves*               *1 egg yolk*
*½ teaspoon grated nutmeg*

**FOR THE ICING**

*2 egg whites*
*2⅔ cups confectioners' sugar, sifted*

Preheat oven to 325°F. Sift the flour, baking powder, salt, and spices into a large mixing bowl. Put the honey, sugar, and butter into a large, heavy saucepan and heat gently together until the sugar has dissolved. Bring the mixture to the boil. Cool to room temperature, and add the lemon juice and rind. Beat one-third of the flour and spice into the cooled honey mixture, add the whole egg and the egg yolk, and incorporate them thoroughly before adding the remaining flour and spice.

Turn the dough back into the mixing bowl and knead it lightly with floured hands until it is smooth and pliable. This dough will be a little sticky, but if it is too soft to handle, knead in a little more flour.

Press the dough evenly into a well-buttered and floured jellyroll pan, about 18 inches by 12 inches, and bake for 40 minutes or until the cake feels firm when pressed lightly with the fingertips. Cool the cake in the pan for about 10 minutes before turning it onto a flat surface. Cut the required shapes, using prepared patterns, then cool the pieces on a wire rack before storing.

To make the icing, whisk the egg whites until they hold a soft peak, then beat in the sifted confectioners' sugar, about 4 tablespoons at a time, beating in each addition thoroughly. Beat continuously until a stiff icing is formed.

To assemble the *Lebkuchen Häuschen,* pipe icing doors, windows, and shutters on the front, back, and sides of the house. When these decorations have dried, lay the base on a tray or board and build up the house with icing cement. Allow the walls to dry before adding the roof and chimney, and leave these to set before completing the decorations with a fresh batch of icing if needed. Sprinkle confectioners' sugar on the base for instant snow.

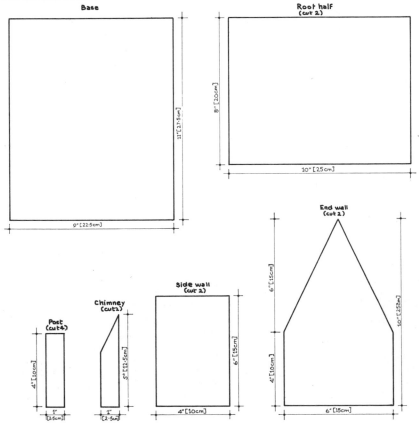

In Sweden a harder biscuit dough, cut before baking, makes the traditional *pepparkaksstuga*. The recipe is a mixture used for Lucia gingersnaps, too, the cookies made in the shapes of people, animals, and trees. The quantities given in the following recipe make the house and plenty of extra cookies—the number will depend on the size of cutters used. Use the tiny fancy cutters for *petits fours* to make miniature decorations.

This dough is very well-behaved in the oven, hardly shrinking or spreading at all. Make accurate cardboard or baking parchment patterns according to the diagram. The windows may be cut out, or applied as decoration.

## PEPPARKAKSSTUGA
*Gingersnap House*

[SWEDEN]        TO MAKE 1 HOUSE AND ADDITIONAL COOKIES

**FOR THE DOUGH**

*¾ cup heavy cream*
*1 generous cup dark brown*
*sugar*
*1 cup molasses*
*2 teaspoons powdered*
*ginger*

*2 teaspoons grated lemon*
*rind*
*1 teaspoon baking soda*
*5 cups flour, sifted*

**FOR THE CEMENT**

*⅔ cup superfine granulated sugar*

**FOR THE ICING**

*1 egg white*
*1¾ cups confectioners' sugar*

Preheat oven to 350°F. To make the dough, whip the cream in a large bowl until it is thick but not stiff. Add dark brown sugar, molasses, ginger, lemon rind, and baking soda and beat well. Add the flour all at once. Stir the mixture with a wooden spoon until it becomes too stiff to manage, then use your hands to blend it until it forms a firm dough.

Roll out the dough thin on a lightly floured surface. Lay the patterns on the dough. Place a ruler on the pattern, lining it up with one edge, and, pressing gently, cut along the edge with a sharp knife. Move the ruler to the next edge, cut, and so on.

Arrange the cut-out dough on heavy baking sheets with buttered wax paper. Brush the dough with water and bake for 20 to 25 minutes. Leave the pieces on the baking sheets for about 5 minutes before laying them carefully on a wire rack to cool. Make sure that each piece is quite flat during cooling as the dough sets hard. When cold, store the pieces in an airtight container until the house is to be assembled. Use the remaining dough to make tiny baked decorations, or plain or fancy cookies.

To assemble the house, melt the sugar for the cement over low heat in a 9-inch saucepan. Dip the edges of the dough pieces in the melted sugar and stick them together. The caramelized sugar sets in an instant, but it is dangerous stuff, so work carefully to avoid nasty burns.

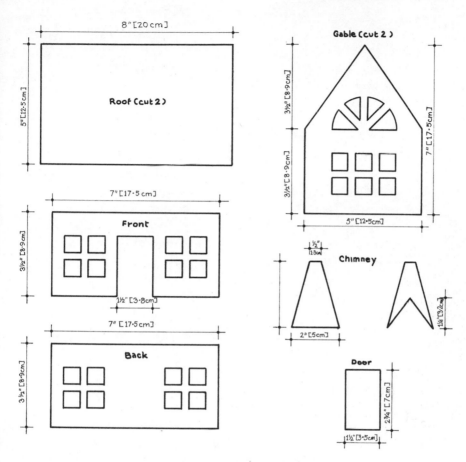

Scale 1cm : 1"

To decorate the *pepparkaksstuga,* beat the egg white until it just holds a peak, then beat in the sifted confectioners' sugar a little at a time until a stiff icing is formed. Pipe decorations on to the house and stick on any other decorations with small blobs of icing.

English Christmas cake, like Christmas pudding, should be made in September or October if it is to mature to its full richness. About 10 days before it is needed, the top and sides are covered with almond paste which is left to dry for about 3 days before the cake is frosted with royal icing. Alternatively, the top only may be covered with almond paste, decorated with closely packed lines of nuts and glacéed fruits, and glazed. The sides of the cake are then covered with a paper frill.

## CHRISTMAS CAKE

2½ cups flour
1 teaspoon salt
1 teaspoon mixed spice
   (commercially
   packaged; or mixed
   ground cloves,
   cinnamon, and
   nutmeg)
1 cup butter
1½ cups light brown sugar
4 large eggs
1 tablespoon molasses

1 tablespoon grated lemon
   rind
1½ cups sultana raisins
1¼ cups dried currants
1½ cups seedless raisins
½ cup candied peel,
   chopped fine
1¼ cups glacé cherries,
   halved
⅔ cup almonds, ground
½ cup brandy

**FOR THE DECORATION**

1¼ pounds almond paste (see page 237)
¾ cup apricot jam

**FOR THE ROYAL ICING**

3 egg whites
5¼ cups confectioners' sugar, sifted
2 teaspoons lemon juice
1½ teaspoons glycerine

Preheat oven to 300°F. Sift together the flour, salt, and mixed spice and set aside. In a large mixing bowl cream together the butter and sugar until very light and fluffy. In another bowl lightly beat together the eggs, molasses, and lemon rind. Gradually beat the egg mixture into the butter and sugar, adding a little flour mixture with the last few additions of egg to stop the mixture from separating.

Sift a few tablespoons of the flour mixture over the fruit, candied peel, and almonds and toss them all together.

Fold the remaining flour mixture into the creamed mixture, then the fruit and nuts, and last the brandy. Mix all these together very thoroughly.

Turn the mixture into a well-greased 8-inch round cake pan, at least 3 inches deep, which has been neatly lined with baking parchment. Make a shallow depression in the center of the cake so that when the mixture rises in the oven the top will be level.

Bake in preheated slow oven for 1½ hours, then lower the heat to a cool 275°F and continue baking for another 2½ hours. The cake is cooked when a warmed skewer plunged into the center comes out clean.

Cool the cake in its pan for 24 hours before stripping off the paper. You may "feed" the cake with 2 or 3 more tablespoons of brandy dribbled over the base before storing it in an airtight container. If the cake is baked well ahead of Christmas, it may be "fed" again about 4 weeks before it is decorated, and returned to an airtight container.

To apply the almond paste, first measure around the outer edge of the cake with a piece of string. Take two-thirds of the almond paste and roll it out on a surface dredged with confectioners' sugar, to a rectangle half the length of the string and twice the depth of the cake in width. Trim and cut in two lengthwise. Knead the trimmings into the remaining paste and roll it out to fit the cake top. Use the cake pan as a pattern, and cut around it with a sharp knife.

Heat the apricot jam with 1 or 2 tablespoons of water and pass it through a sieve. Brush the sides of the cake with this apricot glaze. Fit the two strips of almond paste around the cake and smooth over the seams. Brush the top of the cake with glaze and cover with the remaining almond paste. Roll lightly with a sugar-dusted rolling pin and make sure the joints are neat and well-sealed. Cover the cake wit. a clean cloth and leave it in a cool place for about 3 days to dry the paste a little before icing.

To make the icing, whisk the egg whites until frothy. Stir in the sifted confectioners' sugar, a spoonful at a time, with a wooden spoon. When half the sugar is incorporated, add the lemon juice. Continue adding more sugar, beating well after each addition, until the mixture almost holds a peak. Then stir in the glycerine, which helps prevent the icing from becoming too hard.

To ice the cake smoothly as a base for piped decorations, coat the top and sides on consecutive days so that a clean edge can harden after the first application. A second coat of thinner icing may be applied after 48 hours drying time. (Royal icing remains workable for several days if stored in an airtight container.)

Alternatively, the icing may be used to cover the whole cake with a fluffed, peaky frosting.

Traditional decorations include holly, small sugar or plaster robins, Yule logs, and Christmas trees.

When the icing has hardened sufficiently, the cake should be covered with a clean cloth until it is cut. After cutting, it will still keep for months stored in an airtight container.

Twelfth cake is seldom made now in England for the last day of the Christmas feast, which is a pity if only because it is a very good cake. Traditionally it was not iced, but decorated with glacé cherries, angelica, and other crystallized fruits. Twelfth Night used to be celebrated, often with a play or a masque, before the work of the New Year started in earnest. In the eighteenth and nineteenth centuries a single bean was baked into the cake and whoever found it was called King of the Bean and was assured good luck in the coming year. Earlier still, the customs associated with Twelfth cake appear to have been even more elaborate. Samuel Pepys, writing on January 6, 1666, said:

> "My wife to fetch away my things from Woolwich, and I back to cards to choose King and Queene, and a good cake there was, but no marks found; but I privately found the clove, the mark of the knave, and privately put it into Captain Cocke's piece, which made some mirthe, because of his lately being knowne by his buying of clove and mace of the East India prizes."

The good cake of Samuel Pepys' age would almost certainly have been a heavily spiced yeast-raised mixture. The following nineteenth-century recipe makes a rich, buttery cake which is lighter in color than Christmas cake.

## TWELFTH CAKE

{ENGLAND}                                        TO MAKE 1 CAKE

*1 cup butter*
*1 1/3 cups superfine*
*    granulated sugar*
*4 eggs*
*3 tablespoons brandy*
*2 cups flour*
*1/4 teaspoon grated nutmeg*
*1/4 teaspoon powdered*
*    cinnamon*

*1 1/4 cups dried currants*
*1 1/2 cups seedless raisins*
*1 1/2 cups sultana raisins*
*1/2 cup blanched almonds,*
*    chopped*
*1 dried bean*

Preheat oven to 300°F. Cream together the butter and sugar in a large bowl until pale and fluffy. Mix the eggs with the brandy and gradually beat them into the creamed butter, adding a little of the flour with the last few additions of egg to prevent the mixture from separating. Sift together the flour and spices and fold them gradually into the creamed mixture. Mix in the fruit and nuts and stir until all the ingredients are well distributed.

Spoon the batter into a 12-inch round cake pan, at least 3 inches deep, which has been well greased and lined with baking parchment. Press the bean into the batter. Bake for 3 hours. Rest the cooked cake in its pan for about ½ hour, then turn it out onto a wire rack. When quite cold, strip off the paper and store it in an airtight container.

"A black substance inimical to life" was Robert Louis Stevenson's description of black bun, an invention peculiar to the Scots. It is a fatless, highly spiced fruitcake baked in a rather hard pastry crust, and it should be made well in advance to allow the flavor to mature. Black bun was originally the Scots' Twelfth cake, but it was transferred to Hogmanay, New Year's Eve, after the banning of Christmas festivities by the sixteenth-century church reformers. In the early nineteenth century, huge cakes weighing 16 pounds or more were exported to England and the colonies. The following recipe is faithful to the tradition but moderate in scale.

## BLACK BUN
### New Year Cake

{SCOTLAND}                                        TO MAKE 1 CAKE

**FOR THE PASTRY**

> 2¼ cups flour
> 2½ teaspoons baking powder
> ¼ teaspoon salt
> 6 tablespoons butter

FOR THE FILLING

2½ cups muscatel raisins, pitted

2½ cups dried currants

⅓ cup candied peel, chopped

½ cup slivered almonds

½ cup light brown sugar

2 cups flour

2½ teaspoons baking powder

1 teaspoon powdered ginger

1 teaspoon powdered cinnamon

¼ teaspoon powdered allspice

¼ teaspoon black pepper, freshly ground

5 tablespoons Scotch whisky

5 tablespoons buttermilk or fresh milk

FOR THE GLAZE

1 egg, beaten

Preheat oven to 350°F. To make the pastry, sift together twice the flour, baking powder, and salt, and put them in a bowl with the butter cut into dice. Using your fingertips or a pastry blender, lightly work in the butter until the mixture resembles fine bread crumbs. Add sufficient cold water to make a soft dough.

On a lightly floured surface, roll out two-thirds of the dough and use it to line a lightly greased and floured 8-inch round, preferably loose-bottomed, cake pan.

Put all the fruit, nuts, and sugar for the filling into a large mixing bowl. Sift together twice the flour, baking powder, and spices and add them to the fruit. Toss the fruit and flour together well before moistening the mixture with the whisky and buttermilk.

Spoon the filling into the pastry-lined pan and press the mixture to pack it neatly. Turn the top edge of the pastry lining down over the filling and brush the exposed pastry with water. Roll out the remaining pastry and cut it in a circle which exactly fits the top. Lower the pastry lid onto the cake and press the edges well to seal. With a skewer, make four holes right down to the bottom of the cake. Prick the pastry top all over with a fork and brush it with egg to glaze.

Bake black bun in preheated oven for 2 hours. If the pastry lid shows signs of burning before the cake is cooked, cover the top loosely with baking parchment or foil, removing the cover for the last 10 minutes of cooking time.

Allow the cake to cool in the pan. When completely cold, store it in an airtight container.

Unusual crystallized fruits—pears, watermelon, plums, apricots, and figs, as well as candied citrus peel—are included in Chile's Christmas cake, *pán de Pascua*, which is served with coffee at the end of dinner on Christmas Eve.

## PÁN DE PASCUA
### *Christmas Cake*

{CHILE}                                        TO MAKE 1 CAKE

| | |
|---|---|
| *1 generous cup butter* | *2 tablespoons baking* |
| *1½ tablespoons warm* | *powder* |
| *water* | *1 teaspoon powdered* |
| *2 cups confectioners' sugar,* | *cinnamon* |
| *sifted* | *¼ teaspoon grated nutmeg* |
| *6 large eggs, separated* | *2–3 whole cloves* |
| *1 scant cup seedless raisins* | *2 tablespoons Pisco or rum* |
| *1⅓ cups mixed crystallized* | *1 tablespoon white wine* |
| *fruits, chopped* | *vinegar* |
| *½ cup walnuts, broken* | *1 cup milk* |
| *4¾ cups flour* | |

Preheat oven to 375°F. In a large bowl, cream the butter and warm water until light and fluffy. Gradually beat in the sifted confectioners' sugar, a little at a time. Beat the egg yolks into the creamed mixture. Fold in the raisins, candied fruits, and the walnuts.

Sift together twice the flour, baking powder, and ground spices. Fold the flour into the batter. Add the cloves, Pisco or rum, and vinegar, and mix well together. Beat the egg whites until they hold a peak and fold them gently into the cake. Finally, add enough of the milk to make a mixture which will just drop from the spoon but is not too soft.

Spoon the batter into an 8-inch round cake pan at least 3 inches high, which has been well-buttered and lined with baking parchment. Bake in preheated oven for 15 minutes, then lower the heat to 325°F and bake for 45 minutes more. The cake is fully cooked when a warmed skewer plunged into the center comes out clean.

Let the cake rest in its pan for about 10 minutes before turning it onto a wire rack to cool. Dust with confectioners' sugar before serving.

A popular Christmas season fruit cake in Finland is *Viikunakakku,* a fig butter cake, aptly named for the flavors which give this particularly good cake its distinctive taste.

## VIIKUNAKAKKU
### Fig Butter Cake

[FINLAND]                                      TO MAKE 1 CAKE

*¾ cup butter*
*¾ cup light brown sugar*
*3 large eggs*
*2 tablespoons grated orange rind*
*1½ cups flour*
*1 teaspoon baking powder*
*½ cup dried figs, chopped*

*½ cup seedless raisins, chopped*
*¼ cup walnuts, chopped fine*
*2 tablespoons ground almonds or superfine granulated sugar*
*Confectioners' sugar*

Preheat oven to 350°F. In a large bowl, cream together the butter and brown sugar until pale and fluffy. Beat together the eggs and orange rind and beat them gradually into the creamed butter, adding a little of the flour with the last few additions of egg to stop the mixture from separating.

Sift together twice the flour and baking powder. Toss the figs, raisins, and walnuts in about 2 tablespoons of flour, then stir the fruit and nuts into the remaining flour and mix until they are well distributed. Fold the fruit and flour mixture into the creamed butter and egg mixture.

Spoon the batter into a ring mold, well-buttered and dusted with almonds or superfine granulated sugar. Bake in preheated oven for 40 to 45 minutes. The cake is fully cooked when a warmed skewer plunged into the center comes out clean.

Let the cake rest in its pan for about 10 minutes before turning it onto

a wire rack to cool. When completely cold, dust the cake with confectioners' sugar. Serve in thin slices.

*Pannettone* is literally part and parcel of Christmas in Italy. In December
every year about 200 million of the familiar blue or gold packages of
*pannettone* made by the Motta and Alemagna companies are sold within
the country, and that is not counting the millions more exported all over
the world. *Pannettone* is seldom made at home. In this case the real thing
is the commercially baked product. Italian folklore has it that the recipe
is a secret. Nevertheless it appears in numerous books where details of its
production involve directions of extraordinarily disparate degrees of
complication. The following recipe is one of the simplest.

## PANNETTONE MILANESE
### Milanese Cake

{ITALY}                                          TO MAKE 1 CAKE

| | |
|---|---|
| ½ package active dried yeast | 5 ounces warm milk |
| 3 cups flour | ¼ cup butter, slightly softened |
| ⅓ cup superfine granulated sugar | 3 tablespoons seedless raisins |
| ¼ teaspoon salt | ½ cup candied citron peel, chopped |
| 3 egg yolks | 1 tablespoon melted butter |

Start *pannettone* the day before you plan to bake it, and do not hurry
the dough.

In a small bowl, sprinkle the yeast over 5 tablespoons of lukewarm
water, about 110°F, whisk well and set aside until the yeast has completely dissolved.

Sift the flour, sugar, and salt together into a large, warmed bowl and
make a hollow in the center. Beat the egg yolks with the lukewarm
milk. Add the egg and yeast mixtures to the flour and stir the mixture,
drawing in flour from the sides of the bowl. Beat in the butter, and continue beating until the dough is smooth. Cover the bowl with a damp
cloth or a greased plastic bag, and set it to rise in a warm place until
it has doubled in bulk, about 1½ hours.

Punch down the dough and, using your hand, beat it until it no longer sticks to the sides of the bowl. Cover the bowl tightly with plastic wrap or foil and refrigerate it overnight.

Next day, turn out the dough onto a lightly floured surface and knead it until smooth. Flatten the dough and scatter over it the raisins and chopped citron peel. Knead these lightly into the mixture until they are well distributed. Gather the dough into a ball and place it in an 8-inch round cake pan, well-buttered and fitted with a foil or baking parchment cuff in the fashion of a soufflé dish. Set the dough to rise in a warm place until it has again doubled in bulk. The dough is considered just right when little air bubbles appear on the surface.

Preheat oven to 350°F. Cut a shallow cross in the top of the dough and brush the cake with melted butter. Bake it for about 35 minutes, or until it is firm to touch and a rich golden color. Cool on a wire rack.


At Christmas and New Year few people like to visit friends empty-handed. Homemade cakes have long been appropriate calling gifts, especially in those places where the art of baking is highly esteemed and skillfully practiced. Nowhere has the custom of exchanging cakes been better kept than in the countries that once formed the Austro-Hungarian Empire. When all the sumptuous *tortes* concocted by rival chefs of those far-off days in Vienna are recreated in domestic kitchens, time, trouble, and expense, as well as the artistry of the cook must be weighed in assessing the worth of the resulting offerings. A well-made *dobostorte,* with its many layers of sponge, chocolate butter cream, and glistening caramel, ranks high on all counts.


## *DOBOSTORTE*
### *Chocolate Layer Cake*

[CZECHOSLOVAKIA]                                    TO MAKE 1 CAKE

**FOR THE CAKE**

*1 cup sweet butter*
*1⅓ cups superfine*
*    granulated sugar*
*4 large eggs*

*1 teaspoon vanilla extract*
*1½ cups cake or all-purpose*
*    flour, sifted*

FOR THE FILLING

| | |
|---|---|
| *1⅔ cups superfine granulated sugar* | *½ cup cocoa powder* |
| | *1 teaspoon vanilla extract* |
| *¼ teaspoon cream of tartar* | *2 cups sweet butter,* |
| *8 egg yolks* | *softened* |

FOR THE TOPPING

*1 cup superfine granulated sugar*

Preheat oven to 350°F. To make the sponge layers, cream together the butter and sugar in a large bowl until light and fluffy. Whisk the eggs with the vanilla extract and beat them into the creamed mixture, a little at a time, adding a small amount of the sifted flour with the last few additions of egg to stop the mixture from separating. Fold in the remaining flour.

To bake the sponge in thin layers, generously butter and flour the underside of a 9-inch round cake pan. Spread a layer of the cake mixture about ⅛ inch thick over the upside-down base and bake it in the preheated oven for about 8 minutes. Transfer the cooked sponge layer to a wire rack and repeat the baking procedure to make 7 layers in all.

To make the filling, put the sugar and cream of tartar in a small saucepan with ¾ cup water and stir over low heat. When the sugar has dissolved completely, increase the heat and boil the syrup without stirring to 240° on a sugar thermometer, or until it forms a soft ball when dropped into cold water. Remove from the heat immediately. Whisk the egg yolks until pale and thick and gradually add the syrup, whisking continuously. Continue to whisk until the mixture is cool and has formed a smooth, thick cream. Beat in the cocoa and vanilla extract, then add the softened butter, a little at a time, beating in each addition before adding the next. Chill the filling.

Before making the caramel topping, put the best-looking sponge layer on a wire rack. Heat the sugar with 6 tablespoons water in a small saucepan over low heat and when the sugar has dissolved completely, boil it rapidly, without stirring, until a rich, golden caramel is formed. Pour it immediately over the sponge and, using a buttered knife, mark it quickly into 12 or 16 equal portions. Do not cut right through the caramel.

To assemble the cake, spread all but the glazed layer of sponge with about ⅛ inch of the filling. Stack the layers neatly, ending up with the caramelized top. Coat the sides with the remaining chocolate butter cream and chill the cake before serving.

Finland's Christmas prune cake has a moist topping of puréed prunes and whipped cream.

## JOULULUUMUKAKKU
### Christmas Prune Cake

[FINLAND]                                          TO MAKE I CAKE

**FOR THE CAKE**

¾ cup butter
½ cup superfine granulated
    sugar

2 large eggs
1½ cups flour
I teaspoon baking powder

**FOR THE TOPPING**

8 ounces cooked prunes,
    pitted
I teaspoon grated lemon
    rind

2 tablespoons superfine
    granulated sugar
I cup heavy cream

Preheat oven to 375°F. Cream together the butter and sugar until pale and fluffy. Whisk the eggs and add them, a little at a time, beating constantly until the mixture is thick and creamy. Sift together twice the flour and baking powder and stir it into the creamed mixture. Butter and dust with sugar an 8-inch round flan tin with a raised base. Spoon in the cake mixture, level it lightly, and bake in preheated oven for about 45 minutes, or until it is a light, golden brown. When cooked, a warmed skewer plunged into the thickest part of the cake will come out clean. Turn it onto a wire rack to cool.

To make the topping blend or liquidize the prunes until puréed and combine with the grated lemon rind and sugar.

Fill the hollow in the center of the cake with the prune mixture. Whip the cream until it holds a peak and pipe it around the exposed rim of the cake. Chill well before serving.

Yule log cakes do not appear to have much of a history, but they are certainly popular now in North America, Britain, and especially in France. A roll of plain or chocolate sponge cake, filled with butter cream and decorated with melted chocolate or chocolate butter cream ridged to look like bark, is the usual formula. There is a French dessert version made from chestnut purée mixed with melted chocolate and butter, shaped into a log, ridged with a fork and then chilled. It may be covered with a simple dusting of confectioners' sugar or coated with melted chocolate. I have to confess, however, that having tried several recipes for this sickly confection there is none I would recommend. All were unmanageably tacky. The sponge-based *Bûche de Noël* is another matter. The filling may be well-laced with liquor, or mixed with chestnut purée, hazelnut paste, or chocolate. The possibilities are legion and practical, so the recipe that follows is a basic one which may be elaborated as much as you like.

## BÛCHE DE NOËL
### Yule Log Cake

[FRANCE]                                         TO MAKE 1 CAKE

### FOR THE CAKE

1 cup flour
1 ¼ teaspoons baking
   powder
¼ teaspoon salt
1 tablespoon cocoa powder

4 large eggs
⅔ cup superfine granulated
   sugar
1 tablespoon hot water

### FOR THE FILLING AND TOPPING

½ cup sweet butter
2 ¼ cups confectioners'
   sugar

2 tablespoons cocoa powder
2–3 tablespoons brandy,
   rum, or Grand Marnier

Preheat oven to 425°F. To make the cake, sift together twice the flour, baking powder, salt, and cocoa. Put the eggs and sugar into a large bowl over a pan of hot water and whisk them together until pale and thick. Remove the bowl from the heat and lightly fold in half the flour. Fold in the remaining flour, add 1 tablespoon of hot water, and mix lightly. Pour the batter into a shallow jellyroll pan, 13 inches by 9 inches, lined with baking parchment. Bake in the preheated oven for about 10 minutes.

Turn out the sponge onto a sheet of wax paper cut to the size of the baking tin. Remove the baking parchment and trim off the cake's crusty edges. While it is still hot, roll up the sponge with the paper inside, cover, and set aside until cold.

To make the filling, cream together the butter and confectioners' sugar. Blend in the cocoa and spirits, and beat the mixture until it is light and fluffy.

To assemble the cake, unroll the sponge and discard the paper. Spread one side with about one-quarter of the filling and roll it up neatly. Spread the remaining butter cream over the log. Use a fork to make a ridged pattern like tree bark on the top and sides of the log and circular swirls on the ends like tree rings. Leave the log plain or decorate it with confectioners'-sugar snow and a sprig of holly.

Greece has two New Year cakes. The first, *vasiloppita,* is a plain yeast-raised *brioche* mixture flavored with fresh orange, lemon peel, and aniseed. It is usually made on New Year's Eve, and a gold coin is inserted after baking. The Cypriot version of *vasiloppita* includes blanched almonds. It is cut, with much ceremony, at midnight when the eldest member of the family divides the cake by the number present, plus three extra portions—one for Christ, one for the stranger or visitor, and one for the saint of the day, Saint Vassilios, the Greek Orthodox Father Christmas. The gold sovereign, of course, brings luck to the finder. *Melomacarona,* small spiced honey cakes, are the second New Year treat, invariably homemade in Greece and Cyprus.

# MELOMACARONA
## New Year Honey Cakes

{GREECE}                                    TO MAKE ABOUT 36

4 cups semolina                    1 orange
1 cup olive oil                    ½ teaspoon powdered
1 cup honey, lukewarm                 cinnamon
½ cup superfine granulated         ½ teaspoon powdered
   sugar                             cloves
½ cup brandy                       2 teaspoons baking powder

### FOR THE SYRUP AND GARNISH

1 cup honey
1 tablespoon lemon juice
Sesame seeds or chopped walnuts

Preheat oven to 350°F. Beat together in a large bowl the semolina and olive oil until the mixture is creamy. Add the warm honey, the sugar, and brandy. Grate the rind of the orange into the bowl, then add the juice. Add the cinnamon, cloves, and baking powder. Beat these ingredients together very well into a stiff dough. (If the semolina is rather coarse you may need to add a small amount of flour to stiffen the dough.)

Using your hands, roll heaped tablespoonfuls of the dough into balls, flatten them a little, and arrange them, well-spaced, on cookie sheets lined with baking parchment. With a fork, mark a ridged cross on each ball of dough. Bake them in the preheated oven for about 20 minutes, or until the *melomacarona* are a deep golden brown.

Slide the cakes, with the baking parchment, onto a wire cooling rack and leave them to rest for about 5 minutes before easing them gently off the paper.

Put the honey into a saucepan with ½ cup water and the tablespoon lemon juice and boil together for about 5 minutes. Allow the syrup to cool to lukewarm, dip the cakes in the honey, and arrange them on a serving plate. Pour any remaining honey over them and sprinkle the dish with sesame seeds or finely chopped walnuts. Serve *melamacarona* at room temperature.

# SWEET PASTRIES

Almonds appear in an extraordinary number of the pastries, puddings, breads, biscuits, cakes, and candies made for Christmas. The nut's fine flavor, versatile flesh, and naturally long shelf life are explanation enough for its universal popularity.

One of the best-known almond pastries is *baklava,* with its layers of finely chopped spiced almonds sandwiched between buttery sheets of tissue-fine phyllo pastry. Before the advent of machine-rolled pastry, *baklava* was for big occasions only, Christmas and Easter particularly. Commercial phyllo pastry should not be despised. Much better *baklava* can be made at home with ready-made pastry and fresh almonds than that which is usually sold in coffee shops.

## BAKLAVA
### Almond Pastry

[GREECE]                                    TO MAKE ABOUT 20 PIECES

3 ¼ cups blanched almonds
½ cup superfine granulated
   sugar
1 orange
1 teaspoon powdered cloves
1 teaspoon powdered
   cinnamon

1 pound prepared phyllo or
   strudel pastry
1 cup melted butter
20 whole cloves

F O R   T H E   S Y R U P

>*2 cups granulated sugar*
>*4 inches of cinnamon stick*
>*4 whole cloves*

Preheat oven to 325°F. To prepare the filling, chop the almonds very fine and mix them in a bowl with the sugar. Grate the rind of an orange over the bowl, add the spices, and toss together until well mixed.

Choose a large rectangular baking pan, at least 1 inch deep, which is roughly the size of the pastry leaves—or trim the pastry to fit an available pan. Grease the pan generously with butter and lay a sheet of phyllo in the bottom. Paint it with melted butter and add another sheet. When there are 5 sheets of buttered phyllo in the pan, spread a layer of the nut mixture over them. Top with 5 more sheets of buttered phyllo, another layer of filling, 2 sheets of buttered phyllo, and more filling. Continue placing the pastry and filling in alternate layers, leaving 5 sheets of phyllo for the top. Cut right through the pastry and filling, making intersecting diagonal cuts. Spike each diamond-shaped piece of pastry with a clove. Place the tin on a baking sheet and bake the *baklava* for about 1 hour, or until the pastry is crisp and golden brown.

To make the syrup, put the sugar in a small saucepan with 1½ cups water, the cinnamon, and the cloves. Melt the sugar over low heat, and when it has completely dissolved, bring the syrup to the boil and cook it for about 3 minutes, until slightly thickened but not colored.

As soon as the pastry is taken from the oven, strain the syrup over it and cool it in the pan. When completely cold, store the *baklava* in an airtight container. It keeps well for a number of weeks.

French Twelfth Night cake, *galette de rois,* cake of the kings, is traditionally eaten on the Feast of the Epiphany. There are numerous versions. A plain circle of flaky pastry with a criss-cross diamond pattern scored on top is common in northern France, a simple crown of yeast dough south of the Loire. Elsewhere, two circles of melting puff pastry enclose a rich filling of almond paste, in a version called *Pithiviers* after the town just south of Paris. Pastry shop windows, a picture at any time in France, glitter with shelves of *galette de rois* and *Pithiviers* topped with golden paper crowns. What each of the pastries conceals is a single bean. Whoever finds the bean wears the crown as king for the day and all the family has to fulfill the monarch's wishes. The custom, which in former times led to excesses frowned upon by clerics, is said to be a relic of a pagan feast called the *Basilinda*.

## PITHIVIERS
### Twelfth Night Cake

[FRANCE]                                                    TO SERVE 6 TO 8

| | |
|---|---|
| 5 tablespoons butter | ¼ cup rum |
| ½ scant cup superfine granulated sugar | 1 pound prepared puff pastry (see page 209) |
| 2 eggs | 1 tablespoon confectioners' sugar |
| 1 scant cup ground almonds | |

Preheat oven to 375°F. To prepare the filling, cream the butter, add the sugar, and beat together until light and fluffy. Beat 1 egg and add to the mixture with the ground almonds. When these are well blended, beat in the rum. Set aside.

Roll out half the puff pastry to make a circle about 8 inches in diameter and place it on a greased baking sheet. Heap the filling on the pastry and spread it, keeping a domed shape, to within 1 inch of the edge.

Roll out the second piece of dough to make a matching circle. Beat the remaining egg and dampen the rim of the pastry base with it, then carefully cover with the second circle of dough. Brush the top only, not the edges, with the rest of the egg and chill the assembled pastry for at least 30 minutes.

Decorate the top of the *Pithiviers* with a pattern of curved cuts radiating from the center to within 1 inch of the edge, cutting about halfway through the top layer of pastry. Decorate the edge by making small cuts right through both layers of pastry from the edge for a distance of about ½ inch toward the center. Brush the top again with egg glaze and bake the pastry in the preheated oven for about 30 minutes, or until golden brown. Dust the top with confectioners' sugar and brown under a very hot broiler. Cool on a wire rack and serve cold.

Holland's Christmas pastry also calls for puff paste and almonds and is made twice during the festivities: for Sinterklaas Eve on December 5, when St. Nicholas arrives with Black Peter and gifts for the children, and again for Christmas Eve. For the Sinterklaas feast it is shaped in the initial letter of the family name and called *letterbanket* or *boterletter*, and for Christmas Eve it is made into a wreath or ring, the *Kerstkrans.*

## KERSTKRANS
### Christmas Ring

{HOLLAND}                                    TO SERVE 4 TO 6

1 ⅓ *cups ground almonds*          *Pinch of salt*
½ *cup superfine granulated*          2 *eggs, beaten separately*
   *sugar*          ½ *pound prepared puff*
*Grated rind of 1 lemon*             *pastry (see page 209)*

**FOR THE DECORATION**

2 *tablespoons apricot jam*
*Glacé cherries, cut in halves*
*Candied citron or angelica*
*Toasted almond flakes*

To make the filling, mix together the ground almonds and sugar in a small bowl. Add the lemon rind and salt and mix thoroughly before binding the mixture with 1 beaten egg. On a floured surface, roll the almond paste into sausage-shaped pieces about 1 inch thick. Wrap them in wax paper and chill well.

Preheat oven to 425°F. Roll out the pastry on a floured surface to make a strip about 3½ inches wide and about ⅛ inch thick. Place the rolls of almond paste end to end along the middle of the pastry strip, dampen one side of the strip with water, and fold the dough up over the paste in an overlapping seam. Press along the seam with your fingertips to seal it.

Arrange the filled roll in a ring, seam side down, on a floured baking sheet, and join the ends securely. Brush the ring with beaten egg diluted with a little water, and bake in the preheated hot oven for about 30 minutes or until the pastry is golden brown.

Cool the *Kerstkrans* on a wire rack.

Heat the apricot jam with 1 or 2 tablespoons of water, pass through a sieve, and while the pastry is still warm, glaze it with the jam and decorate lavishly with glacé cherries, leaves cut from candied citron or angelica, and flakes of toasted almond. Eat warm or cold.

*Mandelformar* are little fluted tarts made of almond pastry for Christmas in Sweden. They are baked unfilled and served plain, as shells, or filled with whipped cream topped with raspberry jam. This pastry can also be used as a change from shortcrust mixtures for large flans.

## MANDELFORMAR
### Almond Tarts

{SWEDEN}                    TO MAKE ABOUT 45 TARTS

*¾ cup sweet butter*           *1 teaspoon almond extract*
*⅔ cup superfine granulated*   *1 large egg, beaten*
  *sugar*                      *2½ cups flour*
*1⅔ cups ground almonds*

Cream the butter and sugar in a mixing bowl until light and fluffy. Add the ground almonds, almond extract, and egg and mix well. Sift the flour and work it into the creamed mixture.

Turn the dough onto a lightly floured surface and knead it lightly until smooth, adding a little more flour if necessary. Wrap the dough in wax paper or foil and chill well.

Preheat oven to 375°F. Butter small, fluted tart tins generously. Use your thumbs to line the tins by pressing small lumps of dough over the bases and up the sides. Trim away any excess dough with a sharp knife. Arrange the tins on a baking sheet and bake in preheated oven for about 15 minutes or until the pastry is a light golden color. The exact timing will depend on the thickness of the crust and the number of tarts in the oven.

Invert the tarts on a wire cooling rack and tap the tins to release them. When quite cold, store *mandelformar* in an airtight container. If they are to be filled, top with whipped cream and a small dollop of jam just before serving.

Mince pies are eaten throughout the Christmas season in many parts of the English-speaking world. The earliest mince pies were boat-shaped cribs, sometimes iced, and by the reign of Elizabeth I they had become traditional Christmas fare. The Reformation church banned them as "popish" because their form symbolized the nativity cradle, and their spices the gifts of the Kings. Minced meat is still included in the filling for homemade pies in parts of England and the United States, but it is seldom seen now in the products of commercial bakeries. All that remains of what was once a means of preserving meat is a little shredded suet.

Mince pies are made with puff or shortcrust pastry, in bun or tart tins with shallow cups approximately 2½ inches diameter.

## MINCE PIES

{ENGLAND}                                          TO MAKE 24 PIES

*1 pound puff pastry (see*          *¼ cup milk*
   *(page 209), or 1–1½*            *1–2 eggs, beaten*
   *pounds shortcrust*              *⅓ cup superfine granulated*
   *pastry (see page 210)*            *or confectioners' sugar*
*2 cups mincemeat (see page*
   *235)*

Preheat oven to 400°F. Roll out the pastry on a lightly floured surface to about ⅛ inch thick. Shortcrust pastry may be used a little thicker. Using a cookie cutter or the rim of a drinking glass, cut 24 circles of dough about ½ inch larger than the diameter of the finished pies. (The exact size will depend on the depth of the molds.) Then cut 24 lids exactly the diameter of the molds.

Grease the molds and line them with the larger pastry circles. Put 1 rounded tablespoonful of mincemeat in each pie. Do not overfill or the mincemeat will bubble out during baking. Dampen the edges of the pastry linings with milk and top them with the smaller circles of dough. Seal the two pastry edges firmly together with your fingertips or a pastry crimper.

Brush the lids with beaten egg and bake in preheated hot oven for about 15 minutes, or until the pastry is golden brown. When cooked, allow the pies to settle for about 5 minutes before sliding them out of the tins. Dust the tops with sugar.

Serve mince pies hot or warm, on their own with tea or coffee, or as a dessert with whipped cream or Hard Sauce (see page 236). Cold mince pies will keep for several days in an airtight container and can be reheated in a warm oven.

Finland's Christmas pies, *Joulutortut,* are the subject of much competitive baking. These prune-filled pastries use a very simply made dough.

# JOULUTORTUT
*Christmas Tarts*

[FINLAND]                    TO MAKE ABOUT 24 TARTS

## FOR THE PASTRY

*1½ cups heavy cream*
*1 teaspoon baking powder*
*¼ teaspoon salt*
*3¼ cups flour*
*1 cup butter, softened*

## FOR THE FILLING

*2½ cups prunes*
*½ cup superfine granulated sugar*
*2 tablespoons lemon juice*

To make the pastry, whip the cream until stiff in a large bowl. Sift the baking powder, salt, and flour into the cream and mix thoroughly. Add the softened butter and stir until the dough is well blended. Wrap the pastry in wax paper or foil and chill it well.

To make the filling, cook the prunes in 3 cups water over low heat until they are soft. Drain them and discard the cooking liquid. Remove the pits and purée the prunes by pressing through a sieve or whirling in an electric blender. Add the sugar and lemon juice and mix well.

Preheat oven to 400°F. Roll out the pastry to a thickness of about ¼ inch and cut it into 3-inch squares. Divide the filling among the squares, placing a small mound of purée in the center of each one. With a sharp knife cut from each corner to within ½ inch of the center of the squares. Fold one-half of each corner to the center to form a pinwheel or star.

Arrange the pastries on ungreased baking sheets and rest at room temperature for about 10 minutes. Bake *Joulutortut* in preheated hot oven for about 10 minutes, or until the pastry is pale golden brown. Cool on a wire rack and serve warm or cold.

Coconut cream pie is a Christmas favorite in Puerto Rico.

## TORTA DE CREMA DE COCO
### Coconut Cream Pie

[PUERTO RICO]                                    TO SERVE 6 TO 8

2½ cups milk
2 tablespoons cornstarch
1⅓ cups superfine
   granulated sugar
¼ teaspoon salt
2 large eggs
8 ounces freshly grated
   coconut

1 teaspoon vanilla extract
1 9-inch baked shortcrust
   pie shell (see page
   210)
1 scant cup confectioners'
   sugar

Scald three-quarters of the milk in the top of a double boiler, or in a bowl over a pot of boiling water. Mix the remaining cold milk with the cornstarch, sugar, and salt. Stir it into the hot milk and cook, stirring, until thick and smooth. Cover and continue cooking for another 10 minutes. Separate the eggs, reserving the whites for the meringue, and beat the yolks lightly. Add three-quarters of the coconut to the egg yolks and stir in a little of the hot custard. Add the coconut mixture to the hot custard and cook together, stirring constantly, for about 3 minutes. Remove from the heat and add the vanilla. Pour the coconut cream into the pastry shell.

When the custard is quite cold beat the reserved egg whites until light and foamy. Add half the confectioners' sugar and beat until stiff. Add the remaining sugar and beat until the meringue holds a peak. Pile the meringue on top of the coconut cream and sprinkle with the remaining grated coconut. Serve chilled, in wedges.

An unusual pie made of whole apples moistened with mulled ale is traditionally made at Christmas according to this eighteenth-century recipe.

## BEDFORDSHIRE APPLE FLORENTINE PIE

[ENGLAND]                                        TO SERVE 4

4 large cooking apples,                2½ cups pale ale or good
  peeled and cored                  light beer
3 tablespoons light brown          ¼ teaspoon grated nutmeg
  sugar                               ¼ teaspoon powdered
1 tablespoon lemon rind,              cinnamon
  grated fine                       3 cloves
1 pound shortcrust pastry
  (see page 210)

Preheat oven to 450°F. Arrange the apples in a deep, buttered pie dish of about 3¾-pint capacity. Sprinkle the apples with 2 tablespoons of the sugar mixed with the grated lemon rind.

Roll out the pastry to make a thick crust for the dish and lay it over the apples. Make a hole in the top to allow the steam to escape and bake the pie in the preheated oven for about 30 minutes.

Heat but do not boil the ale along with the nutmeg, cinnamon, cloves, and the remaining sugar. Carefully lift off the pie crust and pour the warm, spiced ale over the apples. Cut the pastry into four pieces and replace one piece over each apple. Serve very hot in bowls, giving each person plenty of the mulled ale. Cold whipped cream may be passed in a separate bowl and, nowadays, creamy natural yogurt would be a refreshing combination with this old-fashioned pie.

Poppy-seed pastry rolls are synonymous with Christmas in Hungary, Poland, and in Vienna, the mecca of the Austrian pastry-makers' art. *Beigli* is the popular Hungarian name for the poppy-seed and walnut pastries which, whether baked at home or bought in a pastry shop or supermarket, are an essential part of the festivities. *Beigli* is served to everyone visiting Hungarian homes between Christmas and New Year, with morning coffee, lunch, and dinner, too. The rite of baking and buying *beigli*, of comparing their respective merits, is a ceremony repeated year after year. Overindulgence in this delicious delicacy brings *beigli*-poisoning, a condition discussed with the same relish as hangovers elsewhere.

# BEIGLI
## Poppy Seed Roll

{HUNGARY}                                    TO MAKE I ROLL

### FOR THE PASTRY

½ package active dried yeast
4 tablespoons superfine
    granulated sugar
¼ cup lukewarm water
¼ cup milk
1 teaspoon vanilla extract
½ teaspoon grated lemon
    rind

½ teaspoon salt
3 egg yolks
2 cups flour
¼ cup sweet butter,
    softened

1 egg
1 tablespoon milk

### FOR THE FILLING

2 tablespoons rum
½ cup seedless raisins
½ cup sweet butter
3 tablespoons honey

1 tablespoon heavy cream
⅔ cup ground poppy seeds
½ teaspoon grated orange
    rind

To make the pastry, sprinkle the yeast and a pinch of the sugar onto the lukewarm water, about 110°F. Let it stand for a few minutes, whisk, and set aside in a warm place until the mixture has almost doubled in volume.

In a large bowl, combine the yeast solution with the milk, vanilla extract, lemon rind, the rest of the sugar and the salt. Stir in the egg yolks. Sift the flour and beat it into the yeast mixture a little at a time. Divide the butter into four pieces, and beat it into the dough one piece at a time.

Turn out the dough onto a floured surface and knead it for about 10 minutes or until it is soft and pliable. Put the dough in a lightly buttered bowl, turn it to grease all over, and leave it to rise, covered, in a warm place.

To make the filling, sprinkle the rum over the raisins and set them aside. Cream together the butter and honey, then beat in the cream. Stir in the ground poppy seeds. Chop the plumped raisins and add them to the mixture along with the grated orange rind. Cook the filling in a small saucepan over low heat for about 10 minutes, or until it is a stiff paste. Set aside to cool.

When the dough has doubled in bulk, turn it out onto a floured surface and knead it lightly. Roll it out to a rectangle about 9 inches by 13 inches. Spread the filling on the dough to within ¾ inch of the edges. Turn over one long side of the rectangle and roll up the dough.

Carefully place the roll, seam side down, on a buttered baking sheet. Brush the exposed dough with the egg mixed with 1 tablespoon of milk and leave it to stand in a warm, draft-free place for about 20 minutes. Preheat oven to 350°F. Brush the roll again with egg and milk glaze and bake it for about 45 minutes, or until the pastry is a rich golden brown. The pastry should have a crackled surface. Cool on a wire rack and serve in slices like a jellyroll.

Maltese molasses rings are another unusual pastry made at Christmastime. Small rings of almost fatless pastry wrap a filling of spiced molasses and semolina. The dough is very lightly baked to contrast with the dark filling, which can be seen through 6 slashes in the top of each pastry.

A variety of fritters and doughnuts are also made for Christmas and New Year. Cornmeal goes into Peruvian *picarones* and *buñuelos navideños* from Ecuador. Yeast-raised doughs are the basis for *olieballen* from Holland and for the *Berliner pfannkuchen,* which are filled with plum or apricot jam and usually served with hot punch.

## BERLINER PFANNKUCHEN
### Berlin Doughnuts

[GERMANY]                                    TO MAKE ABOUT 12

½ package active dried
    yeast
5 ounces warm milk
4 cups flour, sifted
¼ cup melted butter
2 large eggs

Pinch of salt
¾ cup plum or apricot jam
Vegetable shortening for
    frying
½ cup superfine granulated
    sugar

Sprinkle the yeast onto the warm milk, about 110°F, in a large bowl. Whisk the mixture and leave it to stand in a warm place until the yeast has dissolved completely and the mixture is bubbling. Beat in 1 cup of the sifted flour, cover, and leave the mixture to rise in a warm place for about 1 hour. Add the butter, eggs, salt, and the remaining flour and beat the mixture to a smooth dough. Cover and set aside to rise in a warm place until it has doubled in bulk.

Turn the dough onto a floured surface and roll it out thin. Using a circular cookie cutter or the rim of a drinking glass, cut about 24 circles of dough. Put 1 tablespoon of jam in the center of half the circles of dough and cover them with the remaining dough. Press the edges lightly with your fingertips to seal in the filling and leave the doughnuts to rise once more, covered, in a warm place.

Heat the shortening in a deep-fryer or large pot to about 375°F. At this temperature a 1-inch cube of day-old bread will fry to a crisp golden brown in about 60 seconds. Fry the doughnuts, a few at a time so as not to lower the temperature of the fat too much, for about 4 minutes or until golden brown. Turn them over when half done. Drain on absorbent paper and roll the hot doughnuts in superfine granulated sugar. Serve warm.

The dough for Holland's New Year doughnuts is speckled with dried fruit and candied peel.

## *OLIEBALLEN*
### *New Year's Eve Fritters*

{HOLLAND}                                    TO MAKE ABOUT 18

| | |
|---|---|
| ¼ *package active dried yeast* | *3 tablespoons dried currants* |
| *1½ cups warm milk* | *3 tablespoons raisins* |
| *2–2½ cups flour* | *3 tablespoons chopped candied orange peel* |
| *2 tablespoons granulated sugar* | *1 tablespoon grated lemon rind* |
| *½ teaspoon salt* | *Vegetable oil for frying* |
| *2 eggs* | *1 cup confectioners' sugar* |

Sprinkle the yeast over the warm milk in a small bowl. Whisk the mixture and let it stand in a warm place until the yeast has dissolved completely and the mixture has almost doubled its volume.

Sift 2 cups of the flour into a mixing bowl with the sugar and salt. Make a well in the flour and pour in the yeast mixture. Gradually mix in the flour with a wooden spoon. Drop in the eggs and beat the mixture until all the flour has been absorbed. The dough should just hold its shape. If it is too soft, beat in up to ½ cup more flour, adding it a little at a time. Cover the bowl with a damp cloth or plastic bag and leave it in a warm place for about 1 hour, or until it has doubled in bulk.

Punch down the dough and gently mix in the currants, raisins, candied peel, and lemon rind.

Pour the oil into a deep-fryer or heavy pot to a depth of about 3 inches, and heat it to about 350°F. At this temperature a 1-inch cube of day-old bread will fry to a crisp golden brown in about 90 seconds. Make balls of dough, each about 3 tablespoonfuls in size, and drop them into the hot oil a few at a time so as not to lower the temperature of the oil too much. Fry for about 10 minutes, or until the fritters are a crisp golden brown, turning them when half done. Drain the cooked *olieballen* on absorbent paper.

Eat them warm or cool, and dusted with confectioners' sugar just before serving.

*Struffoli alla Napoletana* is an Italian Christmas sweet composed of tiny balls of fried dough soaked in melted honey.

## STRUFFOLI ALLA NAPOLETANA
### Neapolitan Fritters

[ITALY]                                          TO SERVE 8 TO 10

| | |
|---|---|
| 4 cups flour | ¼ teaspoon salt |
| 8 large eggs | 1 teaspoon grated lemon |
| 2 egg yolks | rind |
| 1¼ cups vegetable | 1 cup clear honey |
| shortening | Rind of 3 oranges, grated |
| ½ tablespoon sugar | fine |

Sift the flour into a mixing bowl and make a well in the center. Add the eggs, egg yolks, ¼ cup of the shortening, the sugar, salt, and lemon peel. Using your hands, work the ingredients together into a smooth dough. Shape the dough into small balls about as big as medium-sized grapes.

Melt the honey in a small saucepan and mix in the orange rind.

Melt the remaining shortening in a heavy frying pan and fry the balls of dough, a few at a time, until they are golden brown and cooked through. As soon as they are fried, lift the balls from the fat with a slotted spoon and drop them into the honey mixture.

When all the *struffoli* have been fried and soaked in honey, strain them in a sieve and pile them in conical heaps on a flat serving dish. Serve warm or cold.

Snowballs or *sneeuwballen*, deep-fried balls of *choux* pastry filled with whipped cream and dusted thickly with confectioners' sugar, are another treat for New Year's Eve in Holland. More unusual are Ecuador's *buñuelos navideños*, cornmeal fritters soaked in a spiced syrup.

## BUÑUELOS NAVIDEÑOS
### Christmas Fritters

{ECUADOR}                                                    TO SERVE 4

¼ teaspoon salt                      5 large eggs
2 tablespoons butter                 Corn or soybean oil for
4 tablespoons fine cornmeal             frying
¾ cup flour

**FOR THE SYRUP**

1 cup granulated sugar
4 inches cinnamon stick
1 teaspoon lemon juice
1 teaspoon orange flower water

Put 2 cups water, the salt, and butter into a heavy saucepan and bring to the boil. Sift together the cornmeal and flour, add them to the liquid in the pan, and stir the mixture over low heat until the dough forms a ball. Transfer the dough to a mixing bowl and beat it with a wooden spoon until it is lukewarm. Beat in the eggs 1 at a time.

Heat the oil in a deep-fryer or heavy pot to about 375°F. At this temperature a 1-inch cube of day-old bread will fry to a crisp golden brown in about 60 seconds. Drop tablespoonfuls of the mixture into the hot oil, a few at a time so as not to cool the oil too much, and fry them until golden. Tap the fried balls to release any pockets of trapped oil and drain them on absorbent paper.

To make the syrup, put the sugar in a small saucepan with 1 cup water and the cinnamon stick. Heat together gently until the sugar dissolves, then boil the syrup for a minute or two until it thickens slightly. Remove from the heat, extract the cinnamon stick, and stir in the lemon juice and orange flower water.

Arrange the fried *buñuelos* on a deep plate and pour the syrup over them. Serve warm or cold.

Sweden's *klenäter* are fancy pastry strips, deep-fried and served with jam as a dessert or as a snack with coffee.

## KLENÄTER
### Christmas Crullers

[SWEDEN]                          TO MAKE ABOUT 50 CRULLERS

| | |
|---|---|
| 4 egg yolks | 1 tablespoon brandy |
| ¼ cup superfine granulated sugar | 1 tablespoon grated lemon rind |
| 1½ cups flour | Shortening for frying |
| 3 tablespoons butter | ½ cup granulated sugar |

Beat together in a small bowl the egg yolks and superfine sugar. Sift the flour into a larger bowl, and cut the butter into small pieces over the flour. Using your fingertips or a pastry blender, work flour and butter lightly together until the mixture resembles fine bread crumbs. Add the egg and sugar mixture to the flour with the brandy and lemon rind. Mix well together. Form the dough into a ball, wrap it in wax paper, and chill well.

Turn the dough onto a floured surface and roll it out thin. Using a pastry wheel and a ruler, cut the dough into strips about 3 inches long and ¾ inch wide. The narrow ends may be cut straight or at a diagonal to the sides. Make a long cut down the center of each strip and pull one end through the hole so that when laid flat again each strip divides in the middle into two twists.

Heat the shortening in a deep-fryer or heavy pot to 375°F. At this temperature a 1-inch cube of day-old bread will fry to a crisp golden brown in about 60 seconds. Fry the crullers, a few at a time so as not to cool the fat too much, until light golden brown. Drain them on absorbent paper, sprinkle with granulated sugar, and serve hot or cold.

## PUFF PASTRY
### Basic Recipe

MAKES 2 POUNDS

| | |
|---|---|
| 4 cups cake or all-purpose flour | 12–14 tablespoons ice water |
| 1 teaspoon salt | 1¾ cups sweet butter |
| 1 tablespoon lemon juice | ¼ cup vegetable shortening |

Sift the flour and salt together into a mound on a marble slab or pastry board and make a well in the center of the heap. Put the lemon juice into the well with 6 tablespoons of iced water. Begin to incorporate the flour, using the fingertips of one hand in a light, beating action. As the flour in the middle of the well reaches the consistency of a thick, smooth sauce, gradually add more water and continue to draw in the flour, using the same hand-beating action until about 12 to 14 tablespoons of water have been added, all the flour has been absorbed, and the dough will hold together in a ball.

Knead the dough quickly and lightly to distribute the moisture without allowing the gluten in the flour to develop. Wrap it in wax paper and a damp cloth and rest it in the refrigerator for 30 minutes.

Mix the butter and vegetable shortening by working them together on a plate with a spatula. Shape the fat into a brick, wrap it in wax paper, and put it in the refrigerator to firm up.

Lightly flour the rolling surface and pin. Roll out the dough to a circle about 1 foot in diameter, using light, even strokes from the center outward. Place the chilled fat in the center of the circle, short side facing you, and fold up the dough on the two longer sides to overlap the fat. Seal lightly with the rolling pin. Fold up the dough on the two shorter sides of the fat, overlapping in the center, and seal.

Turn the dough long side facing you, and roll it out to a rectangle about 16 inches by 8 inches. The finished rectangle will have a short side facing you.

Now make the *first turn*. Fold the bottom third of the dough up past the center line and the upper third down on top of it. Lightly seal the edges with the rolling pin and make a shallow dent in the dough with one finger to denote that it has had one turn. Wrap it in wax paper and a damp cloth and return the dough to the refrigerator for 15 minutes.

To make the *second turn,* lay the dough on a lightly floured surface, with the folded edge on your left and the longest sealed edge on your right. Roll it out again to 16 inches by 8 inches, fold in thirds as before, mark with two dents, wrap it up and chill for another 15 minutes.

Repeat the rolling and folding 4 more times, making two turns each of the 4 times. Wrap the finished pastry as before and chill until firm or, better still, overnight.

Use as directed. Wrapped pastry will keep for several days in the refrigerator, longer, of course, if frozen. Thaw frozen pastry slowly and thoroughly in the refrigerator before using.

## BASIC SWEET SHORTCRUST PASTRY

MAKES 2 POUNDS

4 cups cake or all-purpose
   flour
4 tablespoons confectioners'
   sugar
½ teaspoon salt

1 ¼ cups sweet butter,
   softened
2 egg yolks
8 tablespoons iced water

Sift the flour, sugar, and salt together into a large bowl. Add the butter in fairly large pieces and work it lightly into the flour with your fingertips or a pastry blender until the mixture resembles fine bread crumbs.

In another bowl, mix the egg yolks with the iced water. Sprinkle this over the flour mixture and work it in lightly with your fingertips or the blade of a knife until the dough just holds together. Gather it up and press it lightly into a ball. Wrap the dough in wax paper and foil or a plastic bag and chill for at least 1 hour before rolling out. Chilled, wrapped dough will keep in the refrigerator for several days. Use as directed.

For a short savory pastry increase the salt to 1 teaspoon and omit the sugar.

Unfilled pie shells can be baked in advance and stored in airtight containers.

To make a 9-inch pie shell, preheat oven to 400°F. Take about 8 ounces of sweet shortcrust pastry and roll it thin. Cut out a circle about 2 inches wider than the pie pan or flan ring. Using a rolling pin, lift the pastry and lower it onto the pan. Lift the edges gently and press the pastry into shape. Trim the edges.

Line the pastry case with foil or wax paper cut to shape, and weigh it down with dried beans or pastry weights. Bake the shell in the center of the preheated oven for 15 minutes. Remove the beans and foil and bake for a further 5 to 10 minutes, or until the pastry is dry and lightly browned. Allow the pastry to cool a little on a wire rack before removing it from the pie pan.

# COOKIES

Christmas cookies appear to have been made almost exclusively in Europe before settlers brought them to America. Many have become such firm year-round favorites that their festive and regional origins are all but forgotten. The names may change from one continent and country to another but the ingredients are everywhere the same—sugar and spices and eager helpers to lick spoons and lap up crumbs.

The word cookie seems to derive from the Dutch *koekje,* the diminutive of *koek,* cake, and it was still a common term in nineteenth-century England. In Scotland its use continues but the meaning changes to a flat bun. Biscuit, the word now commonest in France and England, derives from the Old French *bescoit,* a flat cake of unleavened bread. It still, in principle, applies to twice-baked goods, and now also to recipes which do not require double-cooking to produce crisp cookies with good keeping qualities.

The Swedish recipe for Christmas gingersnaps, *Luciapepparkakor,* is the one used to make the gingerbread house on page 178, as well as plain and fancy cookies. This Finnish variation is shortened with butter and cream.

## SUOMALAISET PIPARKAKUT
### Finnish Gingersnaps

[FINLAND]                    TO MAKE ABOUT 60 COOKIES

½ cup dark corn syrup          1 tablespoon powdered
½ cup dark brown sugar            cinnamon
½ cup butter                   3–3½ cups flour
½ cup heavy cream              1 teaspoon baking powder
1 tablespoon powdered          ½ teaspoon salt
   ginger

In a large bowl, beat together the syrup, brown sugar, and butter until
the mixture is smooth, then beat in the cream. Sift together twice the
spices, flour, baking powder, and salt, and add them to the creamed
mixture. Work the two together into a stiff dough. Chill the dough
for several hours wrapped in waxed paper.

Preheat oven to 375°F. On a lightly floured surface, roll out the dough
¼ inch thick and, using a cookie cutter, stamp out 3-inch circles. Arrange
them on well-greased and floured baking sheets and bake for about 8
minutes. Rest the cookies on the baking sheet for 2 to 3 minutes before
transferring them to a wire rack to cool. Store in an airtight container.

*Pfeffernüsse* are an almost essential part of Christmas in Germany
where food and family ceremonies are inextricably bound together. The
evocative smell of these spice cookies baking is one of the first thrills
of the festive season.

## PFEFFERNÜSSE
### Spice Cookies

[GERMANY]                    TO MAKE ABOUT 70 COOKIES

½ cup honey                    ½ teaspoon baking powder
¾ cup syrup                    ½ teaspoon powdered
½ cup superfine granulated        cloves
   sugar                       ¼ teaspoon powdered
2 tablespoons butter              allspice
2 cups flour

Preheat oven to 400°F. Put the honey and syrup into a large, heavy saucepan with the sugar and bring the mixture slowly to the boil. Stir until the sugar dissolves, then simmer gently for about 5 minutes before stirring in the butter.

Sift together twice the flour, baking powder, and spices. Gradually beat the flour into the honey mixture a little at a time, and continue beating until the batter is thick and smooth.

Drop teaspoonfuls of the mixture, well-spaced, onto generously buttered baking sheets. Bake for about 15 minutes or until the cookies are light brown in color and firm to the touch. Rest them on the baking sheets for 2 or 3 minutes before transferring to a wire rack to cool. Store in an airtight container.

Cookies cut in fancy Christmas shapes—men, women, angels, pigs, reindeer, horses, cats, trees, stars, and hearts—are made in all the Nordic countries. Sometimes they are left plain, but often they are outlined and decorated with piped white icing. There are dozens of similar recipes to choose from, and small controversies rage over preferences for thin, crisp cookies or thicker, softer ones. This recipe for bishop's pepper cookies makes the softer kind.

## ROVASTINPIPPARKAKUT
### Bishop's Pepper Cookies

{FINLAND}                    TO MAKE ABOUT 30 COOKIES

1 large egg
1 cup superfine granulated
   sugar
½ cup dark corn syrup
1 cup melted butter
¼ cup almonds, chopped
   fine
2½ cups flour
1 teaspoon baking soda

1 teaspoon powdered
   cinnamon
1 teaspoon powdered
   cardamom
1 teaspoon powdered
   ginger
½ teaspoon powdered
   allspice
½ teaspoon salt

In a large bowl, beat the egg and stir in the sugar, syrup, melted butter, and almonds. Beat until well mixed. Sift together twice the flour, baking soda, spices, and salt, and add them, a little at a time, to the syrup mixture, beating until a stiff dough is formed. Chill the dough well.

Preheat oven to 375°F. On a lightly floured surface, roll the dough about ¼ inch thick and, using plain or fancy cutters, stamp out the cookies. Arrange them on well-buttered baking sheets and bake for about 10 minutes, or until they are golden brown and firm to touch. The exact timing will depend on the size of the individual cookies. Let them rest on the baking sheets for 2 or 3 minutes before transferring them to a wire cooling rack.

Use royal icing (see page 180) for piped decorations. Allow the frosting to dry completely before storing the cookies in an airtight container.

Dutch *speculaas* are another much-loved Christmas spice cookie. These are traditionally shaped in carved wooden molds. They take their name from the method of molding the dough—*speculaas* is a corruption of *speculum,* the Latin for mirror. Large cookies, weighing up to 1 pound each, baked as figures of men and women known as "lovers," are decorated with large slivers of blanched almond. Smaller versions of every size down to about 1 inch are also made. When no molds are available, filled *speculaas* are baked in round cake pans with almond paste sandwiched between two layers of dough.

## SPECULAAS
### Spice Cookies

[HOLLAND]                    TO MAKE 1 LARGE OR ABOUT 24 SMALL
COOKIES

*⅓ cup dark brown sugar*
*1 tablespoon milk*
*1 cup flour*
*¼ teaspoon baking powder*
*¼ teaspoon salt*
*½ teaspoon powdered*
*   cloves*
*½ teaspoon powdered*
*   cinnamon*
*¼ teaspoon powdered*
*   ginger*
*¼ teaspoon grated nutmeg*

*1 tablespoon finely chopped*
*   almonds*
*1 tablespoon finely chopped*
*   candied fruits*
*5 tablespoons butter*
*Blanched, slivered almonds*
*   (optional)*
*4 ounces almond paste (see*
*   page 237; optional)*
*1 tablespoon light cream*
*   (optional)*

Put the sugar and milk into a small saucepan and heat gently until the sugar has dissolved.

Sift together twice the flour, baking powder, salt, and spices and put them into a mixing bowl with the chopped almonds and candied fruits. Add the dissolved sugar; cut the butter into small pieces, add it also, and mix well together. Knead the dough lightly until pliable. Chill well.

To make molded *speculaas,* dust the molds thoroughly with cornstarch before pressing the dough evenly into them. Run a sharp knife along the edges of the design to trim off excess dough, then tap out the molded shapes onto a greased baking sheet. Press large slivers of blanched almond into the design before baking. Large figures should be baked in a preheated slow oven, 300°F, for 45 to 60 minutes. Bake small cookies in a preheated moderate oven, 350°F, for 15 to 30 minutes, depending on their size. Cooking is complete when the *speculaas* are golden brown and firm to touch. Cool on a wire rack and store in an airtight container.

To make filled *speculaas*, preheat oven to 325°F. Divide the dough in two. Press one-half into a shallow round cake pan about 7 inches in diameter. Pat it evenly over the bottom and a little way up the sides of the pan. Roll out the almond paste on a surface dusted with superfine granulated sugar to a circle about 6½ inches in diameter, and lay it over the dough in the pan. Press the second piece of dough in an even layer on top of the almond paste. Brush the top with a little light cream and bake in preheated oven for 35 to 40 minutes. Rest the baked *speculaas* in the pan for 2 or 3 minutes before turning onto a wire rack to cool. Store in an airtight container.

Germany's prettiest molded Christmas cookies are *springerle,* made with a decorative board or rolling pin deeply patterned with a variety of festive symbols and pictures. The dough is deliciously flavored with aniseed, and these cookies are best baked several weeks before Christmas because the flavor improves as they mature. Prepare the cookies a day before baking them.

## SPRINGERLE
### Christmas Aniseed Cookies

[GERMANY]                                    TO MAKE ABOUT 40 COOKIES

4 large eggs                          4¼ cups flour
2 cups superfine granulated           1 teaspoon baking soda
   sugar
1 teaspoon whole aniseed,
   anise extract, or
   powdered aniseed*

In a large bowl beat the eggs until pale and fluffy before beating in the sugar, a little at a time. Continue beating until the mixture falls back on itself in a slowly melting ribbon. Beat in the anise extract or powdered aniseed.

Sift together twice the flour and baking soda and beat them into the egg mixture a little at a time to form a firm dough. Knead the dough on a lightly floured surface until it is smooth and pliable, working in a little more flour if it is too sticky. Chill for about 2 hours.

On a well-floured surface, roll out the dough about ½ inch thick. Sprinkle the *springerle* mold or rolling pin generously with flour, tap off the excess, and press the mold or pin firmly into the dough. Cut the patterned dough into individual cookies and arrange them on cookie sheets lined with baking parchment.† Set the prepared cookies aside to dry at room temperature for a day before baking them in a preheated slow oven, 300°F, for about 30 minutes. They are cooked when the tops whiten and the bottoms are slightly golden. Cool on a wire rack and store in an airtight container.

Almond crescents are another Christmas cookie popular in Germany. Czechoslovakia has a very similar almond cookie flavored with vanilla and called *vanillekipfel,* vanilla crescents.

* If using whole aniseed, smear the baking parchment generously with butter and sprinkle it with whole aniseed before arranging the dough on it.
† To make *springerle* without a carved mold or rolling pin, cut ½-inch-thick dough into 1½-inch squares and bake as directed.

## MANDEL-HALBMONDE
### Almond Crescents

[GERMANY]                           TO MAKE ABOUT 36 COOKIES

*1 cup sweet butter*            *2 raw egg yolks*
*1 cup superfine granulated*    *2 teaspoons grated lemon*
*sugar*                          *rind*
*4 hard-boiled egg yolks*       *3 cups flour, sifted*

**FOR THE FROSTING**

*1 egg white*                   *½ cup superfine granulated*
*⅓ cup blanched almonds,*       *sugar*
*chopped fine*                  *1 teaspoon powdered*
                                *cinnamon*

Preheat oven to 325 °F. In a large bowl, cream the butter, then beat in the sugar a little at a time. Cream together until the mixture is very pale and fluffy. Put the hard-boiled egg yolks into a sieve and press them through with the back of a spoon into the creamed mixture. Add the raw egg yolks and lemon rind and mix well. Gradually beat in the flour to form a firm dough.

To prepare the frosting, beat the egg white in a small bowl until it will hold a firm peak. In another bowl mix the almonds with the sugar and cinnamon.

Shape small rolls of the dough about 2½ inches long into crescents. Dip each one into the beaten egg white and then into the almond sugar. Arrange them, spaced well apart, on cookie sheets lined with baking parchment and bake them in the preheated oven for about 12 minutes or until the cookies are firm to the touch. Transfer them carefully to a wire rack. When cold, store *mandel-halbmonde* in an airtight container.


Ratafias are small almond meringue cookies which have been made in England since the sixteenth century, if not earlier. They are named after a Creole liqueur of the same flavor made with almond or peach kernels. The Italian version, *amaretti,* may be even older. They are an essential ingredient of trifle and are often served separately with creams or jellies. This recipe is based on the one given in *The Court and Country Confectioner,* an anonymous English publication of 1772.

# RATAFIAS

TO MAKE ABOUT 100 COOKIES

*5 egg whites*
*2⅔ cups ground almonds*
*2⅔ cups superfine granulated sugar*

Preheat oven to 300°F. In a large bowl, beat the egg whites until they hold a stiff peak. Fold in the almonds and sugar and mix well together to make a soft, sticky dough.

Line several cookie sheets with baking parchment and pipe small blobs of the mixture, about ½ inch in diameter, onto the paper. Use a plain nozzle and space the cookies well apart. Bake the ratafias for about 40 minutes or until they are a pale, pinkish brown and crisp at the edges.

Leave the ratafias on the baking parchment to cool on a wire rack before peeling them off the paper. Allow them to become completely cold before storing in an airtight container.

A few drops of almond extract may be added to the mixture before baking.

*Spritskransar,* the famous Swedish spritz rings, are another piped almond cookie. These have a shortcake texture.

# SPRITSKRANSAR
## Spritz Rings

TO MAKE ABOUT 45 COOKIES

*1 cup butter*                        *1 teaspoon almond extract*
*½ cup confectioners' sugar*          *⅓ cup ground almonds*
*1 egg yolk*                          *2 cups flour*

Preheat oven to 400°F. Cream together the butter and sugar in a large bowl until light and fluffy. Add the egg yolk and almond extract and mix well. Sift together the ground almonds and flour and stir them gradually into the creamed mixture to form a smooth, soft dough.

Using a star nozzle, pipe the mixture into neat rings, 2 inches in diameter, onto cookie sheets lined with baking parchment. Bake in the preheated oven for about 10 minutes, or until the *spritskransar* are golden. Rest them for a minute or two before transferring them to a wire rack to cool. When completely cold, store in an airtight container.

Piped S-shaped cookies are also traditionally made with this dough.

*Syltkakor,* butter leaves, are another Swedish shortcake cookie popular at Christmas time.

## SYLTKAKOR
### *Butter Leaves with Jelly*

[SWEDEN]                                    TO MAKE ABOUT 40 COOKIES

| | |
|---|---|
| 1 cup butter | 2½ cups flour, sifted |
| ½ cup superfine granulated | 1 egg white |
| sugar | ½ cup blanched almonds, |
| 1 egg yolk | chopped |
| ½ teaspoon almond | ¼ cup granulated sugar |
| extract | ½ cup red currant jelly |

In a large bowl, cream together the butter and sugar until light and fluffy. Stir in the egg yolk and almond extract. Gradually add the flour and mix thoroughly. Chill the dough for 2 hours.

Preheat oven to 350°F. On a lightly floured surface, roll out the dough to a thickness of about ⅛ inch and, using a 2-inch round cutter, stamp out circles of dough. Using a smaller round cutter, cut the center out of half the circles of dough. Brush the rings only with egg white and sprinkle them with the chopped almonds and sugar. Arrange the cookies on buttered baking sheets and bake them in the preheated oven for about 10 minutes, or until they are golden. Cool on a wire rack.

When the cookies are cold, sandwich together the plain bases and nutty tops with red currant jelly. Unfilled *syltkakor* keep well for several weeks in an airtight container.

Basel in Switzerland celebrates every festive occasion with an unusual nut cookie which is not unlike the famous *panforte di Siena,* a special occasion confection from Italy.

## BASLER LECKERLI
### Basel Cinnamon Cookies

[SWITZERLAND]                    TO MAKE ABOUT 24 COOKIES

¾ cup honey
1 cup superfine granulated
   sugar
1½ tablespoons powdered
   cinnamon
2 cups flour, sifted
¼ cup kirsch

½ cup blanched almonds,
   chopped
½ cup hazelnuts, chopped
⅓ cup candied orange and
   lemon peel, chopped
   fine
½ cup confectioners' sugar

Preheat oven to 350°F. Put the honey into a large, heavy saucepan with the sugar and cinnamon and cook them together over low heat until the sugar has dissolved. Remove from the heat and stir in half the flour, the kirsch, nuts, and peel. Turn the mixture onto a well-floured surface and knead in the remaining flour. Spread the dough about ¼ inch thick on one or more greased and floured rectangular baking pans and sprinkle the top lightly with flour. Bake in the preheated oven for about 20 minutes or until golden brown.

Turn out of the pans and, while still warm, cut the *leckerli* in half horizontally with a sharp knife. Brush off any excess flour and cut into bars. Dust the pieces with confectioners' sugar and cool on a wire rack. When cold, store in an airtight container.


Caramel-filled coconut cookies are made for Christmas in Peru.


## ALFAJORES DE MAICENA
### Caramel and Coconut Cookies

[PERU]                          TO MAKE ABOUT 25 COOKIES

½ cup butter
½ cup superfine granulated
   sugar
1 egg
1 egg yolk
½ teaspoon vanilla extract
2 cups flour

1 cup cornstarch
1 teaspoon baking powder
1¼ cups natillas piuranas
   (see page 152)
1¼ cups fresh-grated
   coconut

Preheat oven to 350°F. In a large bowl, cream together the butter and sugar until light and fluffy. In a separate bowl, beat together the whole egg, egg yolk, and vanilla extract. Add them to the creamed mixture and beat until smooth. Sift together twice the flour, cornstarch, and baking powder, then add gradually to the creamed mixture. Turn the dough onto a lightly floured surface and knead it lightly until smooth and slightly elastic. Roll it out to about ⅛ inch thick, and stamp out 2-inch circles, using a plain round cookie cutter. Arrange the cookies on cookie sheets lined with baking parchment and bake in the preheated oven for about 12 minutes, or until they are firm but barely colored. Cool on a wire rack.

Sandwich the cookies together with a generous filling of *natillas piuranas* and roll them through the grated coconut so that it sticks to the exposed filling.

Scots shortbread is sent all over the world at Christmas and New Year and the commercial product has become such a popular export that its festive origins are often forgotten. In less affluent times, when fresh butter and white flour were not everyday fare for most people, shortbread was a festive treat, traditionally made and baked in the manner of oatcakes. American cake and pastry flour is softer than the plain flour sold in Britain. This is why Scots recipes invariably include a proportion of rice flour to make the shortbread shorter. Like pastry, shortbread should be handled as little and as lightly as possible, as too much messing about with the dough toughens it. Carved wooden molds are sometimes used to pattern shortbread, but plain circles with hand-crimped edges are more usual.

## *SHORTBREAD*

{SCOTLAND}                                                TO MAKE 8 PIECES

*1½ cups cake flour, or 1*
  *cup all-purpose flour*
  *combined with ½ cup*
  *rice flour*
*¼ teaspoon salt*

*½ cup butter, chilled*
*⅓ cup superfine granulated*
  *sugar*
*1 egg yolk*

Preheat oven to 350°F. Sift together into a large bowl the cake flour (or combined all-purpose and rice flours) and salt. Dice the butter into the flour, then, using your fingertips or a pastry blender, lightly work in the fat until the mixture resembles fine bread crumbs. Blend in the sugar and bind the mixture with the egg yolk to form a stiff dough.

Press the dough lightly into a shallow 7-inch round cake pan lined with baking parchment. Pinch the edges all around, using your finger and thumb, mark into 8 wedges, and prick the shortbread neatly with a fork. Bake it for 40 to 60 minutes or until it is a light, golden brown. Allow the shortbread, which will still be soft, to cool a little in its pan before turning it onto a wire rack. When it is quite cold and crisp, dredge it with superfine granulated sugar and store in an airtight container.

There are countless subtly varied family recipes for the light, fragrant Christmas shortbread made in Greece. It is certainly of ancient origin, and a cake of *kourabiédes* is said to have been mentioned by St. John Chrysostom in one of his sermons. Today it is usually made in the form of individual cookies, each spiked with a clove to represent the gift of spices which the wise men brought to the infant Christ.

The secret of *kourabiédes* is said to lie in beating the butter (which should ideally be goat butter) and sugar by hand for at least half an hour. I think this is a bit of Greek grannies' one-up-womanship, and use an electric beater with perfect results. The following recipe uses *ouzo*. The flavorings of aniseed, fennel, and coriander in this fiery Greek spirit are well tamed by the other ingredients and by baking. If *ouzo* is not available, substitute *pastis* or *arrack* in one of their many forms. There are also equally authentic recipes which leave out the booze altogether and use water and a few drops of rosewater instead.

## KOURABIÉDES
### Butter Cookies

{GREECE}                          TO MAKE ABOUT 40 COOKIES

*1 cup butter*                    *2½ cups flour*
*½ cup superfine granulated*      *½ teaspoon baking powder*
*    sugar*                       *40 whole cloves*
*2 tablespoons* ouzo              *Confectioners' sugar*
*¼ teaspoon vanilla extract*      *Rosewater*
*1 egg yolk*

Preheat oven to 375°F. In a large bowl cream together the butter and sugar until light and fluffy. Beat in the *ouzo,* vanilla extract, and egg yolk. Sift together twice the flour and baking powder and add them to the creamed mixture. Mix well to make a firm dough.

Form rounded tablespoonfuls of the mixture into balls and arrange them on a cookie sheet lined with baking parchment. The mixture spreads very little so there is no need to leave big spaces between the cookies. Press each piece of dough lightly with the ball of your thumb to flatten it in the middle, and spike the center of each cookie with a clove. Bake in the preheated oven for about 20 minutes, or until a light, golden color.

Transfer the *kourabiédes* immediately to a wire rack, and while they are still piping hot, sprinkle them twice with confectioners' sugar and rosewater. When they are completely cold, store them in an airtight container.

There is also a nutty version of these cookies which is made by adding ½ cup of blanched toasted and chopped almonds to the dough.

Another buttery recipe is for *S-Gebäck,* S-shaped ribbons of lemon-flavored shortcake.

## S-GEBÄCK
### S-Shaped Cookies

{GERMANY}                                TO MAKE ABOUT 40 COOKIES

½ cup sweet butter              2 cups flour, sifted
⅔ cup superfine granulated      1 egg white
    sugar                       4 ounces sugar cubes
4 egg yolks
1 teaspoon lemon rind,
    grated fine

In a large bowl cream together the butter and sugar until light and fluffy. Gradually beat in the egg yolks and lemon rind. Beat in the flour, a little at a time, to make a firm dough. Form the dough into a long roll about 2 inches in diameter, wrap it in wax paper, and chill for about an hour.

Preheat oven to 400°F. Shape slices of the dough into ribbons about

4 inches long by ¾ inch wide and ¼ inch thick, and arrange them in S-shapes on a well-buttered cookie sheet. Beat the egg white until foamy and paint the cookies with it. Coarsely crush the lump sugar and sprinkle a little on the top of each cookie. Bake for about 10 minutes, or until cookies are firm but barely colored. Cool on a wire rack and store in an airtight container.

Ring-shaped twists of dough make Sweden's *konjakskransar,* brandy rings.

## KONJAKSKRANSAR
### Brandy Rings

{SWEDEN}                                    TO MAKE ABOUT 75 COOKIES

*1 ¼ cups butter*
*¾ cup superfine granulated sugar*
*3 tablespoons brandy*
*3 ½ cups flour, sifted*

Preheat oven to 350°F. In a large bowl cream together the butter and sugar until light and fluffy. Beat in the brandy and gradually add the flour. Mix thoroughly to make a smooth, firm dough.

On a lightly floured surface, roll the dough into thin ropes. Twist two ropes together, cut into 5-inch lengths, and form each piece into a ring. Arrange the rings on buttered cookie sheets and bake for about 15 minutes or until golden. Rest the brandy rings on their baking sheets for about 5 minutes, then transfer them to a wire rack to cool completely. Store in an airtight container.

*Ruiskakkuja,* sweet rye cookies baked to resemble miniature loaves of sour rye bread, are a traditional offering on the Finnish Christmas coffee table.

## RUISKAKKUJA
### Rye Cookies

{FINLAND}                    TO MAKE ABOUT 35 COOKIES

> ½ cup butter
> 5 tablespoons superfine granulated sugar
> 1 cup rye flour
> ½ cup all-purpose flour

Preheat oven to 400°F. In a large bowl, cream together the butter and sugar until light and fluffy. Sift in the flours and mix well until the mixture looks like bread crumbs. Knead into a firm dough. The warmth of your hands will make a dough without adding liquid.

On a lightly floured surface, roll out the dough about ⅛ inch thick. Using a plain-edged 3-inch cookie cutter, stamp out rounds of dough. Cut a hole in each round, slightly off-center, using a very small round cutter or the top of an extract bottle.

Arrange the *ruiskakkuja* on generously buttered cookie sheets and prick each cookie several times with a fork. Bake them in the preheated oven for about 7 minutes or until lightly browned. Cool on a wire rack and store in an airtight container.

Honey cookies with a crunchy sugar topping are a traditional Christmas treat in Bulgaria.

## MEDENI KURABII
### Honey Cookies

{BULGARIA}                    TO MAKE ABOUT 25 COOKIES

> ½ cup sweet butter
> 6 tablespoons honey
> ⅓ cup superfine granulated sugar
>
> 1 teaspoon baking soda
> 1 egg yolk
> 1 cup flour, sifted
> 4 ounces cube sugar

Preheat oven to 350°F. Melt the butter, and when it is cool but not solidified, in a large bowl mix it with the honey, sugar, baking soda, and egg yolk. Gradually add the flour and mix well to make a firm dough.

The exact consistency of bread sauce is a matter of preference. It may be as soft as mayonnaise or a good deal thicker, and thickened or thinned with more bread crumbs, milk, or cream.

Cranberry sauce to accompany turkey is sold in jars, cans, and freezer packs, but it is not difficult to make. Fresh and frozen cranberries are widely available during the Christmas season. Spiced cranberries are a delicious alternative to the plainer sauce.

## CRANBERRY SAUCE

[UNITED STATES]                                    TO MAKE 1½ CUPS

*1 pound cranberries, fresh or frozen*
*1 cup superfine granulated sugar*

Put the cranberries into a pot with the sugar and 5 ounces water. Bring to the boil, lower the heat, and simmer, covered, for about 20 minutes or until the cranberries are tender. Serve warm or cold.

## SPICED CRANBERRIES

[UNITED STATES]                                    TO MAKE 1½ CUPS

| | |
|---|---|
| *1 pound cranberries, fresh or frozen* | *2 inches cinnamon stick* |
| | *6 whole allspice* |
| *1 cup dark brown sugar* | *6 whole cloves* |
| *1 inch ginger root, bruised* | *¾ cup wine vinegar* |

Put the cranberries into a pot with the sugar, spices, and vinegar. Bring to the boil, lower the heat, cover and simmer for about 20 minutes, or until the cranberries are tender. Fish out the spices and leave to cool. Serve cold.

Spiced peaches and pears pickled in a syrup of sugar and vinegar may be made when the fruits are plentiful and set aside for Christmas eating. They are especially good with cold ham and poultry.

## SPICED PEARS

{ENGLAND}                                        TO MAKE 2 POUNDS

| | |
|---|---|
| 2 pounds fresh, hard pears | 4 inches cinnamon stick |
| 2 cups sugar | 8 whole cloves |
| 1¼ cups malt wine vinegar | 2 teaspoons whole allspice |

Peel, core, and quarter the pears and set them aside in cold water acidulated with 1 teaspoon of vinegar.

Put the sugar and vinegar into a stainless steel or enameled saucepan. Bruise the spices and tie them loosely in cheesecloth. Add them to the pan. Dissolve the sugar over low heat; strain the pears, add to the sugar, and bring to a boil. Lower the heat, cover, and simmer gently until the pears are tender but not mushy.

Using a slotted spoon, lift out the pears and pack them into a large, heated jar. Remove the spice bag from the syrup, and return the pan to high heat. Boil the syrup until it thickens a little, then pour it over the pears. The liquid should cover the fruit. Make an airtight seal for the jar and store the spiced pears in a cool place for at least a month, or until needed.

## SPICED PEACHES

{ENGLAND}                                        TO MAKE 2 POUNDS

| | |
|---|---|
| 2 pounds fresh peaches | 1 inch ginger root |
| 2 cups sugar | 4 inches cinnamon stick |
| 1¼ cups malt or wine | 8 whole cloves |
| vinegar | 1 teaspoon whole allspice |

To prepare the peaches, dip them in boiling water for about 30 seconds and then peel. Cut the fruit in half and remove the pits.

Put the sugar and vinegar into a large stainless steel or enameled saucepan. Bruise the spices and tie them loosely in cheesecloth. Add them to the pan. Dissolve the sugar over low heat, then bring the syrup to the boil and add the peaches. Simmer very gently until the peaches are tender but not mushy.

Using a slotted spoon, lift the peaches out of the syrup and pack them into a large, heated jar. Remove the spices from the pan and return the syrup to the heat. Boil rapidly until it thickens slightly, then pour the syrup over the peaches. The liquid should cover the fruit. Make an air-tight seal for the jar, and store it in a cool place for at least a month, or until needed.

Applesauce is the classic accompaniment to roast pork. In the Caribbean a mock applesauce made with unripe papaya (paw paw in Jamaica), or chayote, is served throughout the islands with roast suckling pig.

## PAW PAW APPLESAUCE

{JAMAICA}                                           TO MAKE 1½ CUPS

*1 pound unripe papaya*
*4 cloves*
*2 tablespoons sugar*
*4 tablespoons lime juice*

Peel the papaya, remove the seeds, and roughly chop the flesh. Put the fruit into a heavy-bottomed pot with 1½ cups water, cloves, sugar, and lime juice. Bring to the boil, cover, and simmer for about 1 hour, or until the fruit is soft and most of the liquid absorbed. Discard the cloves and rub the sauce through a sieve. Serve warm or cold.

Cumberland sauce, a hot mixture of wine and red currant jelly, is de-licious with roast lamb or a hot Christmas ham. Its festive color is an attractive bonus.

## CUMBERLAND SAUCE

{ENGLAND}                                           TO MAKE 2 CUPS

*1 orange*
*4 tablespoons port or red wine*
*1½ cups red currant jelly*

*2 teaspoons lemon juice*
*2 teaspoons powdered dry mustard*
*Salt to taste*

Cut the orange rind into neat julienne strips, being careful to discard any white pith. Squeeze the juice from the flesh and reserve. In a small saucepan heat the port or red wine and strips of orange peel to the boiling point, then reduce the heat and stir in the red currant jelly. Stir over a low heat until the jelly has melted completely. Mix together the orange and lemon juice and dry mustard and stir them into the red currant mixture. Season to taste with salt and serve the sauce hot or cold.

Mincemeat was originally a means of preserving meat without smoking or salting it. It is seldom made with meat now, except in a few strong-holds of tradition, and only the suet remains to remind us of older recipes. Mrs. Beeton's recipe, with its instructions for cleaning the dried fruit, brings home the time-saving virtues of cleaned and packaged currants and raisins brought from the supermarket.

"INGREDIENTS.—2 lbs. of raisins, 3 lbs. of currants, 1½ lbs. of lean beef, 3 lbs. of beef suet, 2 lbs. of moist sugar, 2 oz. of citron, 2 oz. of candied lemon-peel, 2 oz. of candied orange-peel, 1 small nutmeg, 1 pottle of apples, the rind of 2 lemons, the juice of 1, ½ pint of brandy.

*Mode*.—Stone and *cut* the raisins once or twice across, but do not chop them; wash, dry, and pick the currants free from stalks and grit, and mince the beef and suet, taking care that the latter is chopped very fine; slice the citron and candied peel, grate the nut-meg, pare, core, and mince the apples; mince the lemon-peel, strain the juice, and when all the ingredients are thus prepared, mix them well together, adding the brandy when the other things are well blended; press the whole into a jar, carefully exclude the air, and the mincemeat will be ready for use in a fortnight.

*Average cost* for this quantity, 8*d*.

*Seasonable*.—Make this about the beginning of December."

The following modern recipe is particularly good and keeps for over a year. If mincemeat that is stored for long periods dries a little, revive it by adding a little more brandy or rum.

## MINCEMEAT

[ENGLAND]                                        TO MAKE 4 POUNDS

¾ pound eating apples,             1 teaspoon mixed spice
   peeled and cored                  (commercially
1¼ cups seedless raisins               packaged; or mixed
1½ cups sultana raisins                ground cloves,
1¼ cups dried currants                 cinnamon, and
½ pound candied lemon                  nutmeg)
   peel                          ½ nutmeg, grated
½ pound candied orange             ½ teaspoon salt
   peel                          Grated rind and juice of 1
¼ cup blanched almonds                 lemon
1 cup dark brown sugar             6 tablespoons brandy or
2 cups beef suet, shredded             rum

Pass the apples through the coarse blade of a grinder together with the sultana raisins, currants, candied peel, and almonds. Put the ground ingredients into a large bowl with the sugar, suet, spices, and salt. Add the lemon rind and juice, and the brandy or rum. Mix the ingredients very thoroughly together and pack the mincemeat into jars or plastic containers. Make airtight seals, and store the mincemeat in a cool place for at least a month before using.

Three different types of sauce are made to accompany Christmas pudding and each has its particular devotees.

Dr. William Kitchener writing in 1804 gives this recipe for a hot sauce in his famous and much plagiarized *Apicius Redivivus, The Cook's Oracle*. A similar Scots recipe is called caudle sauce.

## PLUM PUDDING SAUCE

[ENGLAND]                                        TO SERVE 4 TO 6

1 teaspoon grated lemon            ½ cup sherry
   rind                          ½ cup brandy
1 tablespoon superfine             ½ cup melted butter
   granulated sugar              Grated nutmeg to taste

Stir the lemon rind and sugar into the sherry mixed with the brandy and slowly stir the melted butter into the mixture. Keep warm over hot water and stir well just before serving in a sauceboat with a ladle. At the last minute sprinkle a little grated nutmeg over it.

Queen Victoria's chef, Francatelli, gives the following instructions for a German custard sauce for plum pudding. It is very like the frothy Italian pudding *zabaglione,* and is served hot.

"Put four yolks of eggs into a bain-marie or stewpan, together with two ounces of pounded sugar, a glass of sherry, some orange or lemon peel (rubbed on loaf sugar), and a very little salt.
"Whisk this sharply over a very slow fire until it assumes the appearance of a light, frothy custard."

Brandy butter or hard sauce is the best-loved accompaniment to Christmas pudding. It should be served well-chilled and can be made in advance.

## HARD SAUCE

{UNITED STATES}                                      TO SERVE 4 TO 6

| | |
|---|---|
| ¾ cup sweet butter | 1 teaspoon grated orange |
| 1 cup superfine granulated | rind |
| sugar | ¼ cup brandy or rum |

Cream together the butter and sugar until pale and fluffy. Beat in the grated orange rind and gradually add the brandy or rum, beating well after each addition. Turn the mixture into a serving dish and chill well.

Marzipan or almond paste is a favorite Christmas sweetmeat brought to the United States mainly from Germany, but popular, too, in other parts of Europe, and an integral part of English Christmas cake. Sugar and ground almonds are the essential ingredients, with eggs and butter appearing in some recipes and not in others. The Danes have pink marzipan Christmas pigs, while Austrians save them for New Year. In Germany, where marzipan appears as almost anything but itself, it is fashioned into brightly colored fruits, flowers, and figures; and in Spain into huge, dragon-like monsters filled with dried fruit.

## LUBECKER MARZIPAN
### *Almond Paste*

[GERMANY]                                TO MAKE 1 POUND

*2⅔ cups ground almonds*
*2 cups confectioners' sugar, sifted*
*Orange flower water or rosewater*

Work the ground almonds and confectioners' sugar into a firm paste with just enough orange flower water or rosewater to make it pliable.

Put the paste into a small saucepan and stir it over a low heat until it no longer sticks to the sides of the pan.

Turn the marzipan onto a sugar-dusted board. Shape it into figures or candies. These may be left, lightly covered, in a warm place to dry a little, or dried in a very slow oven. The marzipan should remain both soft and white.

The next recipe is the one to use for Christmas cake. It can also be tinted with a few drops of food coloring to make candies, stuffed dates, and figures.

## MARZIPAN
### *Almond Paste*

[UNITED STATES]                          TO MAKE 1 POUND

*1 cup confectioners' sugar*          *1 teaspoon lemon juice*
*⅔ cup superfine granulated*          *A few drops almond extract*
*    sugar*                           *1 egg, beaten*
*2⅔ cups ground almonds*

Sift the confectioners' sugar into a bowl and stir in the superfine granulated sugar and almonds. Add the lemon juice and a few drops of almond extract. Mix well, then gradually add enough egg to make a firm paste.

Knead the paste lightly on a sugar-dusted surface until it is smooth. Store the marzipan, well-wrapped, in the refrigerator for up to 2 months.

*Borstplaat* is an indispensable Christmas candy in Holland. It is made in many colors, flavors, sizes, and shapes, and special ring molds are sold in the Netherlands for shaping it. However, round cake pans or the flat lids of cookie tins work just as well. The liquid used may be water, milk, or light cream. Flavorings can be varied by using extracts or by adding cocoa or strong coffee.

## BORSTPLAAT
### Christmas Fondant

[HOLLAND]                                      TO MAKE 24 PIECES

*1 cup granulated sugar*          *A few drops orange extract*
*3 tablespoons light cream*       *A few drops orange food*
*1 tablespoon butter*             *  coloring*

In a small heavy saucepan, stir the sugar and cream together. Heat slowly to the boiling point and cook over low heat, without stirring, until the syrup spins a thread, or registers 240° on a candy thermometer. Remove from the heat immediately and add the butter and a few drops each of flavoring and coloring. Beat the mixture vigorously with a wooden spoon until it thickens and begins to make a scratchy sound. Pour it into a greased pan and leave it to set until cold. When cold, break into bite-sized pieces.

*Turrón* is the Christmas candy of the Spanish-speaking world. The famous *turróns* of Alicante and Jijona are so popular that they are now available all year round. But *turrón* used to be a special Christmas treat, and all the big houses and estates had family recipes for making it. Small bags or packets of *turrón* were distributed on Christmas Eve to the servants and tenants, who in turn brought gifts to the mistress of the house.

The basic ingredients of *turrón* are almonds, sugar and/or honey, and egg yolks or whites. But there are numerous variations—powdered coriander, cinnamon, walnuts, and pine kernels in Spain, hazelnuts and sesame seeds in Mexico. Sometimes the almonds are simply blanched and peeled, sometimes toasted or ground to a paste. Often all three forms are included in a single recipe. A loaf pan will substitute for the wooden mold used in Spain.

## TURRÓN
### Almond Nougat

{SPAIN}                                                          TO MAKE 1 BAR

*1½ cups blanched almonds*
*1⅔ cups superfine granulated sugar*
*4 egg yolks, beaten*
*Almond oil (or a flavorless vegetable oil)*

Leave the almonds as they are or toast all or some of them. Grind at least ⅔ of the almonds to a paste. The remainder may be ground, chopped, slivered, or left whole.

Heat the sugar slowly with 1⅛ cups water in a heavy-bottomed saucepan, and when the sugar has dissolved completely, boil the syrup rapidly for about 7 minutes or until small drops set hard instantly on a cold plate. Remove from the heat and add all the almonds, stirring until the mixture forms a thick paste which leaves the sides of the pan. Stir in the egg yolks.

Line a loaf pan with paper brushed with almond oil and cut neatly to fit. Press the *turrón* into the pan and cover with another piece of oiled paper and a piece of heavy cardboard cut to fit. Weight the top and leave the candy to set in a cool place.

Turn out the bar, remove the oiled papers, and dust the top with superfine granulated sugar. Use a very hot skewer to burn a traditional pattern of crisscross lines on top of the *turrón*.

# DRINKS

If recipe books reflect the world's drinking practices, then punches of varying potency are undoubtedly the most popular Christmas drinks. But books do not exactly mirror our drinking habits, and for the most part people fill their glasses with what they drink on other days. So these recipes are for party drinks, special-occasion brews to be made in quantity for festive gatherings of every kind. There are hot, spiced wines for travelers in cold northern winters, and long, cool punches from places where the sun shines at Christmas.

## JUL GLÖGG
### Christmas Punch

{DENMARK}                                    TO MAKE 1 QUART

2 ¼ pints red wine
2 inches cinnamon stick
4 cloves
8 cardamom seeds
½ cup superfine granulated
    sugar

Rind of ½ lemon, cut into
    strips
½ cup blanched almonds,
    chopped
½ cup seedless raisins
1 cup cognac or armagnac

Put the wine and all the other ingredients except the cognac or armagnac into a large saucepan and stir over low heat until the sugar has dissolved.

Bring almost to the boil and transfer to a serving bowl. Just before serving, add the cognac or armagnac. Set alight with a match, then ladle into handled punch glasses.

## NEUJAHRSPUNSCH
### New Year Punch

[GERMANY]                                    TO MAKE 1¾ QUARTS

> 1⅓ cups superfine granulated sugar
> ¾ pint rum
> 3 pints white wine
> ¾ pint red wine

Soak the sugar in the rum and let it stand for several hours, until the sugar dissolves. Put the wines in a saucepan and bring almost to the boil. Add the sweetened rum and serve immediately.

Wassailing must have been going strong in England long before formal Christmas festivities took root. The word wassail comes from the Old Norse *ves heill,* good health, and a variety of wassailing traditions still survive in various parts of the country. A bubbling wassail bowl greeted the revelers who dragged the Yule log home from the woods on Christmas Eve. Gloucestershire wassailers downed it at New Year, and in the West Country and other fruit-growing areas, wassailing the apple tree survives in a number of noisy ceremonies sometimes known as apple howling and usually occurring on Twelfth Night.

There are many versions of the drink, some of which are made with cider. This recipe for a wassail bowl comes from *The Curiosities of Ale and Beer* by John Bickerdyke. The book was published in about 1860, but the recipe is almost certainly much older.

> "Into a bowl is first placed ½ lb. sugar in which is placed one pint of warm beer; a little nutmeg and ginger are then grated over the mixture, and four glasses of sherry and five pints of beer added to it. It is then stirred, sweetened to taste and allowed to stand covered for two or three hours. Roasted apples are then floated on the creaming mixture and the wassail bowl is ready."

Het pint, the New Year's morning drink of urban Scots, used to be sold from bright copper kettles in the streets of Edinburgh and Glasgow. It is seldom made now, but this recipe is given in *The Scot's Kitchen.*

"Grate a nutmeg into two quarts of mild ale, and bring it to the point of boiling. Mix a little cold ale with sugar necessary to sweeten this and three eggs well-beaten. Gradually mix the hot ale with the eggs, taking care that they do not curdle. Put in a half-pint of whisky, and bring it once more nearly to the boil and then briskly pour it from one vessel into another till it becomes smooth and bright."

Atholl brose is one of those drinks that many people have heard of but few have tried. Its strong associations with New Year's Eve—called Hogmanay in Scotland, where it is a popular gesture of hospitality to first-footers (the first visitors of the New Year) in the Highlands—are excuse enough to give it a whirl. In *The Scot's Kitchen,* F. Marian McNeill says that the following recipe was "made known" by the eighth Duke of Atholl.

"To make a quart, take four dessertspoonfuls of clear honey and four sherry glassfuls of prepared oatmeal; stir these well together and put into a quart bottle; fill up with whisky; shake well before serving.

"To prepare the oatmeal, put it into a basin and mix with cold water to the consistency of a thick paste. Leave for about half an hour, pass through a fine strainer, pressing with the back of a wooden spoon so as to leave the oatmeal as dry as possible. Discard the meal, and use the creamy liquor for the brose."

The proportions suggest that the eighth Duke didn't care to have his whisky messed about with too much.

From the same book comes another recipe served by Williamina Macrae at her angling inn at Lochailort. The quantities called for may seem more suitable for domestic experiment, but the result is more like a pudding than a drink.

"Beat one and a half teacupfuls of double cream to a froth; stir in one teacupful of very lightly toasted oatmeal; add half a cup of dripped heather honey and, just before serving, two wine-glasses of whisky. Mix thoroughly and serve in shallow glasses."

*Advocaat,* a heavy, milkless eggnog, is the New Year's day drink in Holland where it is served from a punchbowl.

## ADVOCAAT
### Eggnog

{HOLLAND}                                                TO MAKE 2 QUARTS

20 egg yolks
1 ⅓ cups superfine granulated sugar
2 pints brandy

**FOR THE TOPPING**

6 egg whites
½ cup superfine granulated sugar

In a large bowl, beat together the egg yolks and sugar until thick and fluffy. Gradually beat in the brandy.

In another bowl beat the egg whites until they hold a stiff peak. Fold in the sugar.

To serve the *advocaat,* fill glasses with the brandy mixture and flip a blob of fluffy egg white on top of each portion.

For Puerto Rico's coconut rum punch, use the liquid from 2 or 3 fresh coconuts plus coconut milk made by straining the grated flesh soaked in water.

## RON CON COCO
### Coconut Rum Punch

{PUERTO RICO}                                         TO MAKE 5½ QUARTS

6 egg yolks
1 ⅓ cups superfine
    granulated sugar
1 pint canned evaporated
    milk

3 pints coconut milk
2 pints rum
Vanilla extract (optional)

In a large bowl, beat the egg yolks and sugar until pale and thick. Gradually beat in the evaporated milk, then the coconut milk, and finally the rum. Add the vanilla, if desired, and chill well.

Beat again immediately before serving in long glasses, with or without ice, as an aperitif or at any other time.

Cola de mono, a Chilean coffee punch served as an aperitif, calls for the local spirit, *aguardiente,* for which vodka is the best substitute.

## COLA DE MONO
### Coffee Punch

[CHILE]                                    TO MAKE 2½ QUARTS

3¼ pints milk                     1 cup sugar
8 cloves                          1 teaspoon grated nutmeg
Rind of 1 orange, cut into        1¼ pints aguardiente or
    strips                            vodka
4 ounces instant coffee

Scald the milk and set it aside to cool. Put 1¼ pints water, cloves, strips of orange peel, instant coffee, sugar, and nutmeg into a saucepan and bring to the boil. Lower the heat, cover, and simmer gently for about 20 minutes. Set aside to cool.

Strain the cold milk and spiced coffee into a large bowl or pitcher. Add the *aguardiente* or vodka, Mix thoroughly and chill well before serving as an aperitif.

Brazil's party punch is a cool, wine-based cup lavishly embellished with fresh fruit.

## PONCHE PARA FESTAS
### Party Punch

{BRAZIL}                              TO MAKE 1½ QUARTS

*1 lemon, sliced thin*
*1 orange, sliced thin*
*½ pineapple, peeled and*
*    sliced thin*
*2 peaches, peeled, pitted, and*
*    sliced thin*
*24 grapes, peeled, seeded,*
*    and sliced thin*

*3 tablespoons superfine*
*    granulated sugar*
*3 ounces maraschino*
*    liqueur*
*3 ounces curaçao liqueur*
*1½ pints red wine*
*¾ pint soda water*

Put the lemon and orange slices into a serving bowl or pitcher. Add the pineapple, peaches, and grapes. Sprinkle the fruit with sugar and set it aside for an hour. Add the maraschino, curaçao, wine, and soda water. Mix well and chill the punch for about 2 hours.

Serve with a large lump of ice in the bowl or jug. Freeze flowers or fruit into the ice for decoration.

Homemade ginger beer—a revelation to those who have only tasted the commercial product—is a popular drink throughout the English-speaking islands of the Caribbean. Start production 2 weeks before it is needed.

## GINGER BEER

{TRINIDAD}                            TO MAKE 2¼ QUARTS

*2 ounces fresh ginger root,*
*    or 2 tablespoons*
*    powdered ginger*
*½ cup lime juice*
*Rind of 1 lime, cut into*
*    strips*

*2 cups sugar*
*3¾ pints boiling water*
*⅓ package active dried*
*    yeast*

Peel and crush the ginger root or substitute the powdered ginger. Put the ginger, lime juice, lime peel, and sugar into a large bowl or pitcher and pour the boiling water over them.

Dissolve the yeast in a small amount of lukewarm water, about 110°F. When the ginger mixture has cooled to the same temperature, add the yeast and stir well. Cover the container loosely and leave it to stand in a warm place for a week. Stir it daily.

Strain the liquid through a fine sieve lined with cheesecloth and pour it into clean bottles. Cork them lightly and leave to stand at room temperature for another 4 or 5 days. Chill well and serve in tall glasses, with or without ice.

Another Christmas drink found in Trinidad and Jamaica is a festive red infusion of sorrel—an annual plant also called rosella, which matures at this time of year. Use 8 ounces whole fresh sorrel, or 1 ounce of dried sorrel sepals for the following recipe. Sorrel syrup is also exported and should be diluted according to the instructions on the bottle.

## SORREL DRINK

{JAMAICA}                          TO MAKE 12 TO 14 SERVINGS

*1 ounce fresh ginger root,*       *2 cups sugar*
*    peeled and grated*            *3¾ pints boiling water*
*    coarse*                       *6–12 ounces dark rum*
*1 ounce sorrel sepals, dried*

Put the grated ginger root into a large bowl or pitcher with the sorrel and sugar. Add the boiling water, stir, and cover loosely. Leave to stand at room temperature for at least 48 hours.

Strain the liquid through a fine sieve lined with cheesecloth into a serving bowl or pitcher. Chill well before adding rum to taste.

In Trinidad cloves, cinnamon, and orange peel replace the ginger.

# SELECTED BIBLIOGRAPHY

Eliza Acton. *The Best of Eliza Acton.* Edited by Elizabeth Ray. London: Longmans, Green, 1968.

Margarette de Andrade. *Brazilian Cookery.* Rutland, Vermont: Charles E. Tuttle, 1965.

Amanda Atha, ed. *Good Housekeeping Home Baking.* London: Ebury Press, 1977.

Elisabeth Ayrton. *The Cookery of England.* London: André Deutsch, 1974.

Margaret Baker. *Christmas Customs and Folklore, A Discovering Guide To Seasonal Rites.* England: Shire, 1972.

Isabella Beeton. *Beeton's Book of Household Management, A First Edition Facsimile.* London: Jonathan Cape, 1968.

Sula Benet. *Festival Menus Round the World.* New York: Abelard Schuman, 1957.

George C. Booth. *The Food and Drink of Mexico.* New York: Dover Publications, 1964.

Bob Brown and Rose and Cora. *The South American Cook Book.* New York: Dover Publications, 1971.

Dale Brown. *The Cooking of Scandinavia.* New York: Time-Life Books, 1969.

Elizabeth Cass. *Spanish Cooking.* England: Mayflower Books, 1976.

Robert Carrier. *Great Dishes of the World.* England: Thomas Nelson, 1963.

————. *The Robert Carrier Cookery Course.* London: W. H. Allen, 1974.

Ann H. Currah. *Chef to Queen Victoria, The Recipes of Charles Elmé Francatelli.* London: William Kimber, 1973.

Elizabeth David. *French Country Cooking.* England: Penguin, 1966.

————. *Italian Food.* England: Penguin, 1975.

————. *Spices, Salt and Aromatics in the English Kitchen*. England: Penguin, 1970.

Enriqueta David-Perez. *Recipes of the Philippines*. Philippines: D. M. Press, 1967.

Peter S. Feibleman. *The Cooking of Spain and Portugal*. New York: Time-Life Books, 1970.

Michael and Frances Field. *A Quintet of Cuisines*. New York: Time-Life Books, 1970.

Theodora FitzGibbon. *The Food of the Western World*. London: Hutchinson, 1976.

Lilli Gore. *Game Cooking*. London: Weidenfeld & Nicolson, 1974.

Károly Gundel. *Hungarian Cookery Book*. Budapest: Pannonia, 1964.

Nika Standen Hazelton. *The Cooking of Germany*. New York: Time-Life Books, 1970.

Robin Howe. *German Cooking*. London: André Deutsch, 1953.

Diana Kennedy. *The Cuisines of Mexico*. New York: Harper & Row, 1972.

Jonathan Norton Leonard. *Latin American Cooking*. New York: Time-Life Books, 1968.

F. Marian McNeill. *The Scot's Kitchen. Its Traditions and Lore with Old-Time Recipes*. Glasgow: Blackie, 1929.

Anna Miadhacháin. *Spanish Regional Cookery*. England: Penguin, 1976.

Prosper Montagné. *Larousse Gastronomique*. English edition, London: Hamlyn, 1974.

Countess Morphy (Marcelle Azra Forbes). *Recipes of All Nations*. London: Michael Joseph for Selfridges, 1935.

Beatrice A. Ojakangas. *The Finnish Cookbook*. New York: Crown, 1964.

Elizabeth Lambert Ortiz. *Caribbean Cooking*. London: André Deutsch, 1975.

Helen and George Papashvily. *The Cooking of Russia*. New York: Time-Life Books, 1969.

Readers Digest Association, ed. *The Cookery Year*. London: Readers Digest, 1973.

Waverley Root. *The Cooking of Italy*. New York: Time-Life Books, 1969.

Sofka Skipwith. *Eat Russian*. England: David & Charles, 1973.

Katie Stewart. *The Times Calendar Cookbook*. London: Hamlyn, 1975.

Nicholas Tselementes. *Greek Cookery*. New York: D. C. Divry, 1956.

Joseph Wechsberg. *The Cooking of Vienna's Empire*. New York: Time-Life Books, 1974.

Sam Widenfelt, ed. *Swedish Food*. Gothenburg: Wezäta Förlang, 1946.

C. Anne Wilson. *Food and Drink in Britain*. London: Constable, 1973.

# Index

Shona Crawford Poole was born of Scots parents at Seaford, Sussex, in 1943. She was educated vigorously at eleven schools, all in Britain, is now a Londoner by choice, and deputy features editor of *The Times*. After an apprenticeship on weekly newspapers, she wrote features for the *Daily Express* before joining *The Times* nine years ago. She travels extensively for work as well as fun, returning home with souvenirs of recipes, food, and cooking utensils. She is married to graphic designer Jasper Partington. They both fly gliders in summer and ski in winter as often as time and funds allow.